4/01

 **St. Louis Community College**

Forest Park
Florissant Valley
Meramec

Instructional Resources
St. Louis, Missouri

*Historic Preservation*
*for a Living City*

HISTORIC CHARLESTON FOUNDATION
Studies in History and Culture

# Historic Preservation for a Living City

HISTORIC
CHARLESTON
FOUNDATION
1947–1997

*Robert R. Weyeneth*

University of South Carolina Press

© 2000 University of South Carolina

Published in Columbia, South Carolina, by the
University of South Carolina Press

Manufactured in the United States of America

04  03  02  01  00    5  4  3  2  1

### Library of Congress Cataloging-in-Publication Data

Weyeneth, Robert R., 1950–
    Historic preservation for a living city : Historic Charleston Foundation,
1947–1997 / Robert R. Weyeneth.
        p. cm. — (Historic Charleston Foundation studies in history and culture)
    Includes bibliographical references and index.
    ISBN 1-57003-353-6 (alk. paper)
    1. Historic Charleston Foundation (Charleston, S.C.)—History.
2. Charleston (S.C.)—Antiquities—Collection and preservation. 3. Historic
preservation—South Carolina—Charleston—History—20th century.
4. Historic sites—Conservation and restoration—South Carolina—Charleston.
I. Title. II. Series.
F279.C447 W49 2000                                        00-008146

*To the memory of my grandparents*
*Merle Lee McGinnis and Velma Louise Gribben*
*Frank Harmon Weyeneth and Huldah Catherine Adamson*
*who kindled my interest in history*

# CONTENTS

# ILLUSTRATIONS

# Maps

# FOREWORD

Historic Charleston Foundation celebrated its fiftieth anniversary in 1997. Lectures, symposiums, and public events scheduled throughout the year recalled the innovative solutions the foundation applied to the historic preservation challenges with which Charleston grappled in the decades that followed World War II. At every one of these events small knots of former trustees, veterans of seemingly innumerable preservation struggles, reminisced about what they had done to protect what they cherished most about their city. They recalled, for example, how they established the nation's first revolving fund and how it fueled the effort that saved Ansonborough, the important historic neighborhood which, without the foundation's intervention, would have disappeared in clouds of urban development dust. At the edges of these conversations current trustees and foundation staff, most of them youngsters when the foundation waged its formative preservation campaigns in the 1950s and 1960s, strained to hear the veterans describe how the citizens of Charleston saved their historic buildings and neighborhoods and, in the process, established a model for the rest of the nation.

One of these sages was Joseph H. McGee, a past president of the foundation's board of trustees and leader of the important preservation initiatives the foundation pursued during the 1970s. McGee often said as the fiftieth anniversary celebration unfolded that the foundation had written a record of its accomplishments in restored houses, rehabilitated commercial buildings, and revitalized neighborhoods. Few, if any, blocks in Charleston's sprawling historic district do not contain handfuls of bronze plaques that recall the energy, capital, and ideas the foundation invested in the preservation of Charleston's threatened buildings and neighborhoods.

The veterans of the city's preservation efforts knew that few of Charleston's remarkable preservation successes had been easy. And they remembered that few were achieved quickly. The revitalization of Ansonborough took nearly two decades. The architectural and commercial revitalization of King Street, the city's most important commercial artery, commenced in the early 1980s with the construction of a new hotel, but only half its length had rebounded some twenty years later. The foundation's trustees knew both the issues and the individuals involved in these and other preservation initiatives intimately, but they began to ask while planning for the fiftieth anniversary events whether the lessons Charleston had learned had been shared with the rest of the nation.

The history of historic preservation in Charleston is familiar to preservation professionals. Its place is prominent in published accounts of the historic preservation movement in America. Charles B. Hosmer Jr., the first chronicler of the historic preservation movement, acknowledged Charleston's leadership during preservation's infancy in *Preservation Comes of Age: From Williamsburg to the National Trust, 1926–1949* (Charlottesville: University Press of Virginia, 1981). More recent narratives have also recognized Charleston's role, among them William J. Murtagh, *Keeping Time: The History and Theory of Preservation in America* (New York: John Wiley and Sons, 1997) and Robert E. Stipe and Antoinette J. Lee, eds., *The American Mosaic: Preserving a Nation's Heritage* (Detroit: Wayne State University Press, 1997). The Charleston experience is sprinkled liberally through these and other books and essays that explore the history and theory of historic preservation and the methods developed to achieve the movement's goals.

There is good reason for that. Charleston was, in many ways, historic preservation's "ground zero." The men and women who proposed the preservation of the city's historic buildings often found themselves grappling with issues and problems for which there were then no known solutions. They created the nation's first historic district in 1931 with a city statute that was a response to the demolition of several significant buildings to make way for two service stations. That ordinance entrusted guardianship of the city's historic buildings to a citizen board of architectural review. To meet other challenges Charlestonians developed many of the techniques which subsequently became the common property of preservationists everywhere.

The story of how a "preservation ethic" took root in Charleston has never been fully told, nor have the many stories of how the city and its citizens channeled their fierce pride in the city's architecture and found, when needed, ways to safeguard it. McGee and the foundation's trustees thought this story was worth telling, and they agreed to support the preparation of a book that would explore why Charlestonians did what they did, how they set preservation goals for their neighborhoods and their city, and how they then achieved them. The book the foundation agreed to pursue would provide, as would the fiftieth anniversary celebration itself, an opportunity to reflect on battles won and lost, a chance to consider how challenges had been met, and an invitation to savor the results of having stood resolutely for the preservation of buildings, neighborhoods, and sites when it might have been easier to relent and allow other alternatives to prevail (as communities throughout the nation had done). McGee and his cohorts thought that a history of preservation in Charleston would show how historic preservation became central to the city's sense of itself and how the city embraced preservation as a way not only to tend its history but also to imagine and then secure its future.

The story that Robert Weyeneth tells in the pages that follow is intended for several audiences. One audience is made up of the veterans of Charleston's preservation movement. They will find here a memorial of sorts to their friends and neighbors. The owners of houses in the historic district and all those who care about the city's unique architectural character and have acted to protect the city from erosive change will find here a chronicle of their remarkable achievement. Their legacy of stewardship has few equals, and we hope that the friends and supporters of historic preservation will find here validation of and commendation for their many good deeds.

Weyeneth has also written for that wider circle of historic preservation experts, professionals, and volunteer board and commission members—the core constituents of historic preservation—who will find here a fuller treatment of the history of historic preservation in Charleston than has heretofore been available. The trustees of Historic Charleston Foundation hope that these readers will find inspiration to meet the daunting preservation challenges that each of them faces. If Charleston was a testing and proving ground, it became a beacon of success for the nation that has from time to time turned to it for ideas and inspiration. For this audience Weyeneth has written an analytical history that invites readers to watch Charleston's preservation ethic, and its civic commitment to preserving the things that link it with its past, unfold. By drawing attention to competing goals and to the alternatives the city faced as it struggled to mediate pride in the past with the need to provide for the future, Weyeneth invites the residents of historic communities everywhere to consider how they might learn from Charleston.

There is another audience for this study of historic preservation in Charleston. Students, new residents of Charleston, men and women new to the preservation movement, and anyone who has ever wondered what difference historic preservation makes in the life of a community will find here a primer in the benefits—social, cultural, and economic—that flow from caring for and respecting what every community inherits from its past. The past matters in Charleston. Because its citizens place a high value on the connections that buildings and places provide with the past, the city is unlike most other American communities. Here the old and the new reinforce and nurture each other. And it is because of this that Charleston wraps its citizens, and those who visit it, in its history and imparts to them messages about the way cities worked in the past and how they should work today. Charleston's embrace has the ability to excite the imagination and to teach lessons about urban scale and balance and how its public realms—its streets, parks, and shared spaces—weave the city into a community. The preservation of the things that connect Charleston to its past allows citizens to recall the history that binds them to each other. Charleston discovered in its determination to save the past a method to secure its future. How Charleston learned that lesson unfolds in the stories that Joseph McGee and the trustees of Historic Charleston Foundation know well and which they invite everyone interested in putting the past to work for the future to savor.

Carter L. Hudgins
*Executive Director*
Historic Charleston Foundation

# INTRODUCTION

One of the many joys of teaching in the public history program at the University of South Carolina is offering our field school on historic preservation in Charleston. The city boasts a rich and elegant architectural heritage dating to the eighteenth century, and today the built environment of Charleston and its nearby plantation landscapes provide a wonderful laboratory for exploring subjects as varied as African-American material culture, linkages between historic preservation and environmental concerns, and preservation without gentrification. As important as anything for a teacher organizing a field course like this, Charleston presents students with an enormous smorgasbord of preservation projects and expertise on which to feast. The city is probably unique among American communities in being blessed with two local preservation groups: the Preservation Society of Charleston, established in 1920 as the Society for the Preservation of Old Dwellings, and Historic Charleston Foundation, established in 1947. Each has its own distinct origins and history, but today both coexist as vital pillars in the nonprofit heritage community, along with the Charleston Museum, one of the first institutions to experiment with preserving the city's architectural legacy. Local government has also long been an important ingredient in the preservation mix of Charleston, beginning most clearly with passage of a seminal municipal ordinance in 1931 during the term of Mayor Thomas P. Stoney and continuing during the administration of Joseph P. Riley Jr., mayor since the mid 1970s. In addition to taking advantage of this wealth of local experience, our public history field school exposes students to the work of federal agencies such as the National Park Service, which manages several historic sites in the vicinity including Fort Sumter National Monument, and to the work of the country's largest nonprofit preservation organization, the National Trust for Historic Preservation, which maintains its southern regional field office in Charleston and operates nearby Drayton Hall as a historic property. The perspectives of all these organizations and agencies—as well as others—make Charleston a marvelous outdoor classroom for teaching about historic preservation. Each in its own way has a place in this book because all have played significant roles in shaping Charleston's preservation history.

The book, however, is first and foremost a history of just one of the players. *Historic Preservation for a Living City* analyzes Historic Charleston Foundation as a case study within the city's preservation movement. When the foundation approached me about taking on the research project as one way to mark its fiftieth anniversary, I was told I should explore the history as I saw fit, "warts and all." This promise of intellectual license made me comfortable about taking on a work of commissioned history, and as the project went forward, ongoing conversations with the foundation have involved not the "warts" in the historical record but the question of how widely the conceptual and historical nets should be thrown. Who will choose to read this book? How "localized" should the story be? On the spectrum of interpretive possibilities that stretches at one end from a purely in-house organizational history to a broadly conceived citywide preservation history at the other, *Historic Preservation for a Living City* occupies a place somewhere in between that might be characterized as a contextual institutional history. The chapter divisions reflect the emphasis on institutional development, but their content concentrates on the evolving philosophy, policy, and practices of the foundation, seeking to understand these within the perspective of local and national developments as appropriate. While future biographers will want to examine in depth some of the towering figures associated with the history of Historic Charleston Foundation—Albert Simons, Robert N. S. Whitelaw, Samuel G. Stoney, Frances R. Edmunds, among others—this book focuses less on individuals, as colorful as they may be, and more on deeds, ideas, and the "work" of the foundation. Readers will discover that in my effort to facilitate an analytical rather than a descriptive approach to the history of the foundation, I have placed some information—for example the names of trustees, officers, and staff members—in a set of appendixes rather than in the text. The book attempts to avoid two common pitfalls that plague traditional institutional histories: the narrative that substitutes chronology for historical analysis and the overly affectionate "puff piece" that highlights organizational success while minimizing failure. I have sought to write a history that will be as informative for residents of Charleston as it will be useful to interested readers elsewhere, on the assumption that the story of the organization deserves to be widely known.

Within a decade of its founding in 1947 Historic Charleston Foundation had embarked on its Ansonborough project, a pioneering urban renewal and preservation initiative that propelled the young organization into the national spotlight in the 1950s and 1960s. The foundation's innovative use of a revolving fund to rehabilitate an entire neighborhood attracted considerable attention within the American preservation movement at the time, and the reputation and influence of Historic Charleston Foundation have continued to grow in subsequent decades. When the success of the Ansonborough project focused concern on the new issue of gentrification, the foundation responded in the 1970s by exploring ways to use preservation to address problems of urban decay and inner-city housing in Charleston's African-American neighborhoods. These efforts to offer a fresh conceptualization of the role of historic preservation in American cities continue today, and they have kept Historic Charleston Foundation in the forefront of the national preservation movement.

In addition to helping broaden the social concerns of American preservationists, the work of Historic Charleston Foundation has anticipated national trends to develop linkages between historic preservation and the environmental movement. While maintaining its time-tested focus on preservation in downtown Charleston, in the 1970s and 1980s the foundation began to address environmental issues of regional importance. Planning and conservation programs associated with this regional perspective targeted metropolitan sprawl and suburban development, open space, and rural and landscape preservation throughout the South Carolina Lowcountry. In all these ways—experimenting with novel financing strategies such as revolving funds, targeting whole neighborhoods for rehabilitation, and enlarging the social and environmental agendas of the national preservation movement—Historic Charleston Foundation has helped to reorient the field of historic preservation from a purely educational focus on house museums to the current view of preservation as a form of urban and environmental planning concerned generally with the quality of modern life. That story is the subject of this book.

The book is organized into ten chapters that are topical, rather than simply chronological, in their focus. Some of the background history, especially preservation activity in the first half of the twentieth century, will be familiar to many readers as it has received considerable previous attention. More recent decades have not been as extensively analyzed, and my efforts here represent an initial attempt to provide perspective from the vantage point of the late 1990s by discovering patterns and meaning among events that many participants will still remember and which subsequent generations of historians will invariably reinterpret. To set the stage for the establishment of Historic Charleston Foundation, the first chapter discusses the early preservation movement in Charleston. Chapter 2 analyzes the creation of the foundation by the Carolina Art Association in 1947 and the first years of the young nonprofit organization in the early 1950s. The acquisition of the Nathaniel Russell House in 1955 was a milestone in the foundation's history, and the story of the Russell House from the 1950s to the present is the subject of chapter 3. The Ansonborough area rehabilitation project is the focus of chapter 4. The fifth chapter examines some of the far-flung activities of Historic Charleston Foundation in preservation planning from the 1960s through the 1980s that included revising the municipal zoning ordinance, helping develop the citywide historic preservation plan, working toward tourism management, and serving as a preservation advocate in the debate over an annex for the federal courthouse. Chapter 6 is a case study in preservation planning that looks at the controversy in the late 1970s and early 1980s over the building of a downtown hotel and convention center. The seventh chapter surveys the foundation's wide-ranging conservation strategies in the 1970s and 1980s that have included the rescue of unique architectural monuments, the development of an easements program, and innovative initiatives in Charleston's predominately African-American uptown boroughs. In the 1970s and 1980s Historic Charleston Foundation embarked on a number of projects beyond the peninsular city—rescuing Drayton Hall and Snee Farm and addressing development issues associated with the James Island Bridge and the Ashley River Road—and these regional and environmental priorities are the subject of chapter 8. The success of the foundation in undertaking such an ambitious institutional agenda reflected, in part, its ability to fund preservation activities; chapter 9 discusses the history of the tours program, Historic Charleston Reproductions, and other ways in which the foundation has been able to finance preservation in the five decades since 1947. The tenth and final chapter assesses the history of the foundation from the per-spective of the 1990s by analyzing how recent projects—the restoration of the Charleston County Courthouse and the Powder Magazine, the Neighbor-hood Impact Initiative and the building crafts training program, the recovery from Hurricane Hugo, the acquisition of McLeod Plantation and the Aiken-Rhett House, and a commitment to African-American heritage preserva-tion—reflected both continuities with previous work and new directions for the organization. The appendixes contain a time line of significant events in the history of historic preservation in Charleston; lists of the trustees, officers, and staff members of Historic Charleston Foundation since 1947; and a compilation of the protective covenants and conservation easements held by the foundation as of 1997. The bibliography provides suggestions for further reading on Charleston architecture, preservation, and history, as well as a guide to general works on preservation history in the United States.

Most of the research for the book was conducted in the files of Historic Charleston Foundation. Especially useful have been the minutes and reports of the board of trustees, its officers, and its committees; correspondence, scrapbooks, staff and consultant reports; and interviews with former and cur-rent officers and staff members. Also helpful were two general circulation publications: *Historic Charleston,* the quarterly newsletter of the foundation since 1994; and *Charleston,* the newsletter of Historic Charleston Reproduc-tions since 1983. Articles from local newspapers—the *Chronicle,* the *Evening Post,* the *News and Courier,* and the *Post and Courier*—proved indispensable in assessing the role of the foundation in civic affairs. Several additional repos-itories were important to the research. The South Carolina Historical Society has a considerable collection of correspondence related to the origins of His-toric Charleston Foundation and the Carolina Art Association in the papers of Albert Simons. Records on the acquisition and management of Drayton Hall are located on-site. Minutes and correspondence of the Friends of His-toric Snee Farm can be found at the Fort Moultrie headquarters of the Fort Sumter National Monument, which now administers Snee Farm as the Charles Pinckney National Historic Site.

I am indebted to a number of people for their guidance and support with this book. At Historic Charleston Foundation I have had many long and pro-ductive discussions with Dr. Carter L. Hudgins, Joseph H. McGee, and Jonathan H. Poston, and I have benefited from fruitful conversations with Eliza Cleveland, Frances R. Edmunds, Betty T. Guerard, Jane P. Hanahan,

Robert A. Leath, Patti McGee, Cornelia H. Pelzer, J. Thomas Savage, Thomas E. Thornhill, Lawrence A. Walker, Mary Pope Waring, and Dr. and Mrs. G. Fraser Wilson. I appreciate the assistance provided by Beth Bilderback and Robin Copp of the South Caroliniana Library; Charles E. Chase and Debbi Rhoad of the City of Charleston Department of Planning and Urban Development; Mary Giles, Sharon Bennett, and Sarah Foss of the Charleston Museum; Stephen Hoffius and Pat Hash of the South Carolina Historical Society; Dr. George W. McDaniel and Meggett Lavin at Drayton Hall; Dr. Alexander Moore, Catherine Fry, Inge O'Reilly, and Barbara Brannon, of the University of South Carolina Press; John Tucker at Fort Sumter National Monument; and W. Scott Zetrouer of the Gibbes Museum of Art. For the challenging task of locating many of the illustrations, I am grateful to Carroll Ann Bowers and Katherine Saunders of Historic Charleston Foundation and to Jim Wigley of the County of Charleston. The maps that trace the evolution of Charleston's historic districts since 1931 may be among the more important contributions of the book, since this information has not been readily accessible heretofore. The maps were produced by the College of Liberal Arts Computing Laboratory at the University of South Carolina from data generously supplied by the City of Charleston Department of Planning and Urban Development; for this assistance I am indebted to Charles E. Chase, Patricia L. Drews, Teri Norris, and W. Lynn Shirley. My thanks to Dr. William J. Murtagh, who suggested to the foundation that I might be a suitable author for their fiftieth anniversary history. Two graduate students in the public history program here at the University of South Carolina, Natalie Harvey and Bradley Sauls, were extremely helpful research assistants. I am especially grateful to my colleagues in the Department of History for granting me release time from teaching to complete the manuscript. And finally to my wife, Leslie Arnovick, thank you for the gift of love that gave me the support to write the book.

Robert R. Weyeneth
*Columbia, South Carolina*

*Historic Preservation
for a Living City*

# Chapter 1

# ANCESTRAL ARCHITECTURE
*The Early Preservation Movement in Charleston*

To UNDERSTAND THE establishment of Historic Charleston Foundation in 1947 and its evolution over the following five decades, it is useful to examine the historic preservation movement in Charleston prior to the 1940s. As in so many other cities, the first stirrings of the preservation impulse were stimulated by the destruction—or threatened destruction—of landmark buildings, structures closely linked with community history whose presence on the cityscape often fostered a sense of civic identity for residents. Charleston faced loss of landmark buildings a number of times in the first years of the twentieth century, and these threats galvanized heritage groups to action and even inspired the creation of a new organization, the Society for the Preservation of Old Dwellings. But in one revealing way the early preservation movement in Charleston was unlike the experience of any other American city. Charleston was the first city in the country to use the zoning process to encourage historic preservation. Through its zoning ordinance of 1931 municipal officials and preservationists sought to marshal public authority to protect historic architecture. The origins of Historic Charleston Foundation in 1947 were rooted in this vibrant local context that spawned both the private campaigns to rescue landmark buildings and municipal government's pioneering preservation ordinance of 1931.

In the twentieth century Charleston has become synonymous with historic preservation, and the new century had barely begun when, in 1902, the National Society of Colonial Dames in the State of South Carolina purchased a small structure known as the Powder Magazine to save it from demolition. The Powder Magazine had long been viewed as an important link with South Carolina's colonial past, having been built in the early eighteenth century along one of the walls of the fortified city to store gunpowder. Shortly after acquiring the historic structure, the Colonial Dames restored it and used the building as the headquarters for the statewide chapter. Subsequently it was opened to the public as a museum.[1] The Daughters of the American Revolution played a similar early role in preserving the architectural legacy of colonial South Carolina when it acquired the Old Exchange Building, a former customshouse and city hall, erected in the mid eighteenth century. The local Rebecca Motte chapter of the Daughters had worked since 1899 to save this imposing building situated at the foot of Broad Street near the Cooper River waterfront, and their campaign proved successful in 1913 when Congress authorized the transfer of the structure from the federal government to the nonprofit organization. The local chapter set up offices in the Old Exchange, and soon after that it was opened as a museum.[2] Both of these early preservation campaigns in Charleston had focused on public buildings dating to the colonial era, and the Society of Colonial Dames and the Daughters of the American Revolution had sought to rescue the landmarks for their educational potential as museums to teach about history, especially the beginnings of American nationalism.

By the 1920s threats to residential architecture, as well as to public buildings, attracted the attention of Charlestonians worried about the pace of change on the cityscape. Two threats loomed largest: the rise of the gasoline filling station and the dismantling of historic homes for their architectural details. To accommodate the growing number of automobile owners in Charleston, oil companies began constructing filling stations in convenient locations around the city, sometimes razing existing structures to make room for the requisite pumps, repair facilities, and rest rooms. Standard Oil in particular sought to break into the Charleston market, and the company quickly found itself at odds with residents concerned about its construction program. In one of the great paradoxes of American preservation history, during the 1920s the Standard Oil Company became the nemesis of Charleston preservationists at the same time that one of its major stockholders and the son of

*The Powder Magazine (ca. 1713), pictured about 1903*
    Early preservation efforts in Charleston focused on saving landmarks of the colonial period like
    the Powder Magazine, purchased in 1902 by the National Society of Colonial Dames. Under
    a long-term lease with the Colonial Dames, Historic Charleston Foundation restored this early
    eighteenth-century storehouse and reopened it as a museum in 1997. Courtesy, HCF.

its founder, John D. Rockefeller Jr., was embarking on his ambitious restoration of Virginia's colonial capital, Williamsburg.

Out-of-town art collectors represented a different kind of threat to
Charleston's residential architecture. Wealthy individuals wishing to furnish
townhouses and country homes in an early American style as well as museums inspired by the vogue for re-creating their galleries as period rooms
found a ready supply of fine interior paneling and ornate exterior ironwork
in Charleston.[3] For their part, Charlestonians were willing to sell the architectural detailing of their old homes for a variety of reasons: they needed the
money to pay taxes, a building was being demolished anyway, their property
was in a deteriorated area occupied by African-American tenants, and the
prices being offered were simply too tempting to resist.[4] A network of local
antiques dealers sprang up to identify potential sources of paneling, mantels,

and balconies for these individual and institutional collectors. For architect Albert Simons, whose voice became one of the most vociferous raised to protest the export of Charleston's architectural legacy, the antiques dealer even more than the oil company was "the greatest menace to the preservation of old buildings."[5]

The first public campaign in Charleston to rescue a private residence from demolition was waged on behalf of the Joseph Manigault House. The three-story brick mansion was built on Meeting Street about 1803 in a neo-classical style for planter Joseph Manigault by his brother, Gabriel Manigault, who designed a number of important Charleston buildings, including the South Carolina Society Hall, the Orphan House Chapel, and probably the Bank of the United States, which serves today as city hall. By the early twentieth century the Manigault property had passed through a number of hands; the mansion itself had been subdivided into a tenement, and a dry-cleaning firm operated on the grounds.[6] Despite this ragged appearance, the impending demise of the building for a Ford automobile dealership inspired a handful of citizens to organize themselves into what became the city's first historic preservation organization. The new group called itself the Society for the Preservation of Old Dwellings, a name that reflected both its immediate concern (saving the Joseph Manigault House) and a prediction of its future role of preserving residential architecture.[7] Its founder and first president was Susan Pringle Frost—a dynamic and unorthodox real estate agent, suffragist, and feminist—who had already established credentials as a preservationist through some of her earlier real estate transactions.[8]

The Society for the Preservation of Old Dwellings was able to rescue the Joseph Manigault House by purchase in May 1920, but ownership of the property proved burdensome and eventually unsustainable for the fledgling organization. The house had been purchased through a bank loan, with pledges of financial support from the society's founding members, most significantly from Susan Frost's cousin Nell McColl Pringle. Even with energetic fund-raising appeals over the next two years and attempts to locate suitable tenants for the Manigault House, the society was unable to meet expenses. In 1922 Nell Pringle and her husband came to the rescue a second time, assuming a personal debt of some forty thousand dollars. To reduce the size of this financial commitment, the Pringles reluctantly sold the Manigault garden to the Standard Oil Company for a filling station and agreed to rent the house to African-American tenants. Beginning in 1928 they tried, briefly, to open

*Joseph Manigault House (ca. 1803)*

The Joseph Manigault House was the first private residence in Charleston saved through a public campaign, and its rescue was an important initial victory for the city's oldest historic preservation organization, the Society for the Preservation of Old Dwellings, now called the Preservation Society of Charleston. Courtesy, The Charleston Museum.

the house as a museum. But these measures could not stave off fore-closure on the Pringle mortgage. Despite several years of efforts to find a new owner and ongoing concern that the spectacular interiors of the Manigault House would be dismantled and sold, the mansion was put up for sale at auction in 1933. It was rescued—for a third time—when a South Carolinian who owned a plantation in the vicinity of Charleston and was the heiress to a major northeastern grocery store fortune purchased it for three thousand dollars and donated it to the Charleston Museum.[9] Shortly thereafter, in 1937, the Standard Oil Company was persuaded to deed its filling station in the former garden to the museum, effectively reassembling the Manigault property.[10]

The Charleston Museum continues to own the property today and operates it as a house museum, one of several in the city that are furnished and interpreted as the homes of important antebellum Charlestonians. The Joseph Manigault House is unique, though, from one perspective: its place in the history of the local historic preservation movement. It was the first private residence in Charleston saved through a public campaign, and its rescue represented an important first victory for the city's oldest preservation organization, the Society for the Preservation of Old Dwellings.

Even before it accepted the donation of the Manigault House in 1933, the Charleston Museum had been playing a significant role in preserving Charleston's architectural legacy. As concern mounted in the 1920s about the sale and export of woodwork and ironwork from old Charleston houses, the museum became an architectural repository of last resort with the support of its director, Laura M. Bragg.[11] Remnants from buildings scheduled for demolition often came to the museum through the intercession of Albert Simons, who seemed always to be on the watch for new construction projects and imminent demolitions. Simons, a Charlestonian trained at the University of Pennsylvania, had studied in Europe and would become the city's leading preservation architect well into the 1970s. Typically, the young architect would communicate with the property owner, arrange to inspect a site personally, and then compile an inventory of features he considered "worthy of salvaging."[12] Simons had no special stake in building the museum collections as such; rather, the salvage effort was a partial solution to what seemed to him an assault on the civic heritage: "It distresses me painfully to see our fine old building[s] torn down and their contents wrecked or what is more humiliating sold to aliens and shipped away to enrich some other community more appreciative of such things than

*In the garden of the Joseph Manigault House, 1936*
  Following the acquisition of the Joseph Manigault House by the Charleston Museum in the
  1930s, the Standard Oil Company was persuaded to donate the filling station it had operated since the 1920s in the former garden. Pictured here are E. Milby Burton, Dick Lewis,
  and Burnet Maybank. Courtesy, The Charleston Museum.

ourselves."[13] Sometimes the Charleston Museum sought to purchase architectural features from vacant buildings that were falling into decay. In some
instances the museum was successful in these negotiations, and at other times
private collectors were able to offer higher prices. The museum also learned to
be wary of local citizens marketing architectural features from buildings in no
danger whatsoever. As Albert Simons warned, "many of our own people . . . are
only too ready to sell anything provided enough is offered."[14] Such salvage work
on the part of the Charleston Museum was clearly not a substitute for preserving whole buildings in place, but in the context of the 1920s and the thriving
Charleston antiques trade it seemed a reasonable stop-gap measure for a problem that did not entirely recede with the coming of the Depression in the following decade.[15]

    Perhaps the most visible role for the Charleston Museum in the city's nas-
cent preservation movement was its participation in the campaign to save the

Thomas Heyward House. Planter Thomas Heyward, who would become one of the South Carolina signers of the Declaration of Independence, built this brick structure on Church Street as his city residence about 1771. Because President George Washington stayed in the townhouse for a week during a visit to Charleston in 1791, it has become known as the Heyward-Washington House. By the late 1920s the first floor of the mansion was in commercial use as a bakery, and rumors were circulating that art collectors were interested in acquiring the contents of the residence. In response, the Charleston Museum agreed to take an option on the Heyward House in 1928, making use of a generous contribution from Mrs. William Emerson of Boston. Frances W. Emerson had become interested in preserving Charleston architecture as a result of a recent visit to the city with her architect husband, Dr. William Emerson of the Massachusetts Institute of Technology. In following years the Boston couple became important backers of preservation initiatives in Charleston. In 1929 a fund-raising campaign in tandem with the Society for the Preservation of Old Dwellings generated half of the purchase price, and the Charleston Museum exercised its option to buy the mansion. Following a major restoration of portions of the house supervised by the architectural firm headed by Albert Simons and Samuel Lapham Jr., the Heyward-Washington House opened its doors to the public in 1931. It is usually considered Charleston's first historic house museum, despite the earlier, abortive effort by the Pringles to open the Joseph Manigault House as a museum. Even with the income from museum admissions, though, the Heyward House remained a constant financial drain on the Charleston Museum. At one point it was seized for nonpayment of taxes but was rescued again by the generosity of Mrs. Emerson, and in 1933 the state legislature exempted both the Heyward and Manigault Houses from further taxation.[16] The mortgage on the Heyward-Washington House was finally paid off in the early 1950s with the assistance of Historic Charleston Foundation.

In the campaigns to save the Joseph Manigault and Heyward-Washington Houses, preservationists in Charleston came to realize that local resources were usually insufficient for projects that involved the purchase of historic properties and their operation as house museums. Despite the harsh rhetoric about the culpability of northern museums, winter tourists, and other wealthy aliens vandalizing Charleston's architectural patrimony, the reality was that out-of-town money was crucial for saving the city's old buildings. And of course it was also true that Charlestonians themselves shared some responsibility for the

*Heyward-Washington House (ca. 1771) with bakery*
By the late 1920s the home of Thomas Heyward, one of the South Carolina signers of the Declaration of Independence, was in commercial use as a bakery, and rumors were circulating that art collectors were eyeing the interior architectural details. With support from the Society for the Preservation of Old Dwellings and Mrs. William Emerson of Boston, the Charleston Museum purchased the property and opened it in 1931 as the city's first historic house museum. Historic Charleston Foundation helped pay off the outstanding mortgage in 1953. Courtesy, The Charleston Museum.

export trade in which many seemed to participate willingly. In a pattern that would come to characterize the history of preservation efforts in twentieth-century Charleston, local preservationists sought out northern capital time and again to rescue historic buildings. In part, the need to seek funds elsewhere reflected demographic and economic shifts in the nineteenth and twentieth centuries that had bypassed Charleston and located centers of growth and prosperity in other regions of the United States. But the reliance on such bene-factors also reflected the fact that many Americans, not just South Carolinians or southerners, could attach significance to the uniqueness and beauty of the city's architectural heritage.

It was to this potential national audience that local preservationists tried to turn when they approached the American Institute of Architects (AIA) in 1930. The AIA had previously commissioned and published a work on the city's historic architecture by Albert Simons and Samuel Lapham Jr. entitled *Charleston, South Carolina* (1927). At the suggestion of Mrs. William Emerson, and with her considerable financial backing, the AIA consented to establish an ad hoc committee to publicize the necessity of preserving Charleston's historic architecture. This blue ribbon committee was composed of both nationally prominent figures in the world of fine arts, whose responsibilities included spreading the word about the threats facing Charleston, and knowledgeable local citizens, whose own efforts over the next couple of years emphasized the ongoing work on behalf of the Heyward-Washington and Joseph Manigault Houses, attempts to discourage Standard Oil from constructing filling stations in historic areas, and the promotion of municipal planning and zoning.[17] In a nod to the situation in Charleston, in 1932 the American Institute of Architects went on record urging museums to avoid the practice of incorporating historic interiors into exhibits, except for those from buildings legitimately on the verge of demolition.[18]

The triumphs and tribulations of the struggle to save the Manigault and Heyward residences during the 1920s and 1930s have become familiar benchmarks in the history of the city's early preservation movement, even as they illustrated the pitfalls of the "museum solution" to historic preservation. There had been prior preservation campaigns in Charleston by the Society of Colonial Dames and the Daughters of the American Revolution, of course, and their efforts had targeted civic rather than residential architecture.[19] But their understanding of historic preservation resembled that of the Society for the Preservation of Old Dwellings and the Charleston Museum: preservation was an educational enterprise carried out with the ultimate goal of establishing museums for the teaching of history. However, saving buildings through purchase and conversion into museums was an enormously expensive undertaking, as the Manigault and Heyward campaigns vividly demonstrated. Use of this strategy could only rescue a handful of the most important landmarks in a community, unless of course one had the resources of a Rockefeller and the drive to create a restored museum village on the scale of Colonial Williamsburg in Virginia.

As crusades to rally public support on behalf of landmark buildings went forward, some Charlestonians had already been exploring other ways to preserve the city's architectural legacy: through keeping historic buildings in use as living and working spaces. As early as the 1910s real estate agent Susan Pringle Frost, who would go on to found the Society for the Preservation of Old Dwellings in 1920, had begun her own efforts to buy, stabilize, and resell modest homes among the slums of St. Michael's Alley and eastern Tradd Street, with an eye to encouraging rehabilitation in the area as a whole. Although by the 1920s and 1930s she was chronically overextended financially, Frost continued to buy and hold properties, restoring them to a livable condition when necessary and often trying to beautify them by adding balconies, gates, and mantels. Her imaginative remodeling efforts took full advantage of the supply of doorways, wrought iron balconies, and other architectural remnants that she had salvaged over the years. Susan Frost's campaign of targeting a succession of houses in a single neighborhood anticipated the modern "area" approach to preservation, which became a potent strategy when linked to the financial mechanism of a revolving fund by Historic Charleston Foundation in the 1950s and 1960s. Her purchases and renovations continued in subsequent decades on Tradd Street, Bedon's Alley, and East Bay Street, almost up to her death in 1960. Dorothy Haskell Porcher Legge was another preservation pioneer who worked privately and effectively to inspire the revitalization of a block of deteriorated eighteenth-century mercantile structures on East Bay Street, beginning with the purchase and restoration of her own residence at number 99–101 in 1931. Her notion of a nonhistorical pastel color scheme for the exteriors subsequently inspired the name Rainbow Row for the picturesque collection of buildings restored in the 1930s, 1940s, and 1950s. In 1936 Mr. and Mrs. Reynolds Brown rehabilitated a kitchen building and courtyard on Church Street at Cabbage Row into a landscaped winter residence for themselves, inaugurating a trend to renovate former outbuildings into substantial private residences.[20] By the end of the decade Frederick Law Olmsted Jr., a keen observer of the American urban scene, was struck by the scale and pace of these private efforts. He was impressed by "the rehabilitation and refurbishing of a considerable number of fine old dwellings and the adaptation of other interesting old structures and their surviving accessories to new uses," developments that seemed to offer "a strong and very encouraging counter-current" to the forces of deterioration and intrusion that were transforming twentieth-century Charleston.[21]

Public agencies were sometimes able to follow the example set by the private sector in adapting historic structures to fresh contemporary uses. With

*Planter's Hotel/Dock Street Theatre, pictured about 1900*
   With federal funds available through the New Deal, the city undertook a significant adap-
   tive-use project at the nineteenth-century Planter's Hotel in the 1930s. The eighteenth-century theater that had once occupied the site was reconstructed within the hotel. The theater
   opened under the management of the Carolina Art Association, and it provided early office
   space for Historic Charleston Foundation. Courtesy, The Charleston Museum.

federal funds available through the New Deal in the 1930s, municipal officials undertook two significant "adaptive use" projects: Dock Street Theatre
and the Robert Mills Manor public housing project. Throughout the 1920s
and 1930s preservationists had worried about the fate of the nineteenth-century Planter's Hotel, but not until Mayor Burnet Rhett Maybank was able to
arrange funding through the federal Works Progress Administration was it
possible to implement a novel idea for the old hotel: reconstruction of the
eighteenth-century theater that had once occupied the site. Between 1935
and 1937, under the supervision of Albert Simons, the interior was fitted
with a period-style theater, using woodwork from the Thomas Radcliffe-
Mitchell King House, which was demolished by the College of Charleston in
1938.[22] Equally innovative was the effort to preserve and integrate historic
buildings into the plan for a public housing complex also erected with New
Deal assistance. The architectural firm of Simons and Lapham, working with

architect Douglas Ellington and landscape architect Loutrel W. Briggs, constructed thirty-four multiunit brick homes in 1939–41 adjacent to several existing historic structures: two antebellum residences on Beaufain Street, the former city jail, and the so-called Marine Hospital built for ailing merchant seamen. The modern housing project was named for Robert Mills, the early federal architect who had added a wing to the city jail in the 1820s and designed the Marine Hospital in the 1830s. Today the Marine Hospital provides offices for the city's housing authority.[23]

Without doubt, the most significant governmental action taken to promote historic preservation in the 1920s and 1930s was the adoption in 1931 of the zoning ordinance, which had an innovative provision to encourage "the preservation and protection of historic places and areas of historic interest."[24] This ordinance was the culmination of seven years of municipal attempts to think systematically about the causes and consequences of urban change in Charleston. Typically, Susan Pringle Frost had been one of the first citizens to wonder how the authority of local government might be used to preserve the city's architectural heritage. In the mid 1920s she had approached Mayor Thomas P. Stoney about drafting a municipal ordinance to prohibit the removal of old ironwork and woodwork from Charleston. But the city attorney could find no legal basis for restricting the rights of private property owners in this way, and nothing came of Frost's proposal. Zoning, on the other hand, seemed to hold out a number of possibilities, particularly since the state legislature had recently authorized municipal governments to enact zoning ordinances if they wished.[25]

It was at the initiative of the Chamber of Commerce in December 1924 that City Council was first urged to implement planning and zoning for Charleston. Both the chamber and City Council studied the issue for several years until April 1929, when a temporary City Planning and Zoning Commission was established. The commission proceeded in fits and starts, unsure how to meet its dual responsibilities for devising a zoning ordinance and evaluating requests for new commercial construction in the historic city, such as the petitions from the Standard Oil Company to build filling stations. The mandate was clarified in October 1929 when City Council established a Special Committee on Zoning, separate from the interim City Planning and Zoning Commission, to draft a proposed ordinance. The Special Committee, under the chairmanship of Alston Deas, who had recently succeeded to the presidency of the Society for the Preservation of Old Dwellings, was able to cobble together a temporary ordinance that prohibited filling stations, automobile repair shops, and factories in a portion of the city south of Broad Street.[26] The committee also recommended professional assistance to prepare a fully adequate ordinance. In October 1930 City Council abolished the interim zoning commission, reconstituted it with new legal authority, and named as the new commissioners the former members of the Special Committee. At the same time the council agreed to seek professional planning assistance from the Morris Knowles firm of Pittsburgh, Pennsylvania.[27]

Staff members of Morris Knowles were dispatched to Charleston in 1930–31, charged with developing both a comprehensive zoning ordinance and recommendations for a city planning document. The consulting firm eventually suggested a set of use and height districts, as well as a "historic district." To formulate ideas for the latter, the Morris Knowles engineers worked with knowledgeable citizens such as Albert Simons to survey and map the location of buildings constructed before the mid nineteenth century. Simons and the planners assumed that these colonial, federal, and antebellum structures were "practically all that is of historic and architectural interest."[28] One of the Morris Knowles reports, presented to the City Planning and Zoning Commission in July 1931, offered predictions about population trends and assessments of where new schools, parks, playgrounds, and transportation routes should be constructed to accommodate orderly growth consistent with "the purposes of the Zoning Ordinance and the City Plan."[29] Special attention was devoted to the future racial distribution of the population and how civic improvements, such as schools and parks, might be used to maintain or direct patterns of residential segregation. "In the South, where separate schools are established for white and negro children," the report observed, the careful placement of public buildings and playgrounds can operate as "an effective influence for the desirable development of the surrounding territory."[30] In spite of its disturbing deference to contemporary racial attitudes, the Morris Knowles report represented one of the earliest attempts in Charleston to consider long-term urban growth from a proactive planning perspective.

Charleston did not adopt a full-scale city plan as a result of the recommendations, but City Council formally ratified a general zoning ordinance in October 1931 that included a small but significant section on historic preservation. While many American cities had been experimenting with both city planning and zoning for some time by the 1930s, Charleston's zoning ordi-

The "Old and Historic Charleston District," established in 1931.

*Gas station, 108 Meeting Street*
    Public outrage about the demolition of three residences on Meeting Street near Chalmers Street by the Standard Oil Company helped Mayor Thomas P. Stoney gain approval for the zoning ordinance of 1931. Standard Oil tried to bolster its public image by employing Albert Simons to design a "colonial revival" filling station with salvaged architectural details. It is shown here in the 1970s. Courtesy, HCF.

nance was novel for its provisions that sought to protect historic architecture. Article X of the ordinance designated a portion of the city as the Old and Historic Charleston District and established a Board of Architectural Review (BAR) with authority over certain types of architectural changes to all buildings in this district. As originally constituted, the BAR was to consist of five members drawn from organizations that offered useful institutional expertise for the new municipal body: the City Planning and Zoning Commission, the local chapters of the American Institute of Architects and the American Society of Civil Engineers, the Charleston Real Estate Exchange, and the Carolina Art Association, a long-established fine arts society that managed the local art gallery. Part-time staff support was provided by the city engineer.[31]

*Frances R. Edmunds Center for Historic Preservation*

Historic Charleston Foundation acquired the gas station at Meeting and Chalmers Streets in the 1980s and converted it to the Frances R. Edmunds Center for Historic Preservation. Courtesy, HCF.

Under the zoning ordinance the Board of Architectural Review had potentially significant regulatory authority over changes to exterior features of buildings in the Old and Historic Charleston District that were "subject to public view from a public street or way."[32] In practice, though, the BAR sought to play an "advisory rather than disciplinary" role, in order to gain acceptance for itself and its mandate.[33] Instead of seeking to impose rulings on citizens sensitive about the rights of private property owners and thereby inciting hard feelings and possibly court challenges to its authority, the BAR operated like "a free Architectural Clinic," dispensing sketches of appropriate alterations and tips on paint colors, for example.[34] While its statutory authority was fairly broad, at least by the standards of the time, the geographical extent of its jurisdiction was actually rather limited, compared with the size of Charleston's historic districts today. The Old and Historic Charleston District established in 1931 consisted of a small portion at the tip of the peninsula, generally south of Broad Street and roughly bounded by East Bay Street, South Battery, and Lenwood and Logan Streets on the west.[35] What was significant about the ordinance was not the size of the historic district but that Charleston sought to target a whole neighborhood, not just individual buildings. This area approach to protection of historic architecture would come to define the modern preservation movement.

From the vantage point of the 1931 ordinance, it is instructive to look back over the preservation concerns of the previous decade in Charleston. Despite all the clamor in the 1920s about the exodus of Charleston paneling and mantels, the 1931 ordinance did not give the Board of Architectural Review any jurisdiction over interior details of a building. The BAR had jurisdiction only over exterior features—if they were visible from a public right-of-way and, of course, if the building was located in the Old and Historic Charleston District. While the Heyward-Washington House was within these boundaries, the Joseph Manigault residence was well outside, and consequently the 1931 ordinance offered the Manigault House no protection in the perilous years prior to its donation to the Charleston Museum. One of the most contentious preservation issues of the 1920s had been the razing of historic structures for the construction of filling stations. Public outrage about the demolition by the Standard Oil Company of three residences on Meeting Street near Chalmers Street had helped Mayor Thomas P. Stoney gain approval for the zoning ordinance.[36] Nevertheless, even after 1931 property owners remained free to raze historic buildings anywhere in the city, including those located within the Old and Historic Charleston District. Not until 1959 did the Board of Architectural Review gain the power to delay demolitions, and not until 1966 did it have authority to prohibit demolitions.[37] As novel as the zoning ordinance was for its inclusion of a section on historic preservation and its focus on an entire neighborhood, it did not fully address the threats that had emerged previously in Charleston.

One measure of the genuine success of Charleston's pathbreaking approach to historic preservation in the 1930s was that so many other cities chose to follow its example in subsequent years. The list included cities as far-flung as New Orleans, Louisiana (1937); Alexandria, Virginia (1946); Winston-Salem, North Carolina (1948); Santa Barbara, California (1949); Georgetown, Washington, D.C. (1950); Natchez, Mississippi (1951); Annapolis, Maryland (1952); Saint Augustine, Florida (1953); Santa Fe, New Mexico (1953); Tombstone, Arizona (1954); and Boston, Massachusetts (1955). By one estimate, by the 1970s more than two hundred American cities had enacted municipal ordinances to preserve historically or architecturally significant private property. Many of these borrowed heavily from the wording of Charleston's original statute, and some even called their efforts "Charleston ordinances." By the 1990s the number of historic preservation ordinances in the United States was estimated at over eighteen hundred.[38]

One question that might be posed is Why Charleston? Why did Charleston produce this pioneering zoning ordinance, as well as the flurry of campaigns on behalf of landmark buildings? Three reasons come to mind: the city's unique architectural environment, the web of family linkages associated with this historic architecture, and the romanticization of the local scene through the Charleston Renaissance. All of these help to explain the origins and vitality of the early preservation movement.

Paradoxically, the urban environment inherited by twentieth-century Charleston reflected both the city's historic wealth and its historic poverty. The slave-based economy of plantation agriculture had made the port one of the wealthiest cities in the English colonies before the American Revolution, and its affluence continued into the first decades of the nineteenth century. The style and construction of Charleston's early buildings reflected the material success of this planter and merchant aristocracy.[39] The poverty that descended on the city following the Civil War persisted well into the twentieth century and had the unintended effect of preserving much of this distinctive cityscape. Because progress and prosperity largely bypassed the city for an extended period of time, Charlestonians did not have the resources to follow the lead of Americans elsewhere who were rushing to replace the old with the new as quickly as possible. It was not until the 1920s that the intrusions of the automobile and the influx of wealthy visitors seemed to pose significant threats to the architectural inheritance.[40]

When early activists took up the preservation banner in response to the pace of urban change, it was often in the hope of protecting places with strong ancestral associations. In a small and parochial community like Charleston in the first decades of the twentieth century, preservation of local heritage was frequently inseparable from preservation of family history. Many early preservationists had a personal identification with the old buildings they wanted to save, and in this way preservation could be a form of celebrating family lineage. The author of an essay about the restoration of the Joseph Manigault House, for example, was described as "one of Charleston's most active and enthusiastic preservationists" by virtue of her "inheritance, interest, and experience."[41] The collective memory of civic conservators inspired their efforts just as it informed their ideas of what constituted meaningful history.[42]

Appreciation of the city's distinctive architecture and history was also fostered by a cultural reawakening in the 1920s and 1930s that has come to be called the Charleston Renaissance. Like regional artistic and literary revivals elsewhere, it drew primary inspiration from the local scene. The books and paintings of Alice Ravenel Huger Smith celebrated the beauty of the historic city and the surrounding Lowcountry, as did the etchings and drawings of Elizabeth O'Neill Verner, whose work often emphasized the aesthetic contributions of vernacular buildings, portraying poverty and dilapidation as picturesque. Alfred Hutty's prints were inspired by the city's grand architectural monuments, scenes of African-American street life, and rural vistas that evoked the Old South. In the opening passage of his novel *Porgy*, a story about the lives of African Americans on the fictional "Catfish Row," DuBose Heyward characterized Charleston as "an ancient, beautiful city that time had forgotten before it destroyed."[43] Artists and writers alike discovered a sentimental charm in the crumbling structures of the old city, and they created images that promoted a powerful, nostalgic aesthetic. The sense of place articulated by the Charleston Renaissance helped to fuel early preservationist sentiment in general and even to motivate several individuals to become active and committed preservationists.[44]

*The Bottle Man*

*Elizabeth O'Neill Verner*

*Elizabeth O'Neill Verner, "The Bottle Man"*

Appreciation of the city's architecture and history was fostered by a cultural awakening in the 1920s and 1930s known as the Charleston Renaissance. Elizabeth O'Neill Verner was among those who found artistic inspiration in the local scene, often emphasizing the aesthetic contributions of vernacular buildings and portraying scenes of poverty and dilapidation as picturesque. Courtesy, The Charleston Museum.

It was against this backdrop of preservation in the 1920s and 1930s that Historic Charleston Foundation emerged in the 1940s. Although the foundation was a completely new organization, a number of the people who served as its trustees in the 1940s, 1950s, 1960s, and even into the 1970s had been deeply involved in efforts to preserve Charleston in the 1920s and 1930s. These men and women had participated in the implementation of the original zoning ordinance, provided leadership for the Charleston Museum and the Society for the Preservation of Old Dwellings in their initial preservation campaigns, and been associated with the Charleston Renaissance.[45] While fresh faces would join these experienced hands to establish Historic Charleston Foundation in 1947, the institutional agenda of the new organization reflected the legacy of the first generation of Charleston preservationists. In the decades following its creation the foundation would build upon this early record of success through efforts to refine the operation of the zoning ordinance, experiment with an area approach to preservation, capitalize on the vitality of the private sector, and address ongoing issues of planning and development. In time Historic Charleston Foundation would also seek to broaden the meaning of historic preservation beyond a reverence for ancestral architecture to a concern for the urban welfare of diverse groups of citizens.

Chapter 2

# The Founding and First Years of Historic Charleston Foundation

THE DECISION TO incorporate Historic Charleston Foundation reflected a novel departure into urban planning on the part of the venerable Carolina Art Association, an organization with roots in antebellum Charleston that had been chiefly preoccupied with the appreciation of the fine arts. By the 1930s and 1940s the Carolina Art Association had begun to turn its attention to issues of civic development. It became increasingly interested in promoting historic preservation and community planning, and the creation of Historic Charleston Foundation in 1947 was the culmination of these efforts.

The Carolina Art Association had led an episodic existence prior to its rejuvenation in the 1930s. Over the course of the nineteenth century its fortunes had ebbed and flowed as it resurrected itself from time to time to mount a public exhibition or offer art instruction in the city schools. It assumed responsibility for the management of the new Gibbes Memorial Art Gallery shortly after its construction in 1905 through a private bequest. The association established an office at the Gibbes and began efforts to acquire a small art collection. Professional guidance came to the Carolina Art Association in 1932 when Robert N. S. Whitelaw was hired as its first full-time director. Whitelaw developed a collections policy that emphasized the work of talented local artists, arranged to show traveling exhibits at the Gibbes, and secured grants and public appropriations to employ a small staff. Robert

Newton Spry Whitelaw was a Charlestonian who had served as the curator of art at the Charleston Museum in the late 1920s; as director of the Carolina Art Association through the 1930s and 1940s he would become the driving force behind the creation of Historic Charleston Foundation.[1]

The energetic Whitelaw was responsible for expanding the educational mission of the association to encompass not just the operation of an art gallery but a concerted campaign to preserve Charleston's unique beauty and surrounding landscape. During Whitelaw's tenure the Carolina Art Association inaugurated a publications program with *Plantations of the Carolina Low Country* (1938), edited by architects Albert Simons and Samuel Lapham Jr. with text by historian Samuel Gaillard Stoney. In time Whitelaw's attention moved beyond the purely aesthetic to focus on planning issues of broad municipal concern. Through what was eventually called the Civic Services Committee of the Carolina Art Association, Whitelaw sponsored studies of community growth, implemented a survey of the city's historic architecture, and proposed a downtown traffic plan. To educate citizens about these issues, he organized a museum exhibit and a series of public lectures on contemporary urban problems at Dock Street Theatre, which the association had begun managing after its reconstruction in 1937 with federal funds from the Works Progress Administration. Historic Charleston Foundation would grow directly out of the urban agenda that Whitelaw established for the Carolina Art Association in the 1930s and 1940s.

By the late 1930s Whitelaw, Albert Simons, and other prominent citizens had become convinced that Charleston's pioneering preservation ordinance of 1931 was inadequate by itself for safeguarding the city's architectural heritage. In their opinion, the dilemma was an absence of municipal planning to respond to the consequences of haphazard urban growth, evidenced by the poor quality and incompatibility of new construction and the press of automobile traffic on the narrow streets of the historic city. "In setting up a zoning ordinance, the community took but one step in the direction of orderly development, but has never advanced to its logical corollary, a comprehensive city plan, nor to the third step, a county or regional plan," Simons argued in 1939.[2] Whitelaw began organizing a small committee of sympathetic and influential citizens to lay the groundwork for a "non-political" city plan, to be developed without the formal participation of municipal government and outside the glare of the public spotlight.[3] The committee members, most of whom would eventually provide the early leadership of Historic Charleston Foundation, included E. Milby Burton, director of the Charleston Museum; John Mead Howells, the New York architect active in the restoration of Portsmouth, New Hampshire, who wintered in a Charleston house he had restored; James O'Hear, a businessman and member of the first permanent City Planning and Zoning Commission; Homer M. Pace, a utility company executive; Sidney J. Rittenberg, an attorney and member of City Council; Albert Simons, architect and member of the city's Board of Architectural Review; Alice Ravenel Huger Smith, an artist and author; Samuel Gaillard Stoney, the historian who had written the text for *Plantations of the Carolina Low Country,* recently published by the Carolina Art Association; and Whitelaw.[4]

The first step for this ad hoc committee was to engage the professional services of Frederick Law Olmsted Jr. Olmsted was the son of the noted nineteenth-century landscape architect and planner, and he was carrying on his father's distinguished Boston practice. In inquiring about Olmsted's availability in December 1939, Whitelaw emphasized that Charleston did not seek to be Williamsburg and that the Carolina Art Association was not interested "in preserving Charleston as a museum piece."[5] Instead, Whitelaw asked Olmsted to assess the pressures of modern growth and articulate possible planning remedies, stressing that the ad hoc committee wished to proceed quietly, even "secretly," to lay the groundwork for developing a city plan.[6] With financial assistance from the Carnegie Corporation, Whitelaw arranged for Olmsted to make a visit of several days to Charleston in January 1940, and the planner delivered his report to Whitelaw and the committee in February and March.[7]

Rather than crafting a formal city plan, Olmsted offered a set of recommendations for potential adoption by government agencies, as well as suggestions that the Carolina Art Association could implement on its own. Olmsted seemed genuinely affected by the picturesque charm of Charleston and impressed by the nascent interest in rehabilitation of historic houses by Charlestonians and by the increasing number of winter residents in the southern city.[8] He fully understood that Charleston was a living city, not a collection of museums, and that his solutions needed to blend old and new as *"functioning integral parts* of a live and ever-changing contemporary community with its face to the future."[9] His report focused on the twin issues of planning community growth and preserving aesthetic and historical values.

Olmsted's major planning recommendation for local government addressed the problem of traffic with two solutions: highways and off-street parking. He urged an east-west truck route that would permit commercial vehicles to move quickly across the city between the bridges over the Ashley and Cooper Rivers. While the partially elevated Crosstown Expressway built in the 1960s had its origins in this suggestion of 1940, Olmsted's original proposal envisioned the conversion of two surface-level streets, such as Spring and Cannon, to one-way roadways. The idea was to speed trucks on their way, keeping them off other streets and relieving the press of traffic elsewhere. On the problem of parking, one traditional remedy had been to widen streets, which often destroyed historic structures. Olmsted urged that streets be used to move traffic, rather than store vehicles, and consequently he advocated the construction of parking lots. As to their attractiveness, they could be walled and bordered by trees to resemble "some of the old gardens," he predicted optimistically.[10]

Olmsted seemed particularly anxious to make Charleston an enjoyable experience for tourists arriving by automobile, and toward this end he recommended that municipal government develop "main routes of pleasure travel in the city."[11] He suggested the construction of efficient north- and southbound roads connecting the Cooper River Bridge directly with the scenic vistas of the Battery. He urged that these drives be located so as to avoid the "unattractive negro sections" that greeted motorists as they approached the city.[12] In turn these roads would be joined to a similar connection with the Ashley River Bridge along the city's west side. The thoroughfares would relieve traffic congestion on Meeting Street, Olmsted promised, and create a round-the-city sight-seeing loop. Olmsted was unmoved by committee members who pointed out that his proposal to cut some of these north-south roadways through existing blocks would destroy picturesque alleys that helped give Charleston its charm.[13]

Although the idea of ramming a tourist corridor through Charleston's tangle of picturesque alleys was never implemented, several of Olmsted's suggestions proved seminal for the Carolina Art Association and its eventual decision to create Historic Charleston Foundation. Realizing that the costs of maintaining historic properties were frequently a reason for their neglect or sale and that lack of architectural knowledge often led to inappropriate alterations, Olmsted recommended establishment of a "permanent agency" to serve as a "central information service" for financial and technical assistance to home owners and investors wishing to undertake historically sensitive rehabilitation work.[14] One mechanism suggested for financing such private rehabilitation was "a long-term revolving fund."[15] As originally proposed, property owners might borrow from this fund at low rates of interest in order

| IDENTIFICATION | ZONE | | | NEIGHBORHOOD | |
|---|---|---|---|---|---|
| Serial No. I A2 1Y | A or K Residence | ☒ | | Favorable | ☒ |
| Borough o ʷft | Commercial | ☐ | | Mediocre | ☐ |
| Street No. | Light Industrial | ☐ | | Adverse | ☐ |
| 27 Kïng St. | Heavy Industrial | ☐ | | Inharmonious | |
| | | | | intrusions | ☒ |
| | Dwelling ☒ | Garden | ☒ | Scenic | ☒ |
| SUBJECT | Church ☐ | Cemetery | ☐ | Isolated | ☐ |
| CLASSIFICATION | Public Bldg. ☐ | Square | ☐ | Extensive | ☐ |
| | Accessory Bldg. ☒ | Park | ☐ | | |
| | Single ☒ | Dwelling | ☒ | Philanthropic ☐ | |
| OCCUPANCY | Multiple ☐ | Abandoned | ☐ | Educational ☐ | |
| | Religious ☐ | Commercial | ☐ | Industrial ☐ | |
| | Historical | | ☒ | Characteristic Type ☐ | Walls ☒ |
| SOURCE OF | Architectural | | ☒ | Spacious Garden ☐ | Fences ☐ |
| INTEREST | Picturesque | | ☒ | Surviving Type Garden ☒ | Piazza ☐ |
| | Construction | | ☒ | Small Garden ☐ | Gates ☒ |
| | Materials b-ick | | ☐ | Ironwork ☒ | Roof ₀lᴀ⅃e ☒ |
| | Interiors | | ☒ | Doorway ☒ | |
| | Trees or Plants of Special Interest ☒ | | | aoᴄᴄᴇ bldqs | |
| | Pre-Revolutionary aₚ 1765 ☒ | | | QUALITY | Mention ☐ |
| PERIOD | Post Revolutionary ☐ | | | RATING | Notable ☐ |
| CLASSIFICATION | Ante Bellum ☐ | | | | Valuable ☐ |
| | Modern ☐ | | | | Valuable to City ☐ |
| | | | | | Nationally Important ☐ |

*Survey card from the architectural survey of 1941*

> Heeding the advice of Frederick Law Olmsted Jr., the Carolina Art Association undertook a survey of Charleston architecture during 1941 with funding from the Carnegie Corporation. Helen Gardner McCormack recorded information on 1,380 historic properties. The project represented one of the first historic surveys in a major American city and one of the earliest architectural inventories to be used in urban planning. Courtesy, Gibbes Museum of Art/Carolina Art Association.

to "reclaim an old house in an appropriate manner," under the supervision of the Carolina Art Association. Proponents expressed hope that this "reconditioning" of older homes would happen all over Charleston, not just in the fashionable areas south of Broad Street.[16] The idea, first suggested by members of the ad hoc committee and subsequently ratified by Olmsted, evolved into the revolving fund for area rehabilitation successfully implemented by Historic Charleston Foundation in its Ansonborough project in the late 1950s and 1960s.[17] One can also find in Olmsted's report the suggestion of using easements to encourage historic preservation. To address the problem of new construction consuming precious open space, Olmsted recommended that the Carolina Art Association agree to accept easements to encourage owners to retain the historic appearance of property.[18]

As a landscape architect, Olmsted voiced special concern about the loss of Charleston gardens for subdivision into building lots, and he thought both easements and tax relief offered possible incentives to preserve open space.

While he was generally skeptical about the constitutionality of the city's authority to police property owners under the zoning ordinance—he urged the Board of Architectural Review to use tactful persuasion rather than compulsion in order to forestall a court challenge—Olmsted thought the board had the potential to be quite effective in preserving the disappearing garden spaces.[19] But for the municipal body to consider where new construction should be permitted (and for it to be convincing with property owners), access to reliable information about the urban geography was needed. Here Olmsted urged the ad hoc committee to "analyze Charleston street by street, house by house, and find out where houses can be put in so we can see where the houses should be saved."[20]

This latter recommendation for a study of Charleston architecture was taken to heart in fairly short order by the Carolina Art Association, and this architectural inventory, along with the creation of Historic Charleston Foundation in 1947, remain the two lasting legacies of Olmsted's work for the association in 1940. Today the process of surveying historic properties and compiling an inventory are considered basic to comprehensive preservation planning, but Olmsted's suggestion was a novelty in 1940. "What in the world do they want an architectural survey of Charleston for?" one New York architect wanted to know. "I thought it was the most photographed, measured and surveyed ten square miles in the world!"[21] To be sure, the historic city had been long admired and extensively depicted on both canvas and film. What Olmsted proposed was a systematic study by experts who would offer comparative judgments about the significance of buildings, open spaces, and street vistas. While some portions of Charleston had been previously surveyed by a few enterprising citizens over the years, no comprehensive inventory of the entire city existed that would permit the evaluations and hierarchical classification scheme that Olmsted envisioned. Ultimately, the citywide list of rated properties was to be used to make decisions about how to plan and what to preserve.[22]

Preparations to implement the survey began in February 1940 shortly after Olmsted's visit, but the actual field work took place during 1941. Again, Robert Whitelaw was able to arrange funding from the Carnegie Corporation for the ad hoc committee's work, this time to employ a temporary staff member for the project. A Charlestonian, Helen Gardner McCormack, who was then the director of the Valentine Museum in Richmond, Virginia, was hired to undertake the survey beginning in January 1941. Over the course of the year McCormack recorded information on a set of custom-made cards for

THIS IS
# CHARLESTON

A SURVEY OF THE ARCHITECTURAL HERITAGE OF
A UNIQUE AMERICAN CITY UNDERTAKEN BY THE
CHARLESTON CIVIC SERVICES COMMITTEE

*Text by*
SAMUEL GAILLARD STONEY
*Revised from the Reports to
the Committee*

PUBLISHED BY THE CAROLINA ART ASSOCIATION
CHARLESTON, SOUTH CAROLINA
FOR THE CHARLESTON CIVIC SERVICES COMMITTEE
1944

*Title page for* This Is Charleston
The Carolina Art Association made public the findings of its architectural survey through an exhibit it organized at the Gibbes Art Gallery in 1942. Interest in the museum exhibit, titled "This Is Charleston," prompted the Carolina Art Association to publish a permanent record in the form of a guidebook with the identical title in 1944. For thirty years this catalog was the definitive touchstone for evaluating the architectural merits of Charleston buildings. Courtesy, Gibbes Museum of Art/Carolina Art Association.

1,380 historic properties that included residences, churches, civic buildings, commercial and industrial structures, gardens, parks and cemeteries, and scenic vistas. Significantly, McCormack also made an effort to survey neighborhoods beyond the Old and Historic Charleston District established by the zoning ordinance in 1931. Over 60 percent of the inventoried buildings were located in boroughs north of Broad Street. In addition to at least one photograph of the property, the cards contained a summary of its current condition and use, its history, and a short bibliography. The cards were then reviewed by Albert Simons, Alice R. Huger Smith, and Samuel G. Stoney, who ascribed the period and style, as appropriate, and its "source of interest," with John Mead Howells making final determinations where consensus was not possible. Only the buildings in the survey, some 1,168, were then rated and placed in one of five categories, based on evaluations of their architectural and aesthetic significance.[23] In sum, the inventory classified 26 buildings as "nationally important," 113 as "valuable to the city," 169 as "valuable," 317 as "notable," and 543 as "worthy of mention."[24] This project in 1940–41 represented one of the first historic surveys undertaken in a major American city and one of the earliest architectural inventories to be used as an urban planning tool.

The findings of the survey were made public by the Carolina Art Association through an exhibit it organized at the Gibbes Art Gallery in the spring of 1942. Entitled "This Is Charleston," the exhibition consisted of a set of thirty-four panels that offered an analysis of the city and its problems (many of which had been exacerbated by wartime preparations), stressing issues of housing, traffic, public health, recreation, and the physical appearance of the urban environment. The statistics, maps, and photographs generated by the newly completed survey emphasized the importance of the city's architectural heritage and recognized the past accomplishments of private groups and public agencies in preserving Charleston. The exhibit concluded with a mirror mounted on the wall and the question Who is responsible for Charleston's future? A series of proposals followed on the need for sound planning to take full advantage of the city's aesthetic legacy, economic base, and labor supply.[25] Through the exhibition, the Carolina Art Association sought to publicize the civic work it had been doing quietly over the last several years and to educate citizens about planning and preservation issues. Few in Charleston besides the ad hoc committee's handful of members had been aware of the community planning initiative on which the association had been embarked since the late 1930s. With the exhibit at the Gibbes the association revealed its new agenda publicly for the first time and asked for support.

The interest stimulated by the museum exhibit prompted the Carolina Art Association to publish a permanent record of the survey in the form of a guidebook with the identical title, *This Is Charleston.* The self-described catalog contained a brief historical essay about Charleston's architecture and historical development that concluded with a plea for its preservation. Most of the book was devoted to illustrations of buildings rated in the top four (of the five) classifications, but appendixes included a complete list of the rated buildings, as well as useful historical maps and a description of the city's zoning ordinance.[26] For thirty years this catalog provided the definitive touchstone for evaluating the architectural merits of Charleston buildings; it was superseded only in 1974 by a planning report commissioned by city government and officially adopted a year later. Unlike the modern planning document, though, *This Is Charleston* is still widely sold in Charleston bookstores, and to date the book has gone through five editions and three reprintings.[27]

During the war years that followed the completion of the survey and the Gibbes exhibit, Robert Whitelaw's committee seemed to lose much of its momentum and sense of direction, despite an ongoing effort to establish its visibility in the community and broaden its membership. The group assumed the title of the Charleston Civic Services Committee in January 1942 but remained under the sponsorship of the private, nonprofit Carolina Art Association.[28] It continued to depend for financial survival on grant support from outside Charleston, and it had an enviable record on that score, evidenced by a sizable twenty-four thousand dollar grant from the Rockefeller Foundation to fund operations between 1942 and 1945. The Civic Services Committee seemed to want to view itself as the "central information service" proposed by Frederick Law Olmsted Jr., but it was never able to define a precise purpose for itself in the early 1940s: should it be a source of assistance to other organizations, a preservation advocacy group, or a permanent "catalytic" planning agency? It struggled, too, with a variety of projects—awakening public interest in planning problems, keeping alive the idea of a revolving fund for rehabilitation, revising the zoning ordinance, designing war memorials, studying postwar issues—and it toyed continually and fruitlessly with the idea of devising an overall city plan.[29]

The most sustained effort during this time was a project Olmsted had suggested to the original committee: the development of a practical downtown parking plan. Through the Rockefeller grant the Civic Services Committee was able to retain George W. Simons Jr., a professional city planner from Florida, for regular consultation, and with his assistance the committee studied how off-street parking might be implemented in the central business district. Throughout 1944 and 1945 committee members analyzed traffic patterns, the financing of public parking lots, the profitability of meters, and the location of "undesirable" neighborhoods that might be cleared of slums while making way for cars.[30] The completed study was presented to City Council in 1945, but no action was taken to establish municipal parking lots. Within a few years, though, a number of private lots had sprung up on downtown streets in several of the recommended locations, essentially implementing portions of the plan.[31]

With the end of the war, the institutional energies of the Civic Services Committee revived to focus on the creation of the "permanent agency" or "central information service" first sketched out by Frederick Law Olmsted Jr. in 1940. To jump-start this effort, the committee invited Kenneth Chorley to speak at Dock Street Theatre as part of its lecture series on urban issues. Chorley was president of Colonial Williamsburg, Inc., at the time and a national figure in the field of historic preservation whose authoritative advice was sought routinely by the federal government (in crafting the Historic Sites

Act of 1935) and by the managers of restoration projects up and down the East Coast from Old Sturbridge Village, Massachusetts, to Saint Augustine, Florida. To prepare for his visit, in the month prior to his talk Chorley dispatched an assistant, Gerald Bash, to Charleston for advice on how his speech could be most helpful to the work of the Civic Services Committee. Delivered in April 1945, Chorley's remarks on "The Challenge to Charleston" emphasized the advantages of creating a foundation similar to the nonprofit Colonial Williamsburg to initiate and coordinate preservation and educational programs. While he admitted the possibility that the Civic Services Committee might simply incorporate itself into a permanent body, Chorley stressed that "The Charleston Foundation" ought to be unaffiliated with any existing civic organization and free from the political control of municipal government. With a broadly representative leadership, the group might undertake an ambitious agenda in providing preservation expertise to private citizens and civic groups, advising public officials on the city's long-term planning, offering educational and entertainment programs for visitors, and acquiring and preserving historic properties. To fund its operations Chorley suggested a variety of sources, including the admission receipts from hypothetical historic sites operated by the foundation, income from properties put to commercial rather than museum use, and gifts and bequests from wealthy benefactors. He was especially keen for the foundation to be given "official status" and made the recipient of public funds raised through a city sales tax and municipal bonds. Many of the recommendations reflected the direct application of ideas from Colonial Williamsburg's museum village to Charleston, as in the emphasis on the acquisition and operation of museum properties, the endorsement of demolitions to "provide a proper setting for your historical and architectural jewels," and the fascination with tourist dollars.[32] Chorley's talk, and its subsequent publication in pamphlet form, helped to precipitate and inform discussion about how a "Charleston Foundation" might shape postwar urban development.

In April 1947 Historic Charleston Foundation was formally incorporated as a nonprofit, educational institution chartered "to preserve and protect buildings of historical or architectural interest and their surroundings, in and about the City of Charleston," but this broad statement of official purpose only hinted at the specific programmatic agenda that its founders had in mind.[33] The organization created by the Civic Services Committee reflected its seven years of experience and experimentation in planning and preservation issues in Charleston. Perhaps the most sobering insight was that public opinion and elected officials in Charleston remained reluctant to embrace one of its major initiatives, development of a formal city plan. Pointing to the difficulties of working with "too many overlapping and conflicting organizations," the challenges of arranging sufficient funding, and the insufficient supply of professional city planners in the country, Robert Whitelaw declared in December 1946 that fashioning a city plan was not "a feasible project"; he explained: "Our theory has always been that although our primary objective is to preserve Charleston architecture, we had first to evolve a plan. We had better accomplish both by reversing the process. If we use the reverse process, much of our selling is already done, as we will be talking not *planning*, towards which there is much resistance, but simply *preservation*, which a large part of Charleston already believes in and is ready to support."[34] While the Civic Services Committee would not completely abandon its commitment to a future plan, Whitelaw argued that it was time to devote its full attention to organizing, funding, and marketing a "Charleston Foundation" visibly dedicated to preservation. Shortly thereafter the adjective *historic* was added to the name of the proposed organization.[35]

As the creation of the Civic Services Committee, Historic Charleston Foundation was established with a philosophy that might be characterized as practical preservation for a living city. The implicit analogy was that cities were biological organisms and could reasonably be expected to grow and therefore change. Frederick Law Olmsted Jr. had stressed the importance of blending the old with the new as "integral parts of a live and ever-changing contemporary community," and this view also shaped the approach of Historic Charleston Foundation: saving historic structures by discovering viable modern purposes for them. Early publicity material explained that the foundation sought "to preserve and use the architecture and history of a living, growing city" and that its purpose "will not be to maintain buildings as museums save in exceptional cases, but to seek when possible to utilize them as living units of the community."[36] When the foundation chose to acquire historic properties, these would be rehabilitated as residences, businesses, civic offices, and even low-cost housing, but not as "static museum pieces."[37] In these ways the working definition of historic preservation for Historic Charleston Foundation would be closer to Frederick Law Olmsted's than to Kenneth Chorley's.

While anticipating that benefactors might wish to give buildings to the foundation, the organization also expected to purchase endangered historic structures through a revolving fund. Most liked the idea of a large capital fund to undertake preservation, but few knew precisely how it should actually operate. Many saw it as a source of low-interest mortgages for properties deemed too risky for conventional financing. To ensure the quality of private rehabilitation, others suggested that the foundation use mortgages through the revolving fund to retain a percentage of ownership in buildings and thereby control architectural alterations. Others saw the revolving fund making loans while also paying a small dividend to stockholders, as one incentive to raising the necessary capital. Throughout the discussions to establish the foundation, reference was sometimes made to the concept of "area planning," suggesting that whole neighborhoods, not just individual structures, might be targeted.[38]

In terms of institutional structure, Historic Charleston Foundation resembled the Civic Services Committee of the Carolina Art Association, with the chief exception that it was a completely independent organization chartered by state government. The foundation was a small, self-elected group composed of leading citizens knowledgeable about Charleston and sympathetic to its goals for historic preservation. It did not have members as such, in the way that the Society for the Preservation of Old Dwellings was a membership organization. Instead, Historic Charleston Foundation was to consist entirely of a board of trustees, numbering between twelve and twenty-one men and women, plus any staff eventually employed.[39] The foundation was established, then, with the structure and independence to function like a business corporation in acquiring and managing property, promoting preservation and education, and operating in a prudent financial manner.

Many of the foundation's first trustees had a long association with preservation in Charleston, and some had been active with the Civic Services Committee. Loutrel Winslow Briggs was Charleston's most influential twentieth-century landscape architect and the author of *Charleston Gardens* (1951). E. Milby Burton was the director of the Charleston Museum and had served on the ad hoc committee organized by Robert Whitelaw to bring Frederick Law Olmsted Jr. to Charleston; he was the author of several studies of Charleston furniture, cabinetmaking, and silversmiths. Banker C. Lester Cannon was the longest-serving treasurer of Historic Charleston Foundation, from 1947 to 1967. Alston Deas had served in the 1930s on the American Institute of Architects' blue ribbon committee to safeguard Charleston architecture, the first permanent City Planning and Zoning Commission, and the first Board of Architectural Review; he was the author of *The Early Ironwork of Charleston*

(1941). Engineer E. Gaillard Dotterer served as the foundation's first secretary. Insurance executive C. Bissell Jenkins Jr. became the first president of Historic Charleston Foundation. Mrs. Percy Gamble (Eliza D.) Kammerer, a patron of the arts, restored the William Branford–Elias Horry House (59 Meeting Street). Attorney Lionel K. Legge was a member of the State House of Representatives and would later serve on the state supreme court. Julian Mitchell, an attorney and banker, had been a member of the AIA blue ribbon committee. Mrs. Victor (Marjorie) Morawetz of New York had taken an interest in preservation issues in Charleston as early as the 1930s, and she served as a trustee well into the 1950s. Homer M. Pace was a utility company executive who had been a member of the ad hoc committee that brought Olmsted to Charleston. Josephine Pinckney was the author of a collection of poems titled *Sea-Drinking Cities* (1927) and of several novels: *Hilton Head* (1941), *Three O'Clock Dinner* (1945), *My Son and Foe* (1952), and *Splendid in Ashes* (1958). Albert Simons had been a significant force for preservation since the 1920s through his initial efforts to stop the export of the city's architectural ornamentation to northern collectors and museums as well as through his role on the AIA committee to safeguard Charleston architecture, the first permanent City Planning and Zoning Commission, the original Board of Architectural Review (on which he served until 1975), and the architectural survey carried out by Helen McCormack; he coedited several books on architectural history including *Charleston, South Carolina* (1927) and *Plantations of the Carolina Low Country* (1938). Alice Ravenel Huger Smith produced writings and paintings that helped define the artistic revival in the 1920s and 1930s known as the Charleston Renaissance; her work appeared in *Twenty Drawings of the Pringle House* (1914) and *The Dwelling Houses of Charleston, South Carolina* (1917), among other publications. William Mason Smith was a New York lawyer and descendant of prominent South Carolina Lowcountry families. New Yorker Henry Philip Staats was a Yale-trained architect who was pivotal in opening the Nathaniel Russell House to the public soon after its acquisition by the foundation in the 1950s. Historian Samuel Gaillard Stoney had served on the ad hoc committee that worked with Olmsted and had provided expertise for the subsequent architectural survey; he wrote the historical text for *Plantations of the Carolina Low Country* and *This Is Charleston* (1944), among other books. Ben Scott Whaley was a lawyer and served as United States Attorney; he became the longest-serving president of Historic Charleston Foundation between 1955 and 1969. As the director of the Carolina Art Association, Robert N. S.

Whitelaw had provided the urban planning vision for its Civic Services Committee and was as responsible as anyone for the establishment of Historic Charleston Foundation in 1947. When these original nineteen trustees held their first meeting in May 1947, they elected Mrs. Lionel K. (Dorothy Haskell Porcher) Legge to the board; she had pioneered in the revitalization of Rainbow Row on East Bay Street and had suggested the concept of house tours as a fund-raising strategy for the foundation. Her election made a total of twenty founding trustees, fifteen men and five women.[40]

Historic Charleston Foundation's first project—fund-raising—began even before it was formally incorporated, and the task dominated its first years of existence after 1947. Plans to establish the foundation proceeded simultaneously with a projected seventy-five-thousand-dollar fund-raising campaign by the Carolina Art Association. Of this amount, twenty-five thousand dollars was to be earmarked to launch the foundation and its capital fund. The association devoted most of its March 1947 magazine to an announcement of the formation of the group and its aims, arguing that "the very richness of the Charleston scene" made the task of preservation too large even for the wealth of existing private and public efforts.[41] Unfortunately, the Carolina Art Association's fundraising campaign fell short of its goal, raising only thirty-five thousand dollars, of which nearly ten thousand dollars was designated for the foundation.[42] Concurrently with this publicity campaign, planning went forward to establish an annual series of historic house tours. These tours would become the longest running program of Historic Charleston Foundation and eventually a major source of revenue, but initially the income did not live up to expectations.[43] In its early years operation of the foundation would depend on a fluctuating stream of tour revenue, as well as on the Carolina Art Association for office space and some limited staff support.[44] In his dual role as a trustee of the new foundation and longtime director of the association, Robert Whitelaw assured his fellow trustees that "The Carolina Art Association laid the basis for the Foundation, created it and can certainly be trusted with its routine management," at least for the short term.[45]

The struggle for financial stability did not keep Historic Charleston Foundation from beginning to play an important role as a preservation advocate in the late 1940s and early 1950s. During these early years the new organization joined in a couple of collaborative efforts with other heritage groups, and it embarked on campaigns to save several architecturally significant properties. The foundation had vowed that it wanted to work with exist-

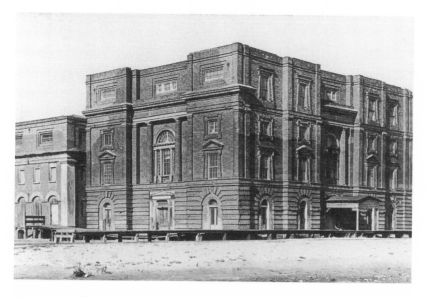

*Bennett Rice Mill (1844)*

Rescue of the Bennett Rice Mill in the 1950s represented the first major preservation victory for Historic Charleston Foundation, in partnership with the Preservation Society of Charleston. In September 1960 Hurricane Donna destroyed much of the structure, and today all that remains is the imposing west facade propped from behind like a Hollywood movie set along the Cooper River waterfront. Courtesy, The Charleston Museum.

ing civic organizations on behalf of the cause of historic preservation, and this commitment was demonstrated in two projects in the early 1950s. In 1952 it joined with the Daughters of the American Revolution to restore the west pediment of the Old Exchange Building, occupied by the local Rebecca Motte chapter of the society. The former customshouse and city hall had been severely damaged during the Charleston earthquake of 1886 and sat largely unrepaired. Half of the cost to restore the pediment was paid by the foundation, the first expenditure of income from its program of house tours. In a second collaboration in 1953 the foundation contributed funds to the Charleston Museum to pay off the outstanding mortgage on the Heyward-Washington House, which the museum had purchased in the 1920s for operation as a historic house museum.[46]

As an advocacy organization, the foundation worked continually to find an effective way to respond to the ongoing problem of demolitions in postwar Charleston. Writing letters of protest did not prevent the demolition of important buildings, as in the cases of the Charleston Orphan House (rated "valuable to the city" in the architectural inventory) and its Chapel (rated "nationally important"), both of which were razed for a Sears, Roebuck department store in 1952–53.[47] One novel educational tactic was publication of an annual "necrology" of Charleston buildings lost during the previous year. In 1953 the foundation featured "a small cross-section of recent destruction," listing as examples the Chapel at the Charleston Orphan House, the north wing of the Bennett Rice Mill, and five residences.[48] Eventually the foundation decided that the trustees as a group should be asked to appear at public hearings when there was a preservation issue at stake.[49] But the real dilemma was that the city's Board of Architectural Review lacked the ability to postpone demolitions; this authority was not granted until the zoning ordinance was revised in 1959.[50]

The foundation's most concerted and successful campaign to save a structure from demolition in the early 1950s was the effort on behalf of the Bennett Rice Mill, an architecturally and historically significant structure on the Cooper River waterfront. The mill was a distinguished example of industrial architecture, built of brick in 1844 in the classical revival style, and the architectural inventory had rated it one of the twenty-six "nationally important" buildings in Charleston. Its harbor-side location and architectural grandeur were a bold statement of the importance of rice in the antebellum economy of South Carolina and the wealth it produced for Charleston. Historic Charleston Foundation participated in the effort to save the rice mill beginning in June 1952, when the structure was condemned as a fire hazard and the current owner, the Seaboard Air Line Railroad, made plans to demolish the building, then being used as a warehouse in the middle of its yards. A campaign of letter writing, resolutions, and petitions on the part of many Charlestonians persuaded the railroad to forestall demolition of the main building (but not its north wing), and the Society for the Preservation of Old Dwellings began a six-year search to identify a viable economic use for the giant old mill. The Preservation Society[51] was forced to abandon this strategy without success in May 1958, and negotiations began again on the fate of the structure, this time with its new owner, the South Carolina State Ports Authority, under the pressure of another municipal condemnation order. In October 1958 the ports authority agreed to lease the mill for five years jointly to the Preservation Society and Historic Charleston Foundation, each of which contributed three thousand dollars toward stabilization

*Inspecting the Bennett Rice Mill, 1958*
> The local newspaper reported on the effort to preserve the mill with this picture depicting citizens inspecting its interior: engineer C. Stuart Dawson; Ben Scott Whaley, Mrs. John P. Frost, and Mrs. Lionel K. Legge of Historic Charleston Foundation; and architect Douglas Ellington. Courtesy, *Charleston News and Courier,* 22 August 1958.

and fireproofing. Regrettably, just two years later much of the structure was destroyed by Hurricane Donna on 11 September 1960.[52]

Today all that remains of the Bennett Rice Mill is its imposing west facade, propped from behind like a Hollywood movie set and isolated in the midst of a large lot used as part of the working port. Because it is difficult now to imagine the impressive antebellum industrial structure that once occupied the site, much less its role in the Lowcountry rice economy, the remnants stand largely as a curious and melancholy monument to Historic Charleston Foundation's first preservation victory. Beginning in the early 1990s, though, the foundation has used the Bennett Rice Mill as part of its innovative building crafts training program to teach historic masonry skills to inner-city youth, and current city plans call for redevelopment of the area with display of the rice mill facade as a central feature.[53]

In these early years impending threats to Charleston's historic architecture instigated many of the foundation's concerns. This reactive approach toward identifying projects would continue, most immediately in 1955 when the foundation took the significant step of purchasing the Nathaniel Russell House. In time the foundation would also experiment with a more proactive approach to preservation, initially in 1957 when the foundation first established its revolving fund for area rehabilitation. The subsequent success of the Ansonborough project would propel Historic Charleston Foundation into the national spotlight and establish it as a pioneering organization. In both its reactive rescue of endangered historic properties and its proactive planning ventures, the foundation was fulfilling the institutional mission envisioned for it by the Carolina Art Association; in the following decades Historic Charleston Foundation would continue this legacy by commissioning important studies of community development, initiating fresh educational and preservation strategies, and embracing a diverse urban agenda that reflected the expanding civic concerns of the late twentieth century.

# Chapter 3

# The Nathaniel Russell House

THE PURCHASE OF the Nathaniel Russell House in 1955 represented a major preservation success for Historic Charleston Foundation and a significant step for the young organization. The acquisition of the stately neoclassical mansion enabled the foundation to rescue an important Charleston residence and to establish permanent offices for itself in a building whose architecture suggested that Historic Charleston Foundation was an institution of means and influence. But the Nathaniel Russell House was more than just an imposing headquarters. The trustees hoped to raise funds for the foundation by operating the mansion as a historic house museum. Beginning in 1956 the public was invited to tour the building and view rooms displayed as the graciously appointed home of a wealthy merchant of the early nineteenth century. In recent years, since its offices have moved elsewhere, Historic Charleston Foundation has committed itself to a museum-quality restoration of the Russell House and to a reinterpretation of the building and grounds as a working urban landscape populated by blacks as well as whites.

Although the Nathaniel Russell House became closely identified with Historic Charleston Foundation—from today's perspective it is difficult to imagine the foundation without the Russell House—its acquisition was hardly a foregone conclusion in 1955. The purchase was both a quick decision made under deadline pressure and an unanticipated departure for an organization that had sought to eschew museums and adhere to the preservation agenda outlined by the Civic Services Committee. The founders had been quite explicit that the purpose of Historic Charleston Foundation was the promotion of preservation in a living city, with operation of museums as a secondary purpose and then only in "exceptional cases."[1] Through its early years the foundation had followed this course, resisting suggestions that it assume responsibility for museums even when buildings were offered at no cost. As early as 1948, for example, the foundation declined the gift of the Washington Jefferson Bennett House at 60 Montagu Street. Mindful of the expense of operating historic house museums like the Joseph Manigault and Heyward-Washington Houses, owned by the Charleston Museum, the trustees debated the merits of the offer but ultimately endorsed the view that "the Foundation was not concerned with House Museums."[2] This decision affirmed an institutional focus on preservation and planning that continued until 1955, when threats to the Nathaniel Russell House moved Historic Charleston Foundation to consider a range of strategies for saving the historic building.

It was clear that the Russell House was both an architectural treasure for the city and a building with significant associations to South Carolina history. Completed in 1808, the mansion was the home of Nathaniel Russell, a Rhode Island native who had come to Charleston in 1765 as an agent for New England merchants and eventually amassed a considerable fortune for himself in the rice and slave trades. Russell's marriage in 1788 at the age of fifty to Sarah Hopton cemented an alliance with a prominent Charleston family, and the elegant townhouse that he and his wife constructed on Meeting Street testified to their wealth and status in postrevolutionary Charleston. As originally built, to a design by an architect who remains unknown, the main house was part of a complex of structures that included a kitchen and laundry building and a stable with carriage house, storerooms, and slave quarters.[3] In the main house was what is today considered "perhaps the most stunning interior architectural feature in the city," a free-standing spiral staircase connecting the three floors.[4] The Nathaniel Russell House has long been recognized as one of the most important examples of residential neoclassical architecture in the United States.

Members of the Russell family lived in the house for almost fifty years, until 1857, when it was purchased by R. F. W. Allston, a successful rice planter who was then the governor of South Carolina. Following the Allston family occupancy, the house became the property of a religious order, the Sisters of Charity of Our Lady of Mercy, which operated a boarding school,

*The Nathaniel Russell House (1808), pictured about 1890*
  Purchase of the Nathaniel Russell House in 1955 enabled Historic Charleston Foundation
  to save an important residence and establish permanent offices for itself. The foundation
  began operating the Russell House as a historic house museum in 1956, and it maintained
  its administrative offices there until 1992. Courtesy, The Charleston Museum.

academy, and offices in the building for close to forty years, from 1870 to 1908, when the house was returned to private residential use by the Mullally and Pelzer families.[5] Historic Charleston Foundation purchased the Russell House from the Pelzer family heirs in March 1955.

  The campaign to acquire the building ranks as one of the most impressive in American preservation history for its quick success in raising a considerable amount of money in a short period of time. Historic Charleston Foundation first involved itself in the Russell House project early in February 1955, when it became apparent that the Pelzer estate might be forced to subdivide the property to make its sale more appealing and affordable to potential purchasers. The house had been on the market for over two years at an asking price of ninety-five thousand dollars, but no buyers had come forward with an interest in taking on the expense of maintaining and staffing an opulent mansion. Worried by the prospect that the house would be severed from its fine garden and historic setting if the property were divided and sold as four separate parcels, the foundation embarked on a campaign to publicize the need to save this piece of Charleston history. The trustees hoped that a private buyer might still be identified to keep the property intact and the house in residential use; significantly, though, they also publicized their own willingness to assume custodial responsibility for the Russell House if it were deeded to the foundation.[6]

The campaign began in mid February with a letter-writing blitz and generous coverage in the local newspapers. Articles emphasized that the foundation lacked the funds to purchase the house and that it was looking for a benefactor to come to the rescue. Through the intercession of Mayor William McGillivray Morrison, the Pelzer estate consented to take the Russell House off the market temporarily for thirty days, until March 11th, and to reduce the price to $65,000 while efforts were made to find an institutional buyer or public use for the property.[7] A benefactor emerged in the form of industrialist Henry Smith Richardson, a winter resident of Charleston and the president of the Vick Chemical Company of New York. Richardson was then in the process of setting up a charitable foundation, and when approached by Historic Charleston Foundation he agreed to an anonymous gift of $32,500, one-half the purchase price, on the condition that the foundation raise the other half through public subscription.[8] Richardson's anonymous pledge was the catalyst for an intensive fund-raising campaign formally announced on March 1st with a deadline of March 11th, the expiry date for the option previously negotiated by the mayor. The task of raising $32,500 in ten days, an average of well over $3,000 a day, was a daunting challenge but was ultimately successful.[9] Among other forms of publicity, the new medium of television was conscripted to the cause of saving the venerable Russell House. A local television station contributed two hours of free programming, and preservationists made their pitches in between amateur musical performances. In total, some one thousand people from all regions of the country donated money for the purchase of the Nathaniel Russell House, including large contributions from Mrs. Victor Morawetz of New York, one of Historic Charleston's founding trustees, who anonymously donated $5,000, and the city's two newspapers, which together contributed $2,500. Historic Charleston Foundation took title to the Russell House, its first historic property, on 24 March 1955.[10]

To organize its management of the Russell House, the foundation established a governing board for the property chaired by Henry P. Staats, an archi-

*Russell House facade*

The Nathaniel Russell House was so closely identified with Historic Charleston Foundation that publicity posters and brochures used an image of the facade throughout the 1950s and 1960s to advertise tours of historic houses. Courtesy, HCF.

tect and founding trustee, that consisted of trustees of Historic Charleston Foundation as well as representatives from City Council, the business community, and its sister organization, the Society for the Preservation of Old Dwellings. To take responsibility for the most pressing tasks at the Russell House, three committees were established at the outset. The Building Committee, chaired by Staats, was to oversee the repair and restoration of the complex of structures for use by the foundation. Maintaining the gardens at the Russell House was the responsibility of the Grounds Committee, chaired by Mrs. Coming Ball Gibbes, who had first been elected a trustee in 1952. The Furnishings and Decoration Committee was charged with setting up museum rooms and offices; this committee was chaired by author and founding trustee Josephine Pinckney. By June, three months after purchasing the Russell House, the foundation was able to convene its annual meeting at its new headquarters at 51 Meeting Street.[11]

Without question the most costly initial task involved repairs and restoration. In a report to the trustees Henry P. Staats estimated that there was over $44,000 worth of work to be undertaken, chiefly interior and exterior painting, carpentry, and repairs to stairways and mechanical systems. To help defray this expense, the foundation again sought financial assistance from a New York benefactor, this time the Avalon Foundation. Avalon offered an anonymous gift in the curiously familiar amount of $32,500, and Historic Charleston authorized $13,000 of its own reserves to fund the full amount of Staats's budget. Work commenced in June and was completed by February 1956 under the supervision of Staats and fellow trustee Albert Simons, whose architectural firm entered into a temporary association to donate their design services for the project. In addition to repairs and upgrading the heating and electrical systems, an effort was made to remove some twentieth-century modifications in order to restore rooms in the main house to their appearance during the Russell family occupancy. The third floor and kitchen wing at the rear were remodeled into residential rental units.[12]

For its part the Grounds Committee, which counted among its members landscape architect and founding trustee Loutrel W. Briggs, worked on a decidedly more limited budget. No thought was given to restoration of the historic appearance of the grounds during the Russell tenure, which would have meant adding a working service yard, for example. Instead the emphasis was on creating aesthetically pleasing gardens. The committee confined itself to pruning overgrown shrubs and trees to open up vistas of the house and grounds. Gifts of camellias and azaleas added a few new plantings intended to bloom during Charleston's tourist season.[13]

Because the Russell House was completely empty when the foundation took possession, one of the most challenging tasks fell to the Furnishings and Decoration Committee, whose chief responsibility was to turn the vacant rooms of the mansion into an appealing house museum that would attract

*New curtains for the Russell House*

In a newspaper article in 1956, Russell House curator Doris Meadowcroft announced that the Furnishings and Decoration Committee had installed new curtains in the reception hall and dining room. In the absence of records about the Russell family possessions, members of the decorating committee had to depend on their own aesthetic judgments about how rooms might have been used and how they appeared. Pictured here are Mrs. Joseph R. Young, Mrs. Thomas R. Waring Jr., and Mrs. Louis R. Lawson Jr. Courtesy, *Charleston News and Courier,* 9 December 1956.

visitors. The challenge of the empty rooms was compounded by the absence of funds to develop a collection of museum pieces through purchase. In light of these formidable obstacles, the achievement of the Furnishings and Decoration Committee was quite remarkable. Using their network of Charleston acquaintances, the committee members arranged for loans from both private collections and local museums and in some cases for the outright gift of furniture and furnishings. As a result of these efforts, the Nathaniel Russell House was ready to receive visitors when it was opened to the public for the first time in its history, in March 1956 to mark the anniversary of the successful public subscription that had made possible its acquisition. Almost eleven hundred people toured the mansion on the first day alone.[14]

The local newspapers devoted considerable coverage to how the Russell House was being decorated, and these stories offer a glimpse of the foundation's early collecting practices. The trustees had established a general policy that furniture acquired for the mansion should date from the period 1750 to 1820, roughly Nathaniel Russell's life span (1738–1820).[15] As to decisions about provenance, style, and placement of furnishings within the house, committee members relied on their own well-developed appreciation for antiques and sophisticated twentieth-century sense of taste. The building's architecture suggested the work of Robert Adam—promotional materials over the years characterized the Russell House as one of the finest Adamesque homes in the country—and an attempt was made to furnish the interior with "fine examples of the work of Robert Adam's contemporaries, Hepplewhite, Chippendale and Sheraton, and highlighted with examples of Meissen, Chinese Export Ware, Wedgewood and 17th century French porcelains."[16] In the absence of family records about the Russell possessions, decorating committees had to depend on their own aesthetic judgments about what rooms might have been used for and how they might have appeared. Thus, the circular pattern of the several oval-shaped rooms in the mansion might inspire the placement of drum tables and globes in these spaces, or the foliage visible in the garden outside the windows might suggest an appropriate color scheme for curtains. In general, committee members sought to locate fine objects associated with wealthy families of the period and to arrange these in ways that suggested the elegant lifestyle of one of Charleston's most successful "merchant princes."[17] Visitors seemed pleased with what they found in the new museum. "Already the aura of its former owner can be felt in the restored rooms," the editor of the women's page for the *Charleston News and Courier* reported, adding that the furnishings were creating "more and more the mood and tempo of those former times."[18] One of the most frequently voiced comments was that Nathaniel Russell would surely feel right at home.[19]

Within a year of purchasing the Nathaniel Russell House, Historic Charleston Foundation had undertaken extensive repairs to the primary buildings, pruned the grounds, furnished a number of rooms with attractive antiques, and established permanent offices for itself in a spacious townhouse. As a result of a well-publicized campaign that had given the young organization good visibility in the community, the foundation had rescued a building significant in Charleston history and in the process acquired its first historic property. There was always the possibility that owning the Russell House would burden the foundation financially, but trustees hoped to minimize maintenance costs and subsidize operating expenses through museum admissions and income from rental units on the property.[20] Helpfully, there was no mortgage to pay off, chiefly due to the two New York benefactors who had made possible the purchase and initial renovation of the property. The Russell House promised not only to pay for itself but also to generate revenue for Historic Charleston Foundation in the coming years.

After the mid 1950s the collections at the Russell House continued to grow, usually as the result of the generosity of Charlestonians rather than any funded strategy of acquisitions. Trustees were among the most consistent supporters of the Russell House in this regard. Many trustees loaned objects for display in the house, and others bequeathed furniture and furnishings. In an unusual tribute to Josephine Pinckney in 1959, friends restored and furnished one of the second-floor bedrooms in her memory. Reflecting the discovery of a valuable Charleston decorative arts tradition, collecting began to emphasize locally produced furniture, rather than just pieces of European manufacture, in the mid 1960s. One of the most important acquisitions came as the result of a purchase in 1975: a painting by George Romney that now hangs prominently above the famous flying staircase.[21]

As a museum, the Russell House gained an enviable reputation as a Charleston showplace, one of only a handful of historic houses in the city that was open to the public on a year-round basis. A tour of its graciously appointed rooms gave residents and tourists alike a glimpse of life inside a grand mansion. Through a corps of volunteer hostesses, visitors were able to learn about the objects and paintings on display and about Nathaniel Russell, a man of "energy, business ability, ambition and good taste."[22] As a result of foundation promotion, the Russell House even attracted the attention of the national press, in stories that extolled the beauty of the restored interiors and their exquisite architectural detailing.[23] The federal government recognized the transcendent historical significance of the foundation property in the mid 1970s, when the Nathaniel Russell House was designated a National Historic Landmark.

In the 1980s two factors coalesced to inaugurate major changes in the management of the Russell House: an expanding role at Historic Charleston Foundation for trained professionals and growing concerns about the physical condition of the historic structure. The increasingly professionalized approach to management of the Russell House can be traced to 1981, when the foundation hired the museum's first full-time, academically trained curator. J. Thomas Savage Jr. was a graduate of the College of William and Mary and the Cooperstown museum studies program; he had come to the Russell House initially as an intern and was subsequently hired as curator. Savage was able to build on the museum collection established in 1955 and its meticulous cataloging over the years by Doris Meadowcroft, a native of England who had arrived in Charleston when her husband was appointed rector of Grace Church; she became the first manager-curator of the Russell House. Savage defined a collections policy that emphasized objects associated with the history of Charleston and the South Carolina Lowcountry, construed broadly to include artistic and social life, as well as political and economic affairs. More recently the museum has focused on acquiring through gift, loan, and purchase artifacts connected with the Russell family and objects used in similar Charleston homes.[24] In the 1980s and 1990s the foundation has been able to apply successfully for outside grant monies that have enabled it to undertake wide-ranging historical and archaeological research projects and employ consultants to advise on technical issues of building conservation. A current institutional goal is accreditation for the Russell House by the American Association of Museums.[25] The curatorial staff was expanded in 1992 to add an assistant curator, Robert A. Leath. One indication of the widening professional reputation of the foundation's curatorial expertise was Tom Savage's appointment in 1993 to the Committee for the Preservation of the White House by President Clinton.

Concern about the structural condition of the Russell House in the 1980s pushed the foundation to begin thinking systematically about conservation issues for the first time since the postpurchase renovations of 1955–56. One immediate catalyst was the wind, rain, and flooding associated with

Hurricane Hugo in September 1989, which caused considerable water damage to the house and its furnishings and necessitated a new slate roof and new heating and air conditioning system. The devastation of the storm, though, was not the only source of structural deterioration evident at the Russell House. As many as seventy-five thousand visitors walked annually through the bottom two floors of the building, and this general wear and tear was harming the historic fabric. Years of deferred maintenance had also taken their toll.[26] "I was shocked to learn that the Russell House needed $1 million to restore it," one Charlestonian confessed in a posthurricane institutional assessment that Historic Charleston Foundation had commissioned for itself. "Why did it go so long without having routine maintenance and restoration?" this citizen wondered.[27] The answer, of course, could be traced to earlier decisions to generate revenue while minimizing expenses.

The year 1992 was an important turning point in the management of the Russell House: Historic Charleston Foundation decided it needed more space for its headquarters and moved out of the Nathaniel Russell House after thirty-seven years.[28] For the first time foundation offices and the museum were separate entities, and the building at 51 Meeting Street could be managed in its entirety as a historic house museum. Toward that end the foundation committed itself to a major restoration of the Russell House. To fund this ambitious initiative the Russell House was designated a primary beneficiary of the Heritage Campaign announced in June 1992. This capital campaign was intended to raise $4 million, of which $1.5 million was earmarked for the Russell House. "After forty years as the Foundation's war-horse—a money-maker, architectural masterpiece and educational center-piece all rolled into one—the Russell House is calling out for help," the director of development argued in one plea for support during 1997. "The conservation of its historic fabric—its bricks, mortar, ironwork, plaster and molding—must receive immediate attention," he warned.[29] Promotional literature for the Heritage Campaign promised that the Russell House would become "a symbol of the Foundation's commitment to the highest standards of restoration, conservation, and education."[30]

The year 1992 was also significant as marking the first "reunion" of Russell family descendants since the early nineteenth century. After being in the planning stages for some time, it came to fruition in November 1992 when almost seventy descendants of Nathaniel Russell traveled to Charleston from across the country. Genealogical research by foundation staff over a six-month period had identified some two hundred living descendants, all of whom were invited to Charleston for a weekend of talks and tours on family history, as well as a display of important family objects from museums and private collections. The reunion provided descendants a chance to learn not only about Nathaniel Russell and his world but also about the programs to conserve his legacy carried on by Historic Charleston Foundation. Because family members were encouraged to bring Russell heirlooms, the curatorial staff at the Russell House had the opportunity to record information on a variety of portraits, miniatures, china, silver, jewelry, letters, and books, including photographs of objects such as pieces of furniture that were too large to transport easily. The reunion furnished valuable information on the whereabouts of important family artifacts, some of which have been donated subsequently to the Russell House collections. The reunion also inspired a committee of descendants to organize a Russell Family Fund designed to raise fifty thousand dollars over a five-year period to support both collections development and building restoration.[31] In these ways the reunion proved to be an imaginative and effective vehicle for research, public relations, and fund-raising.

During 1994 and 1995 a grant from the Getty Foundation enabled Historic Charleston Foundation to undertake a sweeping architectural, archaeological, and documentary assessment of the Russell House, its setting, and its history.[32] A detailed analysis of exterior ironwork, masonry, decorative plasterwork, and composition ornament provided a set of specific recommendations for repair and conservation of important architectural features of the main house, and a microscopic and materials analysis of interior plaster and paint finishes furnished new information about historic decorative patterns and their current condition. A preliminary archaeological survey sampled sites on the entire property, revealing clues about the location of outbuildings and the uses of earlier yards and gardens, as well as information on slave life and household consumption. As part of the Getty project, far-flung archives were scoured as never before for documentary evidence on the property and those who lived there. Assistant curator Robert Leath compiled and edited a two-volume report on Nathaniel Russell's correspondence and newspaper advertisements that documented his business career and growing involvement in trade with Europe, Africa, and Asia. To research how the mansion might have been furnished during Nathaniel Russell's occupancy (since no list of his possessions exists), probate inventories from selected Charleston families who lived in similar homes of the period were consulted, and to understand how

*Archaeology at the Russell House*
    A team of student archaeologists excavate a site adjacent to the original Russell House kitchen and laundry building. Courtesy, HCF.

the house functioned on the property as a whole, documentary sources related to other townhouse complexes and their landscape settings were examined.[33]

    As never before, curators were left with a comprehensive understanding of the original design for Nathaniel Russell's house, how its public and private spaces would have been used, how life and work circulated between the big house and its gardens and service yard, how the building evolved over time under a succession of owners, and what work needed to be done. In addition to providing guidance on the technical conservation of the structure of the house, the research pointed to some tantalizing new interpretative possibilities for the Russell House. Today the foundation has great interest in taking a holistic approach to its reinterpretation, by placing the mansion at the center of an antebellum domestic complex where the lives of both blacks and whites are discussed. One of the most intriguing discoveries to emerge from the recent historical research is that a family slave, the blacksmith Thomas Russell, was convicted and executed for his role as the weapons maker in the abortive Denmark Vesey insurrection, which stunned white Charleston in 1822. The story of Thomas Russell offers a unique opportunity at the Russell House to discuss both the institution of urban slavery and the strategies of slave resistance.[34]

This evolving interpretation of the Nathaniel Russell House emphasizes the point that the management of historic house museums is a process that changes over time. Today grant money has become vital to the operation of museums, and access to these sources of funding makes possible technical investigations and multidisciplinary research that were unimaginable and unavailable in earlier years. Recently curators have been able to turn to the technologies of paint analysis, for example, and to scholarship in historical archaeology, material culture, and landscape architecture to inspire fresh thinking and new questions about historic properties like the Russell House, making research the basis of decisions about building restoration and historical interpretation. The intellectual and political context for supporting historic house museums has also shifted in recent years. The insights of social history have encouraged a capacious approach to the study of the past and an openness to addressing the historical role of all groups of people in museum interpretation. Today the Russell House holds enormous promise for educating the public about southern history and African-American history, and this potential has stimulated renewed interest on the part of Historic Charleston Foundation in acquiring museum properties.[35] Its recent rediscovery of museums represents one important way the foundation is seeking to build on its previous successes at the Nathaniel Russell House and to explore new ways to teach about the past through historic places.

Although Historic Charleston Foundation purchased the Russell House reluctantly under deadline pressure, its acquisition proved extraordinarily fortuitous. For four decades the property housed and funded the foundation, giving it the resources to pursue a far-flung preservation agenda in Charleston and the surrounding Lowcountry. Most immediately, in 1955 the rescue of the Russell House established a track record for the foundation, providing it a recognizable institutional identity and making it a player in civic affairs. With permanent headquarters, a popular museum, and a growing reputation as a successful and effective organization, Historic Charleston Foundation was in a position in 1957 to embark on its next major project—Ansonborough—which would confirm it as a national leader in historic preservation.

# Chapter 4

# ANSONBOROUGH
## *Revolving Funds and Area Rehabilitation*

WITH THE ANSONBOROUGH project, Historic Charleston Foundation dramatically transformed one Charleston neighborhood and brought national recognition to itself and the city of Charleston. Through the innovative use of a revolving fund, the foundation demonstrated the possibilities of a broad areawide approach to historic preservation using a small amount of capital as a catalyst to private investment and restoration. From this standpoint the project was enormously successful: it turned the Ansonborough district into a preservation showplace and represented the first time a revolving fund had been used for area rehabilitation in the United States. But the Ansonborough project eventually raised complicated social questions about residential displacement and neighborhood gentrification, issues that Historic Charleston Foundation would address in subsequent years.

Although an interest in area rehabilitation had helped inspire the creation of Historic Charleston Foundation in the 1940s, it was not until the late 1950s that a formal plan of action was implemented. The initiative launched by the trustees in February 1957 was significant in several respects. First was the breadth of the strategy: the foundation planned to target an entire neighborhood, not just an individual building. Second was the dynamic definition of preservation: historic buildings were to be rehabilitated for contemporary use as parts of a modern city, not converted into museums.

And third was the novelty of its financing: a small fund was to be used to leverage a major private sector investment. All three of these ideas are now widely accepted as indispensable approaches to community revitalization, largely because of the pioneering work of Historic Charleston Foundation in Ansonborough during the 1950s and 1960s.

The trustees finalized an area rehabilitation plan early in 1957 and immediately set about publicizing the venture. The foundation explained to the press and potential contributors that it intended to identify an appropriate area in Charleston for rehabilitation, acquire properties there through purchase or gift, and undertake limited restorations. The nonprofit organization did not intend to become a long-term property holder in the neighborhood; rather it planned to sell its buildings to preservation-minded purchasers interested in taking up residence. If the foundation acquired structures unsuitable for single family use, these might be developed into rental units such as apartments, offices, and stores, with the income put toward other acquisitions. Not everything would be saved: unsightly structures would be torn down to enhance the neighborhood with gardens and open space. As originally envisioned, the foundation's capital was supposed to "revolve" in two ways. Within the neighborhood, monies used to purchase properties were to be returned to the fund upon resale. Following the success of the initial demonstration project, the concept of the revolving fund was to be employed elsewhere, in other neighborhoods. It was not expected that the fund would operate at a profit.[1] One newspaper editorial summed up the foundation plans as an attempt to "lay nest eggs that would encourage private investors to restore entire neighborhoods." The paper applauded the effort, pointing out that "unless Charleston pushes back the slums, the heart of the city will wither while the suburbs bloom."[2]

The foundation anticipated undertaking a certain amount of exterior restoration work on the properties it acquired, but it did not envision major interior restoration or redecoration; those would be the responsibility of purchasers, to be carried out with the oversight of the foundation. All properties sold by the foundation to private purchasers would have protective covenants attached to the deeds; these would be designed to restrict alterations or uses that would compromise architectural integrity. Significantly, though, the foundation did not expect individual property owners to embark on museum-quality restorations. Rehabilitation would preserve significant architectural features, but it was assumed that changes would be necessary to adapt

East Bay
George
Laurens
Society
Wentworth
Hasell
Pinckney
Market

Cooper River

Anson

Calhoun
Meeting
Broad
King

Ashley River

■ Ansonborough neighborhood

N

800   0   800   1600   Feet

*Ansonborough today*

buildings to contemporary use.[3] "We want it quite clear that we are not after more Russell Houses," one foundation spokesman observed in an early announcement about the project. "The properties we hope to reclaim will be used, because it is through their use that they will survive," he explained.[4]

Intensive fund-raising for the area rehabilitation project's capital fund began in earnest in 1957. A goal of one million dollars was established, but initial efforts focused on raising one hundred thousand dollars to inaugurate the plan. As with efforts at the Nathaniel Russell House earlier in the decade, significant financial support came from Henry Smith Richardson, president of the Vick Chemical Company and a winter resident of Charleston. He offered a grant of twenty-five thousand dollars through the Richardson Foundation on the condition that Historic Charleston Foundation raise an additional seventy-five thousand dollars, twenty-five thousand dollars of it locally. Private solicitation and newspaper articles publicized the campaign to Charlestonians, and out-of-town contributions were sought through an elaborate, lavishly illustrated brochure entitled *Charleston, South Carolina: An Historic City Worth Saving*. The booklet argued that Charleston was one of the few cities in the country that had "historic and architectural significance for *all* Americans" and that this heritage was threatened by the forces of progress in "the new industrial South." The case was made visually with images of architectural treasures and lost gems, as well as with a careful exposition of the revolving fund plan. The campaign had raised the money by October 1958.[5]

The revolving fund was established well before Ansonborough was identified as the first target neighborhood. Throughout 1958 the foundation investigated various parts of the city as possible sites for its project. It eventually settled on a residential district near the heart of Charleston comprised of parts of four of the city's historic suburbs: Ansonborough, Rhettsbury, Laurens' Lands, and Gadsden's Lands. After the late 1950s the boundaries of what came to be known as Ansonborough fluctuated, reflecting the purchases and initiatives of the demonstration project. Today, as a result of the foundation's rehabilitation effort and a subsequent revision of the city's zoning ordinance, the area bounded generally by Meeting, Calhoun, East Bay, and Pinckney Streets is known as Ansonborough.[6]

The area was chosen for several reasons, chief among them the rich concentration of historic architecture. Within the six-block core of the district were some 135 colonial and antebellum residences, four churches, and the city's first public high school. Most of the structures dated from the 1840s, as a result of a catastrophic fire in 1838 and the subsequent rebuilding. Because the foundation was looking to "practical contemporary use" of these historic buildings, other factors were also important. Many of the residences were small and medium-sized homes, rather than grand mansions, which made them "adaptable to modern living" and the requirements of young families. The location of the area, close to major shopping thoroughfares, also seemed vital "for the creation of the kind of in-city residential area so necessary to solution of the urban revitalization problems Charleston faces."[7] Urban renewal provided a final rationale for selecting Ansonborough in this experiment in rehabilitation. To the foundation, it appeared to be an area in decline, a place "where tenements and slums were beginning to predominate."[8] One impetus for this transition to high-density, renter-occupied dwellings had been the demand for housing during World War II, stimulated in Ansonborough by the influx of workers employed by the port facilities nearby at the foot of Calhoun Street. Following the war, concern focused on the increasing number of poor blacks in the area. The foundation worried about the "dangers" for Ansonborough "because of the encroachment of negro tenements."[9]

The first property acquired by the foundation became the nucleus of the rental endowment. The so-called Gadsden House (ca. 1800) at 329 East Bay Street was donated to the foundation in December 1958 by Elizabeth Prioleau Gadsden Woodward, who had purchased it the previous June for twenty thousand dollars.[10] In the coming years Mrs. Woodward, a Charleston native, and her husband, Charles Henry Woodward, would become important supporters of Historic Charleston Foundation through this and similar gifts. As residents of Philadelphia, they maintained a winter residence at a plantation in the Charleston vicinity and played active roles in preservation efforts in Philadelphia's Chestnut Hill and on Mount Desert Island, Maine, as well as in Charleston.[11] The Woodwards' gift of the Gadsden House in 1958 included funds for both exterior restoration and conversion of the interior into modern rental apartments. Within five months the two-story kitchen building, which had previously housed two families, had been converted into a spacious, two-bedroom "garden house." Eventually the foundation opened it for public tour in an effort to publicize its fledgling Ansonborough project. The foundation emphasized to the press that the building would not become a traditional historic house museum. In the following year three apartments were completed in the three-story main house, each with "its own warm-air furnace, modern kitchen, and modern tile bath." The foundation anticipated a yearly income of forty-five hundred dollars for its revolving fund from rentals in this property.[12]

The foundation made its first purchases in 1959, when it acquired eight properties clustered at the intersection of Anson and Society Streets in the heart of the six-block core of the rehabilitation project. None of the properties had been on the market when the foundation approached owners in the spring, and negotiations were kept secret until a public announcement was made in July about the foundation's new initiative. For a cost of eighty-seven thousand dollars the foundation purchased houses located at 63, 64, 68, 71, and 72 Anson Street and at 40, 42, and 44 Society Street.[13] A local newspaper hailed the announcement of the purchases as a "wise step in the right direction" and expressed the hope that "this move will encourage private investors to buy property in this and other parts of Charleston, with a view to pushing back urban blight in the midtown area."[14] Within a year three more purchases had been announced—48 Laurens, 56 Society, 66 Anson— at a cost of thirty-four thousand dollars.[15]

The Robert Primrose House (ca. 1817) was the second property donated to the foundation, in July 1960, and its operation as rental apartments became another source of income for the revolving fund. Like the Gadsden House, which was located across the street, the property at 332 East Bay was a grand mansion house well suited for conversion into rental units. The foundation acquired it by gift from the Woodwards, who also contributed funds for exterior restoration. The interior conversion was financed by private donations and foundation funds.[16]

It took about three years for the Ansonborough project to gain enough momentum to get off the ground. By then the foundation had acquired thirteen houses, and the disposition of these properties suggests how the area rehabilitation plan and the revolving fund were operating. Seven of the thirteen houses had been sold by March 1962. The Gadsden and Primrose Houses continued in commercial use, as apartments that generated rental income for the revolving fund. Two properties had been razed, and only two remained unsold. The seven sales included 63, 71, and 72 Anson; 42, 44, and 56 Society; and 48 Laurens. Unsold by March 1962 were 40 Society and 66 Anson. Buildings were razed at 64 and 68 Anson. Almost immediately after the foundation completed its first set of purchases, it had demolished the frame building at 68 Anson Street. This was a small modern structure regarded as without architectural significance and discordant on the street of antebellum homes. Originally the plan was to engineer the resulting vacant lot into an alley, to be christened Foundation Lane, to provide access for out-buildings at the rear of some of the other properties. Instead the lot was added to the property at neighboring 72 Anson Street, giving this residence a spacious triple lot. Restoration work had been undertaken at 64 Anson Street, but it was later razed following extensive storm damage.[17] In short, the foundation was not simply preserving homes in situ; it was actively using historic architecture to construct an aesthetically pleasing neighborhood.

Shrewd marketing helped inaugurate the project and establish its early success. The foundation cultivated the local press, which in turn covered the Ansonborough project extensively. Most of the foundation purchases (and its subsequent sales) were reported in the newspapers, and the foundation used these stories to publicize its efforts. "All of our houses are for sale at any time before, during or after restoration," Ben Scott Whaley, president of the foundation, explained in 1960, offering the foundation's most recent purchases "to anyone who is interested in getting a charming house in a reawakening neighborhood at a very reasonable price."[18] The trustees of Historic Charleston Foundation often set the example by buying homes for themselves in Ansonborough, and this too was reported in the press. The first purchase of a revolving fund property, 71 Anson Street, was made by Peter Manigault, the chairman of the foundation's rehabilitation project.[19]

The foundation organized tours of its Ansonborough properties to stimulate public interest in the demonstration project. The first was held in May 1961 to showcase the adaptive use of the Gadsden and Primerose Houses and the extensive restoration work at 42 and 44 Society Street. Elaborate restoration by the foundation was the exception rather than the rule for revolving fund properties, but it was undertaken in these cases to demonstrate the potential for the entire neighborhood. In general the foundation preferred to undertake exterior restoration of a limited kind, and then only to stabilize a structure or to suggest the appearance of prosperity in Ansonborough.[20]

Conventional advertising was equally effective in marketing homes in Ansonborough. The foundation placed large-format advertisements in local newspapers, illustrated by charming pen and ink sketches and detailed property descriptions. One advertisement from 1961 urged home buyers to "consider living in downtown Charleston . . . in the revitalized Ansonborough

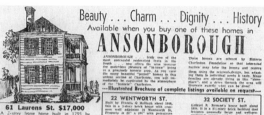

# ANSONBOROUGH

## Beauty ... Charm ... Dignity ... History
### Available when you buy one of these homes in

# HISTORIC CHARLESTON FOUNDATION
51 Meeting St.   —Brokers Protected—   723-1623

## Before You Buy...

CONSIDER LIVING IN

# DOWNTOWN CHARLESTON

You will find living especially convenient and enjoyable in the revitalized *Ansonborough area* ... in the heart of downtown Charleston.

*Consider these advantages:*

● Relatively low-cost, sound property values in area now regaining residential popularity.

● Interesting, attractive and authentic "Old Charleston" design and architecture in historical homes of all sizes, adaptable to the best in modern living.

● Large yards and gardens.

● Within walking distance of King Street shops and theaters, near downtown churches and schools.

*Historic Charleston Foundation*

is a non-profit organization dedicated to the revitalization of residential areas within the City of Charleston. Special emphasis is placed on preservation for modern use of the early American architectural flavor which means so much to our whole community in terms of charm, beauty and a lucrative tourist trade. Currently, The Foundation is offering for sale in connection with its *"Ansonborough Project"* the properties listed below. All are located in this historic borough.

63 ANSON STREET—

66 ANSON STREET—

72 ANSON STREET—

40 SOCIETY STREET—

44 SOCIETY STREET—

56 SOCIETY STREET—

Area approved by FHA. Special advantages offered on renovation under new law.

Information available on other sales and rentals of ante-bellum houses. Brokers protected. For details and appointments to inspect, call

# HISTORIC CHARLESTON FOUNDATION
51 MEETING ST.   RAymond 3-1168

*Advertisements for Ansonborough houses*

Historic Charleston Foundation placed large format advertisements in local newspapers, illustrated by charming pen-and-ink sketches and detailed property descriptions. Courtesy, *Charleston News and Courier.*

area," where they would find reasonable prices, attractive architecture, spacious gardens, and the convenience of easy walking distance to shops, theaters, schools, and churches. Asking prices ranged from four thousand dollars for a small two-story brick house that needed modernization to thirty-three thousand dollars for a recently rehabilitated three-bedroom home set in a spacious garden.[21] A later advertisement described "authentic picture-book houses with all the charm and flavor of Historic Old Charleston" that were "adaptable to modern family living" with their "large yards, roomy interiors and architectural details that lend themselves to imaginative decorations."[22]

The publicity and marketing were intended to identify preservation-minded purchasers who would find Ansonborough a sound investment, make it their home, and undertake the restoration, inaugurating a process designed to encourage other individuals to make similar decisions. Purchasers could buy either from the foundation or from other property owners in the area. For those who purchased from the foundation, protective covenants were attached to their deeds to minimize inappropriate changes. These covenants were to run with the land, binding purchasers and their heirs for seventy-five years. The covenants applied to building exteriors, not interiors, and prohibited alterations, additions, and changes in color or surfacing without the written approval of the foundation. Buyers who later wanted to sell their property were required to give the foundation the opportunity to purchase it prior to contracting with another party. In these ways the foundation sought to effect a demographic and architectural transformation in Ansonborough through transfers of property ownership and a system of preservation oversight.[23]

This residential transformation altered both the economic and racial composition of Ansonborough. Low-income tenants who were often—although not exclusively—African American were replaced by middle- and upper-income residents and property owners who were most often white. Precipitating this kind of social change had been one of the purposes of the Ansonborough venture, and the foundation publicized the transition under way in the mid 1960s in brochures that characterized their project as "the most extensive, concentrated, permanent slum clearance or urban rehabilitation in Charleston by any organization, government or private, since World War II."[24]

While revolving fund purchases continued through the 1960s in the heart of Ansonborough, stabilization of the eastern border of the district received considerable attention. Through the donation of the Gadsden and

Primerose Houses, the foundation had already marked out the commercial thoroughfare of East Bay Street and its surviving mansions as an important line of demarcation. Subsequent acquisitions reiterated the preservation commitment to this corner of Ansonborough. The purchase of the Stephen Shrewsbury House (ca. 1809) at 311 East Bay in October 1962 was characterized by foundation president Ben Scott Whaley as "rounding out our project by tying together our holdings in Anson, Society, and Laurens streets with those on East Bay."[25] The Andrew Moffett House (ca. 1839) at 328 East Bay was acquired through a property trade that saved it from being demolished for a parking lot. By September 1963 it had been converted into three apartments, which the foundation advertised as "combining the elegance of the old with the comfort of the new."[26] The donation of the William Blake House (ca. 1789) at 321 East Bay Street in March 1965 gave the foundation a total of five properties on East Bay between Laurens and Calhoun as a firm anchor for the northeastern corner of Ansonborough.[27]

A precise northern boundary for Ansonborough was delineated by the city's decision in 1964 to build a municipal auditorium on Calhoun Street. As proposed by City Council in May—and approved by voters in the November general election—an auditorium and exhibit hall complex would be constructed on a site bounded by Calhoun, Anson, Alexander, and an extended George Street.[28] As a large municipal project in midtown that required issuance of $3.5 million in bonds, the civic auditorium stimulated public discussion in a way that Historic Charleston Foundation's private purchases in nearby Ansonborough had not. Coverage in the local papers revealed that a close working relationship had developed between Historic Charleston Foundation and city government, particularly with regard to urban renewal and the Ansonborough area rehabilitation project.[29]

In the campaign to persuade voters to approve the bond issue, slum eradication became the persistent theme of advocates of the civic auditorium. Other arguments were made, of course: the auditorium would enhance cultural life in the city; the exhibit hall would attract regional and national conventions; all the activity would benefit the local business climate. As appealing as any argument was that construction would "necessitate demolition of a three-block area of housing that is, for the most part, badly dilapidated."[30] While this area was racially integrated, most press reports characterized it as "a Negro slum."[31] One reporter made a quick visit by car and informed readers that:

A brief tour of the section . . . reveals only a few houses that appear to be sound. But these are also in need of much repair. The narrow streets are filled with Negro children playing, and the predominately Negro residents sit on sagging steps and porches that look dangerously unsafe. Peeling paint, broken or missing window panes, and hard-packed dirt instead of grass contribute to the generally rundown appearance. Clotheslines frequently hang from one house to another. Automobiles steer through what often becomes an obstacle course of dogs, buckets, bicycles, rubber tires, and assorted debris, and stares from those who stand or sit along the streets seem to indicate that few pass through the section.[32]

While the mayor and other advocates of the auditorium promised that landowners would receive fair compensation for their property and that tenants would receive assistance locating housing elsewhere, black and white residents of the affected area were less confident, expressing concern about uprooting families from homes and neighborhood ties, as well as apprehension about the difficulty and cost of moving.[33]

The proximity of the proposed auditorium to the Ansonborough project was crucial for the leaders of both city government and Historic Charleston Foundation. The foundation's area rehabilitation project had been under way for five years by 1964, and construction of the auditorium promised a blockwide geographic and social barrier between Ansonborough and residential districts to the north. This advantage was obvious to the members of City Council who had proposed the auditorium in May, arguing that it would border Ansonborough and give it additional protection.[34] One alderman subsequently observed that the proposed location would inoculate Ansonborough from "invasion by slums."[35] For his part, the president of the foundation thought that "eradication of urban blight in the heart of our community . . . would greatly improve the setting of the six blocks of significant period architecture in which we are working, and help us toward our goal of giving Charleston in-city residential areas which are also tourist attractions of great value."[36] Paradoxically, demolition of one neighborhood would enhance the preservation of another.

While approximately seven hundred people were eventually displaced as condemnation and land acquisition went forward, not all of the buildings at the eleven-acre site were razed. Historic Charleston Foundation decided that

at least four houses on the auditorium site had sufficient architectural interest and structural integrity to warrant rescue, and it decided to incorporate
the buildings into its Ansonborough project through relocation. The foundation purchased the frame houses at 114 Anson Street and 15 Wall Street
for one dollar each from the city, and in March and April 1966 both of them
were moved to a large lot at the southeastern corner of Anson and Laurens
Streets. The empty lot had been created when the foundation chose to raze
the existing building, the former 76 Anson Street, to accommodate the relocated structures. This residence had not been sold in the two years that the
foundation had owned it, and it "didn't seem suitable for restoration,"
explained Frances R. Edmunds, the executive director of Historic Charleston
Foundation.[37] The foundation moved a third frame house, 116 Anson Street,
from the auditorium site in June 1966, although this building seems to have
remained "homeless" for a number of years, propped up on steel beams in
various locations. A fourth house, a challenging three-story brick structure,
was relocated in July 1967 from 86 Anson to 82 Anson.[38] Relocating these
four buildings in 1966–67 rescued the structures from certain demolition,
even as it created streetscapes of a different appearance than had actually
existed. Such "salvage preservation" was an unprecedented move for Historic
Charleston Foundation but one that seemed justified in the context of area
rehabilitation through urban renewal.

The municipal auditorium, completed in 1968, continued to be a source
of controversy, as its appearance attracted critics and defenders. Designed by
Lucas and Stubbs Associates, it was a modernistic monolith, eventually
named for J. Palmer Gaillard Jr., who had actively promoted its construction
as mayor. Critics attacked its massive size and scale as unsuitable for the setting and for the surrounding cityscape. At the Charleston meeting of the
National Trust for Historic Preservation in 1970, architect Philip Johnson
blasted the auditorium, the site of the conference, for violating "every think-
able canon of taste because its scale does not fit its site." In a subsequent letter to the editor Charleston architect and founding trustee Albert Simons,
who had not been involved in designing the auditorium, attempted a rejoin-
der by predicting that "a screen of foliage" would grow and create a transition
"between the domestic scale of the old dwellings and the towering walls [of
the auditorium] which will be flecked with moving sunlight and shadows
from windblown branches." But Simons had an additional argument: "By
replacing a depressed area with a cultural center the auditorium has favorably

*Salvage preservation*
    Utility wires were cut down to allow a two-story frame house to be moved from Wall Street
    to an empty corner lot at Anson and Laurens Streets in March 1966. It was one of four
    houses moved by Historic Charleston Foundation from the site of the new municipal audi-
    torium and incorporated into the Ansonborough project. Courtesy, HCF

affected the future success of neighboring Ansonborough, still striving to achieve its complete reclamation."[39] As a defense of aesthetic design, it was a curious social and political argument, and it reflected the perception of the auditorium complex as a Maginot Line between Ansonborough and residential districts to the north.

By the mid 1970s the foundation's first area rehabilitation project seemed to be a success by most measures. Ansonborough had attracted millions of dollars in private investment, property values had soared, and the tax base had swelled.[40] When executive director Frances R. Edmunds announced the "primary completion" of the Ansonborough project in 1976, she observed, "this is now a stable area with a good real estate market and superior home owners, and this was our goal."[41] Through the 1960s and 1970s the foundation had used its revolving fund to acquire over 60 buildings in Ansonborough, almost one-half of the 135 historic structures estimated to be in the six-block core when the project was launched in the late 1950s. Over this period, restoration work and property improvements were undertaken on some 100 Ansonborough buildings—by the foundation, by purchasers bound by the foundation's protective covenants, and by individual owners electing to follow the foundation's example. One assessment in 1966 suggested that the foundation's original $100,000 investment had stimulated between $1.6 and $2 million of purchases and improvements.[42]

Significantly, by the 1970s few sales involved a role for Historic Charleston Foundation, a development that reflected, as one newspaper observed, "the new popularity of Ansonborough as a good, in-town residential area."[43] The establishment of a neighborhood association for Ansonborough also testified to confidence in the prospects of the neighborhood. Organized in January 1970 to represent the interests of "a contemporary urban residential community," the Historic Ansonborough Neighborhood Association concerned itself with issues of zoning, open space, and beautification, including prodding Historic Charleston Foundation from time to time to clean up the vacant lots it still owned in the neighborhood.[44]

From the perspective of the preservation community, middle-class home owners, real estate brokers, downtown merchants, and the tax collector, Ansonborough had more than fulfilled its promise. It had become a comfortable neighborhood and a sound investment. The experiment had confirmed the promise of a broad focus on area rehabilitation and the catalytic power of well-targeted private investment. But from the perspective of residents who had been forced from the rehabilitated area in the 1950s and 1960s, the Ansonborough project was more problematic. As the executive director of Historic Charleston Foundation observed in the 1980s, Ansonborough seemed in retrospect "a case study in displacement."[45] The success of the project revealed the necessity of confronting the twin issues of displacement and gentrification.[46] Subsequent foundation ventures sought to address these social and economic issues with the same innovation that had characterized the Ansonborough project. Beginning in the early 1970s the foundation moved on to tackle other Charleston neighborhoods. While the focus continued to be area rehabilitation, the new emphasis would be facilitating home ownership for low-income families within their neighborhoods, a subject addressed in a later chapter.[47]

Most immediately, Ansonborough gave Historic Charleston Foundation and its executive director Frances R. Edmunds enormous visibility. The project brought increasing national interest to Charleston's architectural heritage and professional attention to the work of Historic Charleston Foundation as a preservation organization involved in enterprising and effective work. Newspapers and magazines across the country started featuring stories about Ansonborough in the 1960s, under headlines such as "Boston Chamber of Commerce Lauds Preservation Efforts in Charleston," "Inner City Blight Lifted from Historic Houses: A Colonial City Meets the 20th Century," "How Private Money Saved a Slum Area," and "Charleston: Call It Making the City Work."[48] Charleston became an important case study in preservation monographs, and the foundation itself prepared information sheets for national distribution on the creation and management of revolving funds based on its experience. The publication in 1966 of *With Heritage So Rich,* possibly the only government report ever to be released as a coffee-table book, was a significant catalyst to the passage of the National Historic Preservation Act later that year; Historic Charleston Foundation and the Ansonborough project were showcased in one of its chapters.[49] Professional and scholarly societies organized conferences in Charleston to see firsthand the work of Historic Charleston Foundation with revolving funds and area rehabilitation.

Perhaps the best indication of the arrival of Charleston on the national scene was its hosting of the annual conference of the National Trust for Historic Preservation in November 1970, coordinated by Historic Charleston Foundation. Over sixteen hundred people gathered in Charleston for the meeting of the nonprofit National Trust, the country's largest private preservation organization, chartered in 1949 to promote historic preservation in the United States. Among the five days of presentations, receptions, and tours on the general theme of "Preservation in Our Changing Cities," the foundation's activities and especially its Ansonborough project were prominently featured. An entire panel discussion was devoted to the subject of "The Charleston Story," and one of three "tours of preservation techniques" took visiting preservationists into Ansonborough to see "the methods used to bring back from slum" this section of the city.[50] Tour brochures informed visitors that in Ansonborough they would see "adaptive use on an area-wide scale" and explained the role of Historic Charleston Foundation in assuming "the financial burden of 'showing the way' to practical modern use of fine old buildings."[51] In a lengthy essay in the conference program, Frances Edmunds also highlighted the success of the Ansonborough project, stressing its lessons for preservationists all across the country: the feasibility of similar area reha-

*"The Charleston Story," National Trust for Historic Preservation*
> The Ansonborough project brought wide attention to Charleston's architectural heritage
> and the work of Historic Charleston Foundation. The best indication of the arrival of
> Charleston on the national scene was its hosting of the annual conference of the National
> Trust for Historic Preservation in November 1970. An entire panel discussion was
> devoted to "The Charleston Story," with presentations from Peter Manigault, Frances R.
> Edmunds, Dr. George C. Rogers, and Joseph H. McGee. Courtesy, *Charleston Evening
> Post,* 6 November 1970.

bilitation projects elsewhere and the utility of revolving funds for stimulating preservation by the private sector.[52]

As suggested by her role at the Charleston meeting of the National Trust, by 1970 Frances Ravenel Smythe Edmunds had established herself as both a formidable force for preservation in Charleston and an important figure in the American preservation movement. Her association with Historic Charleston Foundation had begun soon after the organization's founding, and the evolution of the foundation over the following four decades directly reflected the confidence of her personality, the authority of her operating style, and the tenacity of her vision for preservation. As one acquaintance explained: "Frances came from a family that was confident about dealing with anything, so she didn't hesitate when she was asked to be the executive director of a new preservation organization. . . . She would take on anybody. Charleston wouldn't begin to look the way it does today if it hadn't been for her willingness to make enemies anywhere. Practically speaking, she saved the city and put it back on the map."[53] At the time of her retirement in 1985

Frances Edmunds was regarded as the most influential woman in Charleston (the mayor was considered the most influential man).[54] A native Charlestonian, she was the daughter and granddaughter of a line of prominent attorneys and the great granddaughter of an early historian of Charleston who is often credited with introducing the city and its heritage to the world—and to Charlestonians.[55] The future foundation director had been educated at Saint Timothy's School in Catonsville, Maryland, and at the College of Charleston, and she subsequently gained valuable experience working as a newspaper reporter and later as a real estate agent. She married attorney S. Henry Edmunds, became the mother of three daughters, and in 1948 at the age of thirty-one she volunteered to serve as a "hostess" during the inaugural season of Historic Charleston Foundation's spring house tours. In fairly short order Frances Edmunds assumed responsibilities as the director of tours, the first paid staff position at the foundation.[56] Her organizational and promotional skills gave the tours a firm financial footing—eventually they proved one of its most successful fund-raising efforts—and Frances Edmunds soon found herself in charge of the entire organization, in a position variously labeled executive secretary, director, and ultimately executive director.

Frances Edmunds oversaw the establishment of the revolving fund in 1957 and the selection of Ansonborough as the foundation's first area rehabilitation project in 1959, and from this experience in Charleston she emerged as an important national commentator on the value of adaptive use of historic buildings.[57] When the National Trust met for its annual conference in San Diego in 1971, the year following its meeting in Charleston, the organization recognized Frances Edmunds with its highest honor, the Louise du Pont Crowninshield Award. The award acknowledged her work with Historic Charleston Foundation, not just in Ansonborough but also in other preservation planning initiatives in the 1960s that included a major revision of Charleston's zoning ordinance, a significant expansion of the historic district, and a successful program to beautify the city's financial and legal center along Broad Street. These and other preservation planning projects from the 1960s through the 1980s are the subject of the following chapter.[58]

Chapter 5

# LET THE OLD EXIST IN
# HARMONY WITH THE NEW
*Preservation Planning*

THROUGH PRESERVATION PLANNING Historic Charleston Foundation sought to anticipate change and weave it into the historic fabric of Charleston in ways that would enhance the quality of modern urban life. The foundation played a wide-ranging role in preservation planning in the 1960s, 1970s, and 1980s by working to augment municipal authority, participating in long-term planning, and acting as a preservation advocate. The foundation attempted to strengthen the authority of municipal government by proposing revisions to the zoning ordinance, expansions of the city's historic districts, and extensions of the enforcement powers of the Board of Architectural Review. In an effort to adopt a proactive approach to urban growth, the foundation initiated, funded, and contributed its expertise to architectural and planning studies intended to take a comprehensive, long-term look at issues such as beautification and revitalization, tourism management, and transportation development. As an advocate and watchdog, the foundation assessed the impact of public works and private-sector ventures and sought to encourage sensitive development and compliance with preservation regulations. Historic Charleston Foundation's projects in preservation planning in the 1960s, 1970s, and 1980s were far-flung, and it is useful to look at a sample of the most significant and more visible of them over this thirty-year period.

## URBAN RENEWAL AND AREA REHABILITATION

The foundation's first sustained initiative in preservation planning focused on urban renewal, in the Ansonborough project. As fund-raising proceeded for the revolving fund in the late 1950s, trustees briefly considered a simultaneous initiative. They sought the advice of planner Carl Feiss, whom they brought to Charleston for a three-day visit early in 1959. Feiss told the trustees that he was skeptical about the ability of a revolving fund to actually "revolve," or at least to revolve rapidly enough to effect urban revitalization beyond a limited area. He recommended that the foundation expand its focus and develop a comprehensive preservation plan for the whole city. He urged trustees to undertake an architectural inventory in order to update the 1941 survey by the Carolina Art Association, supplying current information on structural condition and market value and expanding its geographical breadth.[1] He wanted particular attention paid to the "grey areas" of the city that had architectural character but lacked the financial resources to halt deterioration. Feiss argued that with an inventory like this in hand, the foundation would be in a position to formulate a conservation plan that could be presented to municipal government for implementation. However, the risks associated with the nascent Ansonborough venture discouraged trustees from taking on an ambitious additional project. Feiss's suggestion was eventually adopted, but not until the 1970s.[2]

Instead, urban redevelopment became the initial focus of the foundation's preservation planning efforts. Removing blight had, of course, provided a primary rationale for both the privately financed Ansonborough project and the adjacent, municipally funded auditorium. Historic Charleston Foundation began a search for ways to supplement local funding with federal dollars, which seemed to be flowing out of Washington, D.C. in a growing torrent in the 1950s and 1960s, joining with city officials and the Chamber of Commerce to try to divert some of this flow to Charleston. However, these joint efforts were repeatedly rebuffed by voters, who seemed to prefer a limited role for government in these matters. The state supreme court had ruled that South Carolina cities lacked the authority to condemn private property for resale to private redevelopers, making the cities ineligible to participate in federal urban renewal programs. Efforts to extend this authority to local government failed

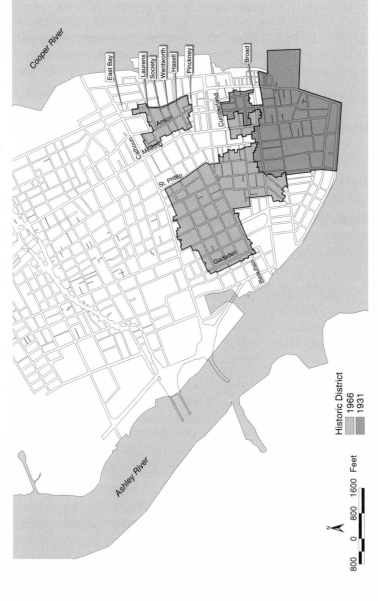

*The 1966 expansion of the "Old and Historic Charleston District."*

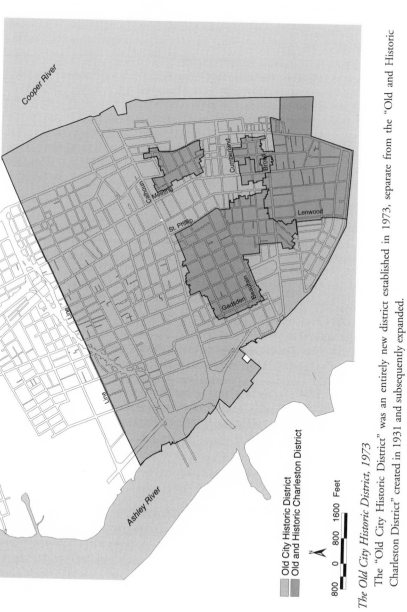

*The Old City Historic District, 1973*

The "Old City Historic District" was an entirely new district established in 1973, separate from the "Old and Historic Charleston District" created in 1931 and subsequently expanded.

Old City Historic District
Old and Historic Charleston District

800  0  800  1600  Feet

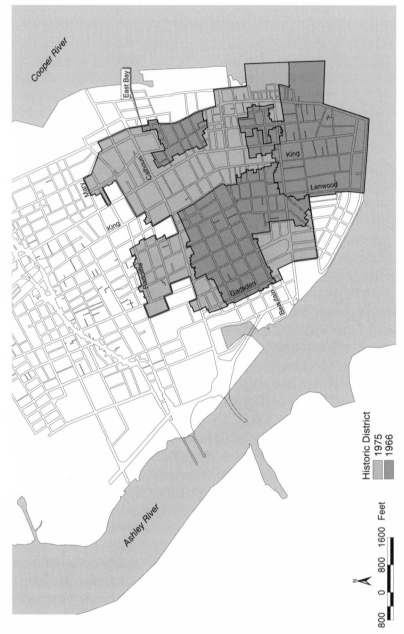

The 1975 expansion of the "Old and Historic Charleston District."

Historic District
1975
1966

N

800   0   800   1600   Feet

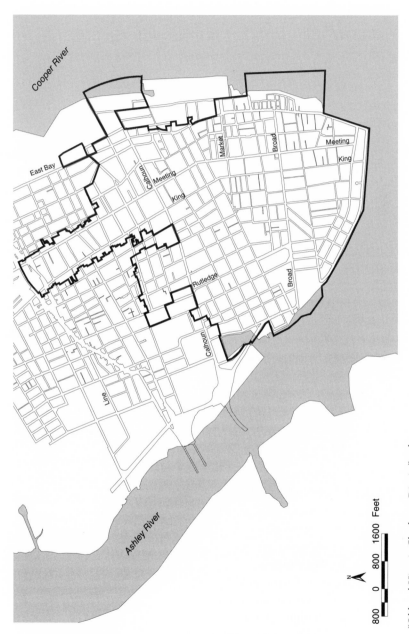

*The "Old and Historic Charleston District" today.*

in several elections from the late 1950s through the 1960s.[3] Eventually the foundation decided to pursue redevelopment funds on its own as a way to establish an urban renewal program for the city. With a salary provided by Mr. and Mrs. Charles Henry Woodward of Philadelphia, who had previously donated houses and funds to the Ansonborough project, Historic Charleston Foundation hired an expert on federal programs as a staff member in July 1966. Formerly with the redevelopment authority in Philadelphia, the new planner, Peter J. McCahill, was described by a local newspaper as someone "familiar with the rabbit warrens of the federal government treasury as it relates to urban renewal funding."[4] One of the first projects was a multiyear effort to devise a master plan for redevelopment of the old City Market using federal beautification and improvement funds.[5] For the most part the foundation continued to make the Ansonborough area rehabilitation project the focus of its urban renewal interests, and in the 1970s it expanded the concept to uptown boroughs, such as Wraggborough and Radcliffeborough.[6]

## REVISING THE ZONING ORDINANCE IN 1966

Zoning had long been an important mechanism by which historic preservation influenced development in Charleston, and in time Historic Charleston Foundation's focus on urban renewal was joined by a campaign to strengthen the zoning ordinance. In the process the foundation emerged as the pivotal architect of the first significant revision of the city's preservation ordinance in 1966, thirty-five years after the pioneering statute was adopted. The ordinance had remained almost unchanged since 1931. A small but valuable modification had been made in 1959, when the Board of Architectural Review (BAR) was given the power to delay for up to ninety days the demolition of any building constructed before 1860 within the city limits. This measure was intended to allow a window of opportunity for private-sector preservationists to devise a permanent alternative to demolition. Previously the Board of Architectural Review had no authority even to comment upon pending demolitions. The BAR was also given power to review exterior alterations to any building constructed before 1860 within the city limits, an expansion of its authority beyond the original Old and Historic Charleston District.[7] The modification of the zoning ordinance in 1959 was important for finally bringing the issue of demolition under the oversight of the Board of Architectural Review and for extending limited BAR authority throughout the city, but it did not anticipate either the pressures of growth in the 1960s or the pace of demolition outside the Old and Historic Charleston District.

The wide-ranging revisions to Charleston's preservation ordinance in 1966 significantly expanded the powers of the Board of Architectural Review and the geographical area over which that authority was exercised. The size of the Old and Historic Charleston District was tripled, and preservation review in this enlarged area was tightened. In perhaps the most important change, the Board of Architectural Review was given the power to deny, not just to delay, demolition of buildings. This authority extended to an expanded Old and Historic Charleston District that encompassed portions of the city stretching as far north as Calhoun Street and included Historic Charleston Foundation's ongoing rehabilitation project in Ansonborough.[8] In addition the new ordinance sought to formalize and professionalize BAR procedures by instituting a preapplication review of major projects, requiring applications to include drawings and photographs, establishing a process of public notification of agenda items, and setting up a publicly accessible archive of application materials and board decisions. The terms of office and composition of the Board of Architectural Review were changed as well to provide for staggered, limited terms and to increase the number of board members from five to seven (to allow the mayor to appoint two people who "have demonstrated outstanding interest and knowledge in historical or architectural development within the city").[9] The effect of these changes was to create a more powerful Board of Architectural Review that was also more professional in its deliberations, more publicly accountable for its decisions, and somewhat less vulnerable to political pressure.

By furnishing a set of specific recommendations for revision of the zoning ordinance, Historic Charleston Foundation played an enormously influential role in updating the ordinance in 1966. A year or so earlier the foundation had embarked on a study of how zoning was used in other cities to encourage historic preservation. As Joseph H. McGee, the attorney who undertook the study, explained: "In the years since 1931 many other American cities have enacted this type of municipal ordinance, and probably the majority of them have built upon the Charleston law, in fact many have copied it almost word for word. This has given us an opportunity, however, to study changes made by the other cities and an idea of how we could improve ours through the experience of other areas."[10] As the research went forward on this national survey, the city's Planning and Zoning Commission initiated its own assessment of the adequacy of the entire municipal zoning ordinance, of which historic preservation was only a small part. "This presented us a unique opportunity to influence changes in the Zoning Law," the foundation attorney observed in a report to the trustees prior to public hearings on the proposed changes.[11] As it turned out, the zoning ordinance adopted in August 1966 incorporated almost all of the foundation recommendations: the enlarged historic district, the power to deny demolition, the formalization of procedures, and the changes in board composition and terms. In one long-term suggestion the foundation recommended "classification" of all buildings outside the Old and Historic Charleston District. Under such a plan the city would compile a list of architecturally significant buildings, consult with owners, and then extend to these landmarks the same degree of protection as buildings in the Old and Historic Charleston District were given. It was a novel and pioneering suggestion, largely untried in the United States at the time. (In 1975 a system for classifying buildings was adopted in Charleston.) In only two areas were the foundation recommendations not adopted. The effort to curb "demolition by neglect" by requiring owners to maintain their property was less coercive than recommended. In addition the foundation wanted to make subject to review all exterior alterations, not just alterations visible from a street or public thoroughfare as in the old ordinance, but this change was not made.[12]

This effort to revise the zoning ordinance illustrated one important way in which Historic Charleston Foundation participated in preservation planning. Initiating its own studies and contributing its findings and expertise on a pro bono basis, the foundation sought to be a catalyst in the formulation of sound public policy. By 1966 it had effected the first major revision of the city's seminal preservation ordinance and a dramatic expansion of the Old and Historic Charleston District.

## Beautifying Broad Street

Downtown revitalization would become the goal of preservation planning and a number of development ventures in the 1970s and 1980s. One of the earliest of these efforts focused on Broad Street, the city's financial and legal center. Through the Broad Street Beautification Plan, Historic Charleston Foundation took the lead in coordinating an extensive face-lift of an architecturally impressive four-block stretch of Broad Street dominated by eighteenth-, nineteenth-, and twentieth-century commercial buildings. The 1966

## BROAD STREET BEAUTIFICATION PLAN

SPONSORED BY
HISTORIC CHARLESTON FOUNDATION

A FACE LIFTING FOR A BUSINESS DISTRICT, PROBABLY AMERICA'S OUT STANDING COMMERCIAL STREET IN TERMS OF HISTORICAL IMPORTANCE COMBINED WITH ARCHITECTURAL VALUES.

*Beautifying Broad Street*
One of the earliest efforts at downtown revitalization focused on Broad Street, the city's financial and legal center, in the late 1960s. Overhead utility wires were removed, and property owners were encouraged to remove inappropriate signs and to paint with historic colors. Courtesy, HCF.

revisions to the zoning ordinance had placed Broad Street within the Old and Historic Charleston District, and the foundation's program was established two years later to revitalize the area through beautifying the streetscape and enhancing the appearance of buildings. With grant support from the America the Beautiful Fund and technical assistance from Historic Charleston Foundation, Broad Street property owners and tenants were encouraged to paint facades in historic color schemes and remove inappropriate signs. Research undertaken on each building also permitted the placement of informative historical plaques. The city and local utilities cooperated to

remove overhead wiring by placing electrical and telephone lines underground and to upgrade landscaping through tree plantings. While beautification would seem a modest goal in comparison with subsequent revitalization
programs, the Broad Street plan showed the opportunities for collaboration
between preservationists and downtown interests and reaffirmed a commitment to the viability of downtown even in an era of suburban expansion.[13]

THE HISTORIC PRESERVATION PLAN OF 1974

Through a grant from the state historic preservation office, city government
set out in 1971 to develop a comprehensive preservation plan for Charleston.
Historic Charleston Foundation lent its support to this civic initiative by supplying technical assistance, participating in planning meetings over a three-
year period, and advancing specific proposals, most notably the wording for
a potential height ordinance. The origins of this municipal project can be
traced back to the late 1950s, when consultant Carl Feiss was brought to
Charleston to advise the trustees of Historic Charleston Foundation as they
were embarking on the Ansonborough rehabilitation project. At the time
Feiss had recommended an architectural survey of Charleston as the basis for
developing a comprehensive historic preservation plan. In 1971 the city's
Planning and Zoning Commission brought Feiss back to implement his proposal, and the so-called Feiss-Wright-Anderson plan was presented to the city
as its historic preservation plan in June 1974.[14] Many, but by no means all, of
its recommendations were adopted by City Council between 1974 and 1978.

At the core of the preservation plan was the most elaborate inventory yet
undertaken of historic structures in Charleston. Planners cast their net
broadly to include buildings on the entire peninsula south of Highway 17,
known locally as the Crosstown Expressway.[15] Remarkably, both the exteriors
of buildings and the architectural features of interiors were investigated by the
survey teams. The results of this field work were evaluated by a panel of outside experts, who compiled a list of 2,288 buildings divided into four categories of architectural merit: exceptional, excellent, significant, and
contributory. These classifications were designed to indicate both architectural importance and preservation potential. For example, "exceptional"
buildings were of the highest design quality and were recommended for
preservation and protection at all costs. In contrast, "contributory" structures
had contextual value in giving character to the settings of buildings ranked in
the higher categories.[16] The inventory was adopted as an official city docu-

ment in June 1975, but not before it was amended to delete the "contributory" classification, despite the plea of the alderman who argued that dropping one of the four classifications recommended by the consultants would represent "invading a carefully worked-out plan."[17] Adoption of the amended historic architecture inventory placed the structures listed in the three official categories (designated 1, 2, and 3) under the authority of the Board of Architectural Review and established a repository of architectural information to inform decisions about development.[18]

Perhaps the most far-reaching recommendation to come out of the Feiss-Wright-Anderson study was the set of proposals to replace the existing Board of Architectural Review with a historic preservation commission. The consultants' report proposed that the new commission have broad authority to buy and sell property, operate a revolving fund, establish protective covenants, and hold conservation easements, among other powers. The recommendation seemed inspired by the success of the private-sector initiatives of Historic Charleston Foundation, especially in Ansonborough, but the public body would also have the power to use eminent domain for preservation purposes. Ultimately, though, no action was taken to replace the Board of Architectural Review with this commission.[19]

More successfully, one of the most significant changes to result from the historic preservation plan was the height ordinance. The idea was initially suggested by Historic Charleston Foundation; it was incorporated into the preservation plan proposed in 1974 and eventually adopted by City Council in 1978. To study the issue of height and high-density development in Charleston, the foundation had contracted in 1972 with a pair of Philadelphia consultants, Edmund M. Bacon and John Bower. Their recommendations included a fifty-foot height limit for all new structures in most areas south of Calhoun Street, with exceptions made for designated commercial and industrial areas, where ninety-foot height limits were set. Advocates argued that the proposed zoning ordinance would preserve the architectural quality of Charleston's streetscape and skyline while minimizing the overcrowding, traffic congestion, and expensive municipal infrastructure associated with high density development.[20] "Density is the greatest mistake that urban areas have made, to stack families and offices on top of each other," foundation president Thomas E. Thornhill maintained. "The quality of life has always been hurt when buildings get taller," he warned.[21]

The historic preservation plan of 1974 incorporated the foundation's height ordinance as one of its major recommendations, but the idea attracted considerable public criticism. Opponents contended that high-rise development was a desirable way to build the local economy and augment the municipal tax base and, to judge from the experience of other cities, was inevitable in the late twentieth century.[22] "Are you going to stifle future business growth?" demanded one opponent, who argued that height limitations would "place a ceiling on the value of property" and make new construction unprofitable.[23] Action on the height ordinance was postponed for four years, until December 1978, when City Council adopted a revised ordinance that divided the city into nine height districts, each with its own restrictions on new construction. The area covered by this ordinance—all of the city south of Mount Pleasant Street—was considerably larger than that covered in the foundation's original proposal, but the restrictions were more nuanced, reflecting the compromises that had been necessary to find popular support.[24] Thomas Thornhill, who had worked hard for passage of a height ordinance as president of Historic Charleston Foundation, summarized the reasons that citizens had spent so much time debating the need for the ordinance in the 1970s. Contrary to conventional wisdom, Thornhill explained, the height ordinance was not designed simply to preserve charming views of Charleston's historic skyline and streetscape, and it was certainly not intended to halt new construction in the historic district. Rather, it sought "to provide for orderly growth" by establishing a framework through which an old city could "continue to exist in harmony" with new economic development.[25]

The planning process of the 1970s produced a viable height ordinance and a historic preservation plan sanctioned by broad public support; municipal authority in historic preservation was extended in other ways as well in the 1970s and 1980s, chiefly through expanding the sphere of BAR review. The Old and Historic Charleston District continued to offer the most protective control in the city: approval from the Board of Architectural Review was required for demolition or relocation of any building and for repairs, alterations, and additions visible from a public right-of-way. The Old and Historic Charleston District encompassed most of the city below Calhoun Street but also a few neighborhoods above it, including the historic suburbs of Radcliffeborough and Wraggborough. Not quite as much protective control existed in the separate Old City Historic District, which had been established to encompass much of the rest of the city south of Line Street and was extended beyond the peninsular city in 1990. In the Old City Historic District approval from the Board of Architectural Review was required for demolition and relocation of buildings older than seventy-five years of age or rated in categories 1, 2, or 3 in the city's architectural inventory.[26] Approval was also required for all new construction visible from a public right-of-way and for repairs and alterations to buildings older than one hundred years or rated in categories 1, 2, or 3. And in a third area even further to the north, between Line and Mount Pleasant Streets, approval from the Board of Architectural Review was required for demolitions and relocation of buildings older than seventy-five years of age or rated in categories 1, 2, or 3.[27]

To outsiders it seemed a chaos of multiple jurisdictions and complicated restrictions, but the system reflected the evolution of Charleston's zoning ordinance and Board of Architectural Review from the 1960s through the 1980s. As the historic and architectural significance of uptown neighborhoods had come to be appreciated, the police power of the Board of Architectural Review had been extended progressively north up the peninsula. In the resulting pattern the most protective control was exercised over the enclaves nearest the Battery and the fewest restrictions applied in areas farthest north.

## TOURISM MANAGEMENT

Only comparatively recently has tourism been perceived as a mixed blessing for Charleston. Throughout the 1960s local newspapers excitedly applauded the number of out-of-town visitors streaming into Charleston, and a flurry of development studies examined strategies for boosting the role of "the travel industry" in the local economy. By the mid 1970s tourism had become the city's leading source of revenue: visitors were coming to Charleston in ever increasing numbers, and they came during all seasons of the year, not just for the southern spring and its spectacular displays of flowers.[28] This success precipitated questions about the impact of tourism on the quality of residential life in the city, especially for those who lived in the favored tourist destinations, among the grand homes and charming lanes at the southern tip of the peninsula. "The traffic of the once serene city boggles the mind," one citizen complained, "and the side effects of a successful tourist industry unravels [sic] one's nerves."[29]

Beginning in the late 1970s the city began concerted efforts to manage, not just to promote, tourism. A series of ordinances sought to specify the streets in the Old and Historic Charleston District where horse-drawn carriages and tour buses could travel, the size of buses and the number of their passengers, and where the vehicles could begin tours and pick up passengers. The popularity of the horse-drawn carriages eventually inspired requirements that horses wear "diapers" and that operators mop up urine spilled on city streets. To enhance the educational possibilities of the tours, the city enacted an ordinance requiring guides to pass a test on Charleston's history and architecture.[30]

The most elaborate attempt to manage tourism in the 1970s and 1980s was the construction of what came to be known as the Visitor Reception and Transportation Center. The idea had been conceived by Frances Edmunds and was formally developed in a *Tourism Impact and Management Study* prepared by the Barton-Aschman consulting firm for Charleston County and released in February 1978.[31] While Charleston already had a modest tourist information center housed in the historic Arch Building on Calhoun Street, Mayor Joseph P. Riley Jr., who had been elected in 1975, wanted a multipurpose tourist complex that would help support several of his urban initiatives.[32] Eventually the favored location for the complex became Wraggborough, along a stretch of upper Meeting Street some distance from the historic area. One goal for the proposed visitor center was to exert more guidance on how tourists used the city. As suggested by its name, the center was intended both to orient visitors and to serve as a transportation hub from which people would be encouraged to walk or ride trolleys into the historic area. Large buses would drop all passengers at the visitor center, and private automobiles would be discouraged from navigating city streets by providing ample, inexpensive parking as well as advice that Charleston was best experienced on foot. Part of the orientation would stress that Charleston was a living city, not a museum village like Williamsburg, and that people actually lived in the restored homes.[33]

In supporting a location for the visitor center in Wraggborough, Mayor Riley hoped the facility would achieve a second important goal: revitalization of the business district along upper King Street. Proponents were recommending, in addition to the visitor-transportation hub, construction of a complex of hotels, restaurants, shops, an office building, a parking garage, and a relocated Amtrak and bus station, all on a two-block area of former railroad warehouses bounded by Meeting, John, King, and Mary Streets. Some visionaries described the area as a potential museum district for the city. Across Meeting Street from the proposed site was the Charleston Museum's new building, then under construction, and nearby were two of its historic house museums, the venerable Joseph Manigault House and the recently acquired Aiken-Rhett House. Establishing a railroad museum was also suggested because the site for the visitor center was already a National Historic Landmark significant for its association with South Carolina's early railroad history.[34]

A final role for the visitor center emerged in the controversy over a hotel and convention center that had been proposed for lower King Street in the mid 1970s, shortly after Mayor Riley had taken office.[35] The mayor's plan for a hotel complex stimulated enormous opposition largely because of concern about the potential adverse impact of tourism. In the eventual resolution of this contentious issue, the city was required to implement the recommendations in the 1978 tourism study, which included establishment of a visitor reception center. In the end, the mayor was able to go forward with the hotel complex, and he could argue that the downtown convention center would not in fact bring too many tourists to Charleston because a midtown visitor center would shift tourists from downtown residential neighborhoods into new areas, such as Wraggborough and its museum district, shops all along King Street, and a new park planned on the Cooper River, among others.[36] The construction of this latter project, Waterfront Park, went on in tandem with the Visitor Reception and Transportation Center during the 1980s. Historic Charleston Foundation pushed for both projects as useful ways to manage tourism while enhancing the urban environment. In the case of Waterfront Park, the foundation also contributed fifteen thousand dollars toward the costs of its construction.[37]

The politics surrounding the hotel and convention complex—which was called Charleston Place when it was completed in the mid 1980s—affected who was involved in the planning for the Visitor Reception and Transportation Center. The mayor excluded the Preservation Society of Charleston because the society had been vigorously opposing the hotel development and was then, in 1980, in the process of suing the city to stop it. The mayor informed the society's president that he had "no intention whatsoever" of involving the city's oldest preservation organization, because he had found them "unreliable and completely impossible to work with" on the hotel-convention complex.[38] By contrast, Historic Charleston Foundation, which had endorsed the hotel project, was invited to participate in the planning and construction of the visitor center. The foundation worked closely with the city's consultants, suggesting modifications in the size and retailing operations and loaning its name in support of the $3 million bond issue that voters approved in November 1987.[39] The foundation also proved instrumental in resolving the issue of the project's impact on the National Historic Landmark buildings at the site, making the argument that "demolition by neglect" threatened the extant freight warehouses and that an adaptive-use project such as the visitor center would provide "needed stabilization."[40] The protracted controversy over the hotel-convention center delayed completion of the visitor center, as did Hurricane Hugo, which destroyed one of the main buildings at the site in 1989, but the visitor center and transportation pavilion opened in May 1991 after fourteen years of planning. Construction since then has surrounded the site with an office building, a parking garage, a hotel, restaurants, a railroad museum, and a music hall and entertainment complex, and upper King Street in general seems to be in the midst of an economic resurgence.[41]

THE CALHOUN STREET CORRIDOR STUDY

A particularly good example of how preservation had become a proactive form of urban planning was the *Calhoun Street Corridor Study,* a land-use plan initiated by Historic Charleston Foundation in 1988. Anticipating that Calhoun Street would undergo significant changes in the coming decades, the foundation asked the city to commission a study of long-range development options for this major downtown artery. The immediate impetus was a zoning application to build a McSleep Inn at the site now occupied by the new public library. But Calhoun Street also faced long-term development pressure in the form of projects slated for each end of the thoroughfare (the terminus of the James Island Bridge on the western end and an aquarium and a tour boat facility at the eastern end), as well as expected growth at two adjacent institutions, the College of Charleston and the hospital complex at the Medical University of South Carolina. The city consented to the request of Historic Charleston Foundation, declared a temporary zoning moratorium, and contracted with outside planning firms for the study, with funding provided in part by the foundation.[42]

The final report offered a set of recommendations for the development of Calhoun Street as a "gracious and functional urban boulevard." With a tripartite goal of accommodating growth, managing tourism, and preserving the historic scale and ambiance of the thoroughfare, the consultants laid out a block-by-block analysis of how this might be accomplished through new public amenities, sensitive private development, municipal design review, and formation of a coalition of public and private parties to ensure implementation of the plan. In general, the report tried to outline compatible land uses for the diverse corridor, while recommending beautification measures to give the street a distinct identity and articulating appropriate design concepts rooted in the city's architectural legacy. In this way the report sought "an integrated approach to sensitive preservation and appropriate development." City Council approved the report in concept in January 1989.[43]

PRESERVATION ADVOCACY: THE FEDERAL COURTHOUSE ANNEX

One of the most dramatic illustrations of the role that Historic Charleston Foundation played in preservation advocacy was the controversy in the 1980s over construction of an annex for the federal courthouse. The debate focused on both the design and the location of the proposed addition, and the conflict eventually reached the highest levels of preservation review in the United States. The seven-year-long controversy was unusually drawn-out—and the foundation was by no means the only preservation organization involved—but the battle over the annex reflected how the foundation participated as an important player in the civic debate over a major public works project.

The fight began when the General Services Administration (GSA) proposed the construction of a federal courthouse annex adjacent to the United States Post Office building, where all federal court facilities were then housed, in order to accommodate the increasing number of United States district judges posted to Charleston. The original plan called for a three-story, twelve-thousand-square-foot structure to be built on the site of a neighboring park, which the GSA characterized as "under-utilized" space. The local newspaper announced the plans in February 1980 and predicted that the new facility would be completed within two years, "barring any holdups."[44] As preliminary planning and congressional funding went forward, the size and cost of the courthouse annex dramatically expanded into a thirty-three-thousand-square-foot structure that included two courtrooms, judges' chambers, jury rooms, and offices for federal marshals and probation personnel. At that point a firestorm of protest broke out.[45]

Initial concerns focused on the exterior design of the annex, especially its scale and stylistic compatibility for Charleston. "It looks like a silo to store grain on the way to the Soviet Union," the state historic preservation officer declared in 1982 at one meeting set up by the General Services Administration to solicit comment from preservationists prior to finalizing a design.[46] In her role as executive director of Historic Charleston Foundation, Frances Edmunds voiced similar comments. "No one envisioned the mass that we see here," she observed, adding that "the park has become a little decoration."[47] Subsequent redesign by the General Services Administration in 1983 did not allay concerns about visual impact or the loss of park space, and ultimately Historic Charleston Foundation moved to a public position of "unequivocal opposition to the proposed exterior design" with its "monolithic proportions."[48]

The location, as much as the design, of the annex intensified the fight. The annex was proposed as an addition to the United States Post Office, one of the four historic buildings that defined the "Four Corners of Law" at the intersection of Meeting and Broad Streets. The Four Corners of Law was both the urban heart of modern Charleston and one of the most significant concentrations of historic architecture in the United States. The location was "the very epicenter" of Charleston's historic district, and it was surrounded by fifteen buildings designated as National Historic Landmarks and hundreds of structures listed on the National Register of Historic Places. "These buildings were carefully and deliberately designed to respect the traditions of the city, to be distinguished and to be a part of and contribute to the beauty and integrity of Charleston," Frances Edmunds observed at one public hearing in a plea that the General Services Administration find a design with more "grace and meaning" for "an historic area unequalled in this country."[49]

Because the courthouse annex was a federally funded undertaking, the controversy about its location and design was eventually reviewed by the Advisory Council on Historic Preservation, a presidentially appointed agency charged with oversight of the impact of federal projects on historic buildings. While findings of the Advisory Council are not legally binding on a federal agency, its recommendations can often be instructive in pointing the way to resolution.[50] Members of the Advisory Council convened in Charleston in December 1983 to review a scaled-down, two-story 22,700-square-foot plan and to listen to arguments that the project's environmental impact statement had failed to assess the seismic impact that sinking a foundation would have on nearby historic structures. Mayor Riley urged that an alternative location be found for the courthouse, at the nearby site of a former supermarket. This property was subsequently purchased by the city in order to hold it for the courthouse, and the city even proceeded to have schematic designs prepared for the site. Despite an Advisory Council recommendation that the General Services Administration build elsewhere or redesign, the GSA announced in

May 1984 that it would go ahead and build at the park adjacent to the Post Office because of the expense and delay that construction at a different location would entail. Also significant in the decision was the insistence of federal judges that the new annex be physically linked with the existing court facilities in the Post Office building.[51]

The decision ignited threats of court suits and even congressional action to defund the project entirely, but by the end of the year a compromise had been achieved among preservationists, city officials, federal judges, and GSA administrators. The catalyst for compromise was a "footprint" for the new building sketched on the back of a paper napkin during a meeting at a Columbia restaurant between Judge Solomon Blatt and Joseph H. McGee of Historic Charleston Foundation. The annex would be built just south of the Post Office as originally proposed, but it would be situated differently on the site, far back from Meeting Street. This setback would have the effect of leaving space for a sizable park in front of the building and a smaller park at the south end of the property, rendering the new structure invisible from the historic intersection at the Four Corners of Law. With a compromise secured on the location, attention turned to working out the details of the exterior appearance of the building. Agreement was eventually reached on a contemporary design by Goff Associates that incorporated materials and colors similar to those in the old Post Office. A groundbreaking ceremony was held in August 1986, and the completed federal courthouse annex opened in 1988.[52] A local newspaper characterized it as "a handsome structure in harmony with its surroundings."[53]

The controversy over the annex attracted enormous attention in Charleston during the 1980s, and it triggered activity at the highest levels of the American preservation system, when the Advisory Council on Historic Preservation became involved because agreement could not be worked out at the local level. The compromise that was eventually devised may have been influenced by the recommendations of the Advisory Council, but it was certainly shaped by the persistence of Charleston's preservation community—Historic Charleston Foundation and others—working with public officials at the federal, state, and municipal levels. It was an especially visible debate that illustrated well the decisive role preservation organizations such as the foundation played in making the case that modern planning decisions must take into account Charleston's unique design and architectural legacy.

In all of these examples—preservation advocacy related to a major public works project, planning studies of transportation corridors and visitor centers, architectural inventories, and revisions to municipal zoning ordinances—we see many of the forms that preservation planning can take, as well as some of the ways that Historic Charleston Foundation participated in efforts to weave change into the historic urban fabric. One of the most intense and intractable debates about the proper balance between preservation and development was the controversy in the late 1970s about a downtown hotel and convention center, the subject of the next chapter. Subsequent chapters will examine the role of Historic Charleston Foundation in preservation planning in uptown boroughs and beyond the peninsular city.

## Chapter 6

# THE "BATTLE OF CHARLESTON"
## *The Controversy over Charleston Place*

THE PROPOSAL TO build a hotel and convention center in the heart of the city ignited a fierce debate in Charleston in the late 1970s and early 1980s that divided public opinion locally and attracted considerable attention nationally. Just within the confines of Charleston's preservation community, the debate precipitated a schism between existing organizations, kindled new groups of opponents and proponents, and even incited an attempt to topple the leadership of the Preservation Society of Charleston. Historic Charleston Foundation played a significant, although less vocally confrontational role, a stance that opponents of the hotel complex criticized as prodevelopment and supporters defended as pragmatic. As in many cities contemplating similar proposals for new construction, the vortex of the storm involved the familiar issue of what balance ought to be struck between preservation and development. But because this was Charleston—and all sides maintained they were working to ensure the preservation of the city—the debate came to focus on the meaning and definition of preservation in a living historic city.

The driving force, more than anyone, behind the hotel and convention center in the mid 1970s was the newly elected mayor, Joseph P. Riley Jr., who had made the rejuvenation of King Street, the city's longtime retail thoroughfare, a centerpiece of his campaign. Toward this end a downtown revitalization plan prepared by Barton-Aschman Associates had recommended construction of a hotel and convention center at the King Street site formerly occupied by a Belk department store. In July 1977 Mayor Riley announced that a developer had been located for the project, Theodore B. Gould of the Holywell Corporation of Washington, D.C., and several months later architects revealed detailed plans for the project.[1]

The design proposed in October 1977 would go through various permutations over time (as would the name for the project), but the initial plans called for a 419-room, nine-story hotel surrounded by a four-story perimeter wing occupied by hotel suites, retail shops, and a "quality" department store. The reduced-height perimeter was intended to lessen the visual impact of the nine-story center block from the street level. A penthouse nightclub and elevator shaft would occupy a central tower 114 feet tall, approximately ten stories. In addition to the privately developed hotel and shopping complex, the proposal envisioned city assistance in constructing a convention center capa-

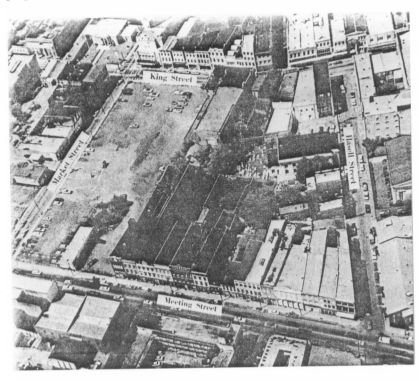

*Aerial view of site proposed for the hotel-convention complex*
Courtesy, *Charleston Evening Post,* 19 February 1979.

ble of seating twelve hundred banquet guests and an adjacent 750-car parking garage. The site itself would extend well beyond the former department
store property to encompass almost the entire block bounded by King, Market, Meeting, and Hasell Streets, and this expanded setting would necessitate
demolition of historic structures. The original price tag was placed at $30
million for the private developer and $10 million for city government, but
these figures rose with both the ongoing process of redesign and the infla-
tionary pressures of the late 1970s.[2]

To its proponents, the hotel-convention "complex," as it was initially
styled, offered a number of benefits to the city. First and foremost in the
minds of the mayor and Kenneth A. Gifford, the director of downtown revitalization, the project would be the catalyst for transforming lower King
Street into a thriving business district. A commonly cited estimate predicted
$70 million of spin-off development. Proponents also pointed to augmenta-
tion of the municipal tax base, the consequent reduction of residential property taxes, promotion of the tourist industry, and creation of employment
opportunities, first with temporary construction jobs and eventually with
over six hundred permanent positions.[3] Although the city would agree to
undertake construction of the parking garage and convention center, the cost
to taxpayers would be nothing, city officials maintained, because the lease of
these facilities to the developer would amortize the necessary revenue bonds.
The so-called Gould proposal seemed to hold out the promise of downtown
revitalization with minimal risk to the public treasury.[4]

Misgivings about the project began to surface in the fall of 1977, shortly
after the architects made their plans public. Few people doubted the need to
revive King Street or the utility of developing a vacant department store site.
But the magnitude of the development proposal and its long-term impact on
the historic district raised questions. Initially the apparent absence of public
input attracted criticism. To many it appeared that the early and enthusiastic
interest of Theodore Gould in the King Street property had hijacked the nor-
mal planning process, skewing the city's feasibility studies and encouraging
what some saw as the developer's take-it-or-leave-it attitude toward consultation and redesign. Subsequently the issue of demolition became a focus of
preservationist concern. The Gould proposal called for the city to clear sites
on King Street for the convention center and on Meeting Street for the parking garage. In the case of the garage, the rears of a number of Meeting Street
buildings were to be razed, while the facades would be spared to preserve the

*Two sketches of Charleston Place*
The first sketch uses a trick of perspective to minimize the height and mass of the then current proposal for the hotel-convention complex. The view is from the corner of Market and Meeting Streets with Market Hall on the far right. The *News and Courier* printed the drawing in order to blunt the impact of the second sketch, circulated by the Save Historic Charleston Fund, which shows a view from the same vantage point with the hotel-convention complex towering over Market Hall. Courtesy, *Charleston News and Courier,* 26 May 1978.

appearance of the existing streetscape.[5] The Preservation Society of Charleston became one of the most persistent critics of "facadism" as a form of preservation. William McIntosh, the society's president, warned that it would not accept "the precedent of saving only facades."[6]

For its part, Historic Charleston Foundation issued a lengthy statement on the hotel and convention center in December 1977, setting out a position that might be described as nonoppositional. Like many preservationists in Charleston immediately following the announcement of the Gould proposal, the foundation chose to express neither support nor opposition, but rather preferred to identify a set of concerns that it expected to be addressed. The foundation pointed out that the most important components of the project were the proposed high-quality department store and the associated shops, which would serve residents by replacing abandoned stores and providing a "keystone" for a revitalized shopping district. While supporting construction of a new hotel and the architectural effort to shield it "behind compatibly scaled retail spaces," the foundation suggested that the size of the 419-room proposal was "too large" and recommended a 350-room structure instead. The foundation was then in the midst of its campaign for a municipal height ordinance and consequently also voiced reservations about the height of the hotel exceeding ninety feet. The foundation urged a reduction in the size of the parking garage by one-third to accommodate five hundred cars. This would permit preservation of entire front sections, not just facades, of the Meeting Street buildings that it claimed were long "recognized as Charleston's finest collection of cast iron commercial structures." From the foundation's standpoint, the most controversial aspect of the Gould proposal was the convention center: its capacity suggested an intention to attract large gatherings to Charleston that would "dramatically increase the already challenging number of tourists by creating a new convention industry." For the foundation, then, the issues were both the massive architectural scale of the project for the historic district and a questionable commitment to promoting tourism. The foundation urged further studies to assess the impact of the hotel-convention complex on downtown Charleston.[7]

An outstanding legal question provided the means for the first sally of what came to be known as the "Battle of Charleston." Four preservation organizations joined a suit filed against the city in January 1978 designed to test the legality of the project's private-public partnership. Parties in the suit included the Preservation Society of Charleston and two neighborhood organizations, the Charlestown Neighborhood Association and the Harleston Village Association. None of the three opposed the concept of a downtown hotel and shops; rather, each questioned the size of the undertaking and the nature of the city's financial commitments. A fourth party to the suit was a newly formed organization, the Save Historic Charleston Fund, which opposed the concept of the project in its entirety.[8] Historic Charleston Foundation chose not to take part in this legal skirmish. At issue was the propriety of the city's involvement in a private development, essentially whether or not the city could issue bonds to build a convention center and garage associated with a private development and whether or not it could condemn private property for use by a private developer. Although a circuit court ruled in favor of the city, finding that the venture was an appropriate redevelopment project, in August 1978 the state supreme court declared the city's contract with the developer an invalid use of eminent domain.[9]

While this test case was making its way to the state supreme court during 1978, a federally mandated review process was also going forward. Because the city had received a federal grant for the purpose of acquiring land for the convention center and parking garage, the controversy over the project eventually came under the jurisdiction of the Advisory Council on Historic Preservation.[10] Members of the Advisory Council came to Charleston in January 1979 to tour the site and take public testimony. At the hearing, Historic Charleston Foundation went on record with conditional endorsement of the project, subject to review of all aspects of the plan by a panel of architects that the foundation offered to bring to Charleston. Foundation president Joseph H. McGee explained that the judgment represented the "near unanimous" agreement of the organization's thirty trustees, but he was quick to point out that "the circumstances are unique and the endorsement should not be considered as a precedent" that the foundation would support new construction in the historic district in the future.[11]

The foundation brought three architects to Charleston from Boston, New York, and Washington, D.C., shortly after the Advisory Council meeting, and it released their report in February 1979 with the hope that its recommendations would be "a catalyst for new and improved design."[12] While commending the concept of the project and the effort "to line the perimeter of the site with low-rise structures," the report recommended that more be done to reduce "the visibility of the high-rise element" by eliminating two or three stories (of the twelve stories then under consideration) and not widening Market Street. On the issue of appropriate design elements, the architects admitted that "there is no 19th century precedent for a high-rise structure, a department store, or a convention center" but urged that a redesign pay more attention to "the special architectural character of King Street" and its store-fronts. It was also suggested that an art deco movie theater directly across the street from the proposed convention center might profitably be reused "as a large meeting room/auditorium."[13] Local newspapers, which had been gener-ally supportive of the hotel-convention center, editorialized that "possibilities of reconciliation emerge very strongly from the recommendations" and urged the mayor to intervene with the developer. "That is all the foundation asks, and it is not asking too much," the paper argued.[14]

From these public consultations and from negotiations directly with the parties involved, the Advisory Council crafted a memorandum of agreement that was formally ratified in July 1979. Signed by the mayor, the developer, officials of the two federal agencies making grants to the city, the state historic preservation officer, and the Advisory Council, the agreement acknowledged the "adverse effect" on the historic district of "Charleston Center," as the complex had come to be known. But the Advisory Council maintained that the benefits outweighed the costs and set out a number of stipulations to mit-igate the damage, to be monitored throughout the design and construction phases by state and federal preservation officials. The memorandum required the rehabilitation of the front forty feet of nine Meeting Street buildings, with their facades to be restored at municipal expense and low-interest loans offered to owners for appropriate interior rehabilitation.[15] One of the most significant provisos required the city to implement a comprehensive tourism management plan to minimize the impact of visitors and their cars on the his-toric district through establishment of a visitor information center in a mid-town location, a river-front park to siphon tourist activity elsewhere, and a shuttle service and system of restrictive parking permits.[16]

The memorandum of agreement in 1979 did not bring the controversy to a close. Historic Charleston Foundation had been instrumental in facili-tating the Advisory Council process, but other preservationists were unhappy with the nature of this resolution. Spearheaded by the Preservation Society of Charleston, a lawsuit was filed to deny the city the use of crucial federal grant money. The suit made its way through the federal courts in 1980 but proved unsuccessful by December 1980, effectively marking the end of legal redress for opponents.[17] The story continued, though, with more unexpected turns.

Theodore Gould and his Holywell Corporation obtained preliminary approval from the Board of Architectural Review (BAR) to begin site preparation in mid 1981, but his financing for the project had collapsed by early 1983. As committed as ever to the project, Mayor Riley moved quickly to assemble a new partnership of developers and to arrange an attractive financial package in order to construct what was now being called "Charleston Place." In December 1984 the BAR gave "interim final approval" for the newly designed project, an eight-story, 450-room hotel and conference center that was four stories lower than the last Gould design and much reduced in scale and mass. Both Historic Charleston Foundation and the Preservation Society of Charleston expressed satisfaction with the redesign presented by the new developers. Ground breaking for the hotel occurred in early 1985, and the $75 million Charleston Place development opened for business in September 1986.[18] The city's public garage rose behind the facades and first forty feet of the stores along Meeting Street, amid a warning from one local newspaper that "facadism is a trend to be watched and avoided" lest Charleston become "a kind of Disneyland of false fronts."[19] The city successfully sold these storefronts to private investors for commercial use in 1987 and 1988. Three years after Charleston Place had opened, the city's revitalization director claimed that more than one hundred businesses had moved into the King-Market-Meeting Street area.[20]

The years of controversy, court action, charges, and countercharges caused turmoil within the ranks of established preservation organizations, spawned new groups of self-styled activists, and dominated public discourse and private conversation in Charleston in the late 1970s and early 1980s. One out-of-town commentator characterized it as "a preservation controversy that has become almost as hysterical as it is historical."[21] While the torrent of words was often full of vindictive, misleading, or unsubstantiated claims, the tumult represented a debate rooted in competing visions of how to define the meaning and purpose of preservation in Charleston.

The mayor, the city's two major newspapers, many business interests, and Historic Charleston Foundation adopted a capacious view of historic preservation. "Preservation means many things—many of which are obvious," Mayor Riley asserted during the early stages of the controversy. "One of the things it also means in a city like Charleston is keeping a central business district alive and helping it return to the degree of activity, attractive appearance and economic health that is important to a city."[22] Charleston suffered from "classic Main Street sickness," he argued, and the hotel and convention center was the remedy.[23] A national newspaper that covered the Advisory Council hearing suggested that Historic Charleston Foundation's support for the hotel and convention center represented a "new approach" to historic preservation: "accepting the new if it harmonizes with the old"; the state historic preservation officer, who had taken heat for the role he had played in the Advisory Council's review process, concurred that "an imaginative mix of historic preservation and new building" was the key to urban revitalization.[24] From this perspective, preservation in a living city like Charleston represented a negotiation of interests, informed by sensitivity to the historic setting and sympathy to economic realities.

The leadership of the Preservation Society of Charleston took a far less accommodationist approach toward new construction in the historic district, and this venerable organization assumed the lead in opposing the mayor and the developer, filing lawsuits to stop the project and staking out a position of "pure" preservation by opposing demolition of historic structures as a matter of course. Although the society supported a hotel on the vacant King Street site, it did not endorse the block-sized complex of Theodore Gould, which it characterized at one point as the product of "politics and big-city development greed" and the result of "a local authority in league with a high pressure developer."[25] The executive director of the Preservation Society and several society presidents became some of the mayor's most vocal critics as the debate wore on; they were unafraid to issue frank opinions questioning mayoral character and motives—and earned considerable mayoral enmity in return. One consequence of the society's unyielding stance was a remarkable attempt in the spring of 1979 to topple its leadership by packing the membership rolls with proponents of the hotel and convention center, followed by running an alternative slate of candidates in the traditionally uncontested annual election of officers. All firm proponents of the hotel complex, this slate—many of whom were brand-new society members—was derided as "the business slate" in society literature and decisively defeated. A subsequent opinion poll specifically on the hotel issue showed that the membership of the Preservation Society opposed the project by a margin of 62 percent to 38 percent.[26]

Members of the Preservation Society had a variety of reasons for their opposition to the hotel and convention complex, but in general their views reflected deep and genuine feelings about the incompatibility of massive new construction for the historic district, anxiety about the future of Charleston neighborhoods, and reservations—even hostility—to the prospect of a tourist-based economy. One citizen explained why the hotel development had galvanized such vehement opposition: "Charleston Center has been the lightning rod for every piece of horse dung and every tourist that knocks on the door asking to go to the bathroom," referring to the horse-drawn carriage tours and visitors who seemed to think the city is a collection of house museums rather than private homes.[27] The popular perception of conventions reenforced many of the concerns about tourism, with images of drunken conventioneers stumbling around downtown and through quiet residential streets. (As these concerns emerged, proponents began to speak of the project as a conference center rather than a convention complex.) Traffic jams, increased commercialization, and demolition of historic buildings raised more general issues about the livability of the city, particularly in the comfortable neighborhoods in the vicinity of downtown. "We're speaking not just about saving one block, but about preserving a way of life of the people of Charleston," Henry F. Cauthen Jr., executive director of the Preservation Society, maintained in one public forum expressing a widely shared apprehension.[28] To many, residential Charleston seemed on the brink of being transformed into a commercialized tourist mecca like the French Quarter in New Orleans.[29]

The organization that focused more heat than light on the debate was the Save Historic Charleston Fund, a small group of residents and part-time residents who banded together in January 1978 to denounce the development in no uncertain terms. Styling themselves "conservative preservationists" who were picking up the ball because existing groups were divided and "did not oppose the whole complex," the Save Historic Charleston Fund committed itself to opposing all aspects of the development.[30] As R. de Treville Lawrence explained in an early volley directed at Mayor Riley, the project was "a massive dose of medicine that would kill the patient instead of revitalizing him."[31] In a subsequent interview with the *Los Angeles Times* he suggested that the development "makes about as much sense as putting a Holiday Inn in the middle of a redwood forest."[32] The critique seemed to be based on a profound distrust of change of any sort: Charleston was a unique and special place, and residents would be better off if the city were left undiscovered. "I think we ought to stay low key and not attract too many people and not turn Charleston into a Disney World," one supporter of the Save Historic Charleston Fund explained.[33]

While it joined with other preservation organizations in various suits, the Save Historic Charleston Fund was probably most effective—its adversaries would say irresponsible—in directing enormous national attention to the local controversy through mass mailings to preservation organizations, public officials, and newspapers in anticipation of the Advisory Council findings. Frequently apocalyptic in tone ("America's Most Pressing Preservation Crisis in 1979"), the broadsides resonated with people across the country who were familiar with the simple dichotomy (and classic conflict) between developer and preservationist.[34] Typical of the press response was the West Virginia paper that editorialized about "the mayor's nightmarish project" that was being "vigorously opposed by Charlestonians of taste and refinement."[35] A journalist writing for the bimonthly magazine of the National Trust for Historic Preservation saw that there were more complicated and subtle questions involved in the controversy. It was not "one of those open-and-shut issues like a fast-food joint threatening to wipe out a pilgrims' cemetery," he observed. Indeed, he concluded that Charleston's debate reflected "the tough choices facing preservationists these days" about how welcoming they should be to change.[36]

The success of the Save Historic Charleston Fund in garnering attention for its views inspired hotel proponents to establish their own publicity apparatus, the Downtown Residents for Charleston Center. The group was organized in October 1978 to counter the growing adverse national publicity and to facilitate approval for the project in the impending federal environmental and preservation review process. Using arguments that had become well-known to most Charlestonians, the organization assembled a slick twelve-page promotional brochure and distributed ten thousand copies to preservationists throughout the country and to regional and national newspapers. The brochure declared that "Charleston Center is a Catalyst to Preservation" because it was "the rare project that contributes to preservation and the economy." Images and text were used to make the case for the shabbiness of downtown, the possibilities for revitalizing 233 endangered buildings, and the nonintrusiveness of the proposed hotel and convention center on the historic city. With both local and national audiences in mind, the brochure raised the delicate issue of tourism, welcoming affluent visitors (those "'upscale' individuals who patronize first-class hotels such as the one planned for Charleston Center") and holding out the threat of "a lower economic class of tourists" who drive rather than fly when they travel, do not appreciate museums or historic preservation, and prefer a "family-style motel." The brochure explained pointedly that the developer was more than willing to lease the property for a motel if he could not get his hotel.[37] The publicity paid off, and the Downtown Residents for Charleston Center disbanded shortly after the Advisory Council ratified the memorandum of agreement on the project. In its press campaign the organization had appealed to the country's traditionally well-heeled preservationist constituency with a tale of appropriate development rescuing a historically charming city.

The "Battle of Charleston" took place because the hotel and convention center represented a development project on a magnitude never before seen in Charleston—and because so many people felt passionately about the uniqueness of their city. It was striking how many residents said they did not want Charleston to become like someplace else—either a typical big city or a tourist-infested historic city—as they deliberated strategy and tactics and debated the balance that ought to exist between preservation and development, continuity and change, resistance and accommodation. In the decade that followed the opening of Charleston Place, lower King Street did indeed undergo a significant transformation, as trendy retail outlets proliferated in the vicinity of the luxury hotel. When Saks Fifth Avenue finally opened for business in a new building on an adjacent corner, one of the original goals of the revitalization project was also realized: bringing a "quality" department store to King Street. As recommended by the consulting architects brought in by Historic Charleston Foundation, the vacant Riviera movie theater across the street from the hotel was eventually restored and adapted for use as an additional conference site, offices, and a shopping complex.[38] From the standpoint of the current economic health of downtown, the hotel and meeting facility seems to have lived up to the hopes and expectations of proponents.

Nevertheless, a clear consensus has not yet emerged about the proper balance between preservation and development, and perhaps none can, as places such as Charleston engage in an ongoing search for a formula to keep city centers viable in an age of continuing suburban expansion. Tourism has become a potent force in the Charleston economy over the last several decades, and it has kept alive many of the questions associated with the original convention center proposal of the late 1970s, especially as fresh plans for hotels continue to be advanced in the historic city. It is also worth noting that, despite all the fury of the "Battle of Charleston," the debate occurred among a relatively small group of people who lived in downtown and midtown. Uptown Charlestonians were conspicuous by their silence. Many of the issues at stake in the controversy—courting wealthy tourists, establishing upscale stores, maintaining a way of life—did not seem to animate the great majority of these citizens. Their concerns lay elsewhere. The next chapter will examine the conservation programs of Historic Charleston Foundation, some of the most innovative of which targeted the pressing urban concerns of people in uptown neighborhoods.

Chapter 7

# KEEPING SOUND THE LEGACY
## Conservation Strategies and Programs

THIS CHAPTER EXAMINES conservation programs and strategies implemented by Historic Charleston Foundation in the 1970s and 1980s. These
diverse efforts ranged from the challenges of conserving unique and architecturally significant properties to pioneering initiatives that sought to couple historic preservation with issues of urban decay and social justice. One
architectural treasure, the Edmondston-Alston House on Charleston's Battery,
was conserved through the venerable strategy of adaptive use as a museum. The
foundation also engaged in the practice of "fire-fighting," a crisis-management
approach to conservation in which a building of architectural merit was purchased, usually to forestall impending demolition or inappropriate use, and
then resold to an appropriate buyer. Such preservation-through-purchase efforts
have long been employed by heritage organizations throughout the country,
and Historic Charleston Foundation made use of them when it was deemed
advantageous. In its conservation programs between 1970 and 1990 the foundation also embarked on important new directions, developing a successful
easements program and experimenting with ways to use historic architecture to
meet vexing urban needs, such as inner-city housing. Mindful of one of the
consequences of its Ansonborough project—residential displacement—the
foundation began to target low- to moderate-income African-American neighborhoods for assistance. These conservation initiatives in uptown Charleston

reflected a broadening social agenda for the foundation that would eventually come to shape the priorities of the national preservation movement as a whole. Historic Charleston Foundation had pioneered with area rehabilitation projects during the 1950s and 1960s and in responding to their legacy in the 1970s and 1980s would again offer a fresh conceptualization of the role of preservation in modern urban life. The foundation was in this way breaking new ground for the American preservation movement as a whole.

### EDMONDSTON-ALSTON HOUSE

Through an agreement designed to preserve the historic integrity of a grand water-front mansion and to generate income for Historic Charleston Foundation, the foundation undertook the operation of the Edmondston-Alston House as a museum beginning in 1973. The house had been built in 1828 for merchant Charles Edmondston and was remodeled ten years later by its second owner, planter Charles Alston. The three-story regency-style residence had since

*Edmondston-Alston House (1828), second floor piazza*
Through an agreement designed to preserve the architectural integrity of a grand waterfront mansion and to generate income for Historic Charleston Foundation, the foundation operated the Edmondston-Alston House as a museum from 1973 to 1989. Courtesy, The Charleston Museum.

remained in the hands of Alston family descendants.[1] In the early 1970s the current owners, Mr. and Mrs. Charles H. P. Duell, offered Historic Charleston Foundation the use of the first two floors of their home with its furnishings as a year-round house museum. In inviting the foundation to consider the idea, the Duells noted that they had thought about converting the bottom floors into apartments but had concluded: "The rooms are large and elegant, with 14 ft. ceilings on the second floor; we feel it would be a shame to split them up in order to add the necessary facilities for modern living. Rather than do a butchering job, we feel that there is an opportunity to maintain the architectural integrity of the house, provide a complement to the Russell House and the Heyward-Washington House in the immediate vicinity (the three together spanning nearly a century of history) and at the same time produce additional income for the foundation and contribute somewhat to maintaining this demanding property."[2]

The Duells and Historic Charleston Foundation negotiated an initial two-year agreement that was subsequently extended for another fourteen years. The family continued to live on the third floor, and the foundation managed the lower floors as a historic house museum open daily to the public. In 1990 the Middleton Place Foundation, a nonprofit educational trust previously established by the family, assumed full management of the Edmondston-Alston House, which continues to operate as a museum.[3]

WILLIAM GIBBES HOUSE

Preservationists use the term fire-fighting to refer to potential conflagrations requiring swift attention in order to avert irreparable damage or impending demolition of a historic structure. It is a kind of rescue conservation, precipitated by crisis and focused usually on a single building. Historic Charleston Foundation was called upon to fight its share of fires, and one of the most significant in the 1970s and 1980s involved the William Gibbes House at 64 South Battery. Constructed about 1772 for a wealthy merchant and planter, the large wooden structure was prominently situated to be viewed from the Ashley River as boats approached Gibbes's three-hundred-foot wharf.[4]

The immediate threat to the residence by the 1980s was the prospect of its sale for multifamily, rather than single family, use.[5] When the house was put on the market, various developers expressed interest in subdividing the property into condominiums or converting it for use as a private club or restaurant and inn. To avert this possibility, Historic Charleston Foundation took an option on the property in May 1984. "We were disturbed that it was going to be subdi-

*William Gibbes House (ca. 1772)*

In an important fire-fighting mission, Historic Charleston Foundation succeeded in maintaining the William Gibbes House at 64 South Battery as a single-family residence by taking an option on the property in 1984 and selling to a preservation-minded purchaser in 1986. Courtesy, The Charleston Museum.

vided for some use other than private occupancy," executive director Frances Edmunds explained. "We don't want to see that happen to the residential area in which the house has such an important historic place."[6] The foundation identified a preservation-minded purchaser the next year, and the property was resold in February 1986. On closing, the new owners conveyed to Historic Charleston Foundation an easement that ensured the structure's continued residential use and protected its historic interiors as well.[7]

## THE EASEMENTS PROGRAM

One of the most effective conservation strategies employed by Historic Charleston Foundation has been its easements program. Inaugurated in October 1982, this program was modeled on the successes of a similar program operated by Historic Savannah Foundation. A conservation easement enables a nonprofit organization such as Historic Charleston Foundation to protect the historic fabric of properties in private ownership, while property owners who donate easements receive certain tax benefits. In essence, an easement is a partial interest in a piece of property that takes the form of a set of restrictive covenants attached to a deed. A facade easement, for example, might specify that an owner will not alter the exterior architectural character of a building, and an open-space easement might stipulate that an owner will not construct new buildings or subdivide property. Landscape features and building interiors can also be protected through conservation easements. Because the terms of an easement run with the property in perpetuity, binding all subsequent owners, easements can be an enormously effective form of conservation. For owners there are several advantages: an immediate tax deduction for the gift (of the restriction on uses that may be made of the property in the future) and the knowledge that in the long term heirs will be obliged to preserve historic features of the property. From the standpoint of Historic Charleston Foundation, accepting the donation of an easement guarantees conservation without the burden and expenses of property ownership.[8] Jonathan H. Poston was hired in 1982 to begin the easements program and to work with Frances Edmunds on a range of other preservation projects. He holds a master of arts degree in historic site administration from the College of William and Mary and a law degree from the University of Richmond. Poston was the first attorney on the foundation staff and the second professionally trained director of its Preservation Division, following Gregory B. Paxton in the position.

One measure of the success of the easements program was the growing number of property owners who chose to become involved. Not surprisingly, the inauguration of the program in 1982 stimulated a flurry of interest. The foundation accepted 8 easements in 1982, 23 in 1983, and a record 44 in 1984. The number of easements donated fell off by the late 1980s in part because of changes in federal tax law, and over the last ten years of the program the foundation has accepted an average of 3 per year. By 1997, fifteen years after starting the program, Historic Charleston Foundation held a total of 139 easements, the largest number of easements held by any South Carolina organization.[9]

AREA REHABILITATION: WRAGGBOROUGH AND RADCLIFFEBOROUGH

Historic Charleston Foundation embarked on its first area rehabilitation project in the boroughs north of Calhoun Street in the 1970s. As in the earlier Ansonborough venture, the focus was neighborhood revitalization through his-

*8 and 6 Judith Street, Wraggborough*
> Use of the revolving fund to purchase 6 Judith Street in 1972 marked the beginning of Historic Charleston Foundation's efforts "to move into a marginal neighborhood with the express purpose of renovating for low income tenants." Courtesy, HCF.

toric preservation, but this time the goal was also home ownership without displacement. Through the use of its revolving fund, federal grant money, and the "sweat equity" of residents, the foundation sought to use a combination of historic rehabilitation and new construction to facilitate neighborhood stabilization and property ownership for moderate- and low-income families. In the 1970s and 1980s the foundation targeted two uptown neighborhoods, first Wraggborough and then Radcliffeborough.

At the time of the foundation's area rehabilitation initiative Wraggborough was a predominately African-American neighborhood with housing stock in severely deteriorated condition. Wraggborough was one of Charleston's historic suburbs and encompassed much of the area east of Meeting Street between Calhoun and Mary Streets. The foundation had made its first foray into uptown as early as the 1960s, when it had engaged in some firefighting to rescue three historic mansions, two on the upper stretches of East Bay Street and one, at 44 Charlotte Street, that would become the nucleus for the subsequent area project.[10] It was not until the early 1970s, though, that the foundation identified Wraggborough as a neighborhood appropriate for one of its rehabilitation ventures.

The purchase of the handsome house at 6 Judith Street in September 1972 marked what the foundation called its "first effort to move into a marginal neighborhood with the express purpose of renovating for low income tenants."[11] This property, acquired for twelve thousand dollars, had all of its original interior intact, but considerable work was needed to bring the structure up to code. The foundation planned to restore the exterior to be "a source of pride and encouragement to the neighborhood" that would demonstrate to both home owners and landlords the possibilities of rehabilitating older structures for contemporary use.[12] The house at 6 Judith Street was sold in 1976, at which time the foundation had purchased and restored the exterior of a nearby property at 36 Chapel Street. The foundation acquired another house, at 9 Judith Street, in 1977. The exterior was restored, and the residence was advertised at an asking price of sixty-five thousand dollars to a buyer who "preferably plans to live in the house." The property was sold in 1985 after completion of additional exterior work that was funded through a grant from the state historic preservation office.[13]

In the disposition of these four Wraggborough properties—44 Charlotte, 6 Judith, 36 Chapel, and 9 Judith—Historic Charleston Foundation was applying the time-tested concept of its revolving fund: acquiring the larger houses in a carefully chosen target area, restoring at least the exteriors of the homes, and reselling them with protective covenants. This approach had several advantages: it relied solely on the funds of the foundation and, consequently, gave the organization maximum flexibility in its choice of properties, potential buyers, and the extent and quality of architectural restoration. While this foundation activity stimulated a bit of private investment, the effort seemed to have had only limited impact. In the fall of 1976 executive director Frances Edmunds confessed some frustration with the Wraggborough experiment after four years. "We have not been able to find suitable smaller houses for resale to black owners," she admitted, adding optimistically, "but I believe we can."[14]

Beginning in 1977 the venture in Wraggborough involved several separate but related programs, a "three pronged approach" as the foundation's first director of preservation, Gregory B. Paxton, once characterized it.[15] The earlier revolving fund activity was to be supplemented with two additional initiatives: the Judith-Chapel Street project and the Home Ownership Program. The

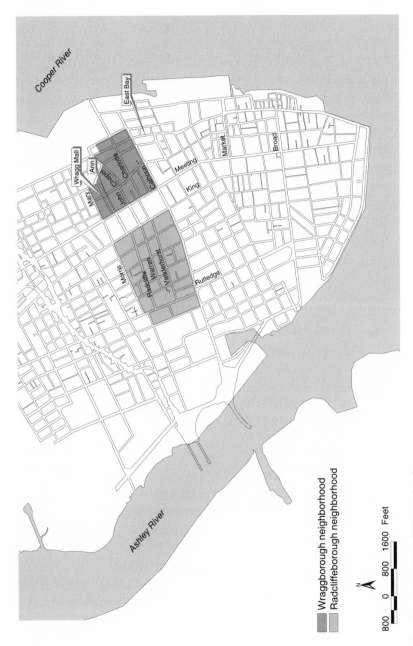

*Wraggborough and Radcliffeborough today.*

Judith-Chapel Street project was an unusual departure for a preservation organization: its purpose was construction of twenty-seven new townhouses as "infill" among the historic structures of Wraggborough. Individual two- and three-bedroom units were to be built for moderate-income families on a 1.8-acre parcel that had been assembled from adjoining lots between Judith and Chapel Streets. Although the townhouses would represent new construction, their design was "to reflect the quality and form of Charleston architecture in a contemporary manner." An architectural competition selected a design by the Heyward and Salmons firm of Columbia.[16] The foundation hoped that the Judith-Chapel Street project would demonstrate the possibilities of well-conceived modern architecture while also helping to stabilize and revitalize a neighborhood without displacing current residents. "We believe that the development of compatibly designed housing to complement historic neighborhoods will become an increasing trend, and in this project we seek to blend the best of the old with the best of the new," Frances Edmunds explained.[17] Planning for the infill project had begun in 1977, but the project was delayed for some time because of the state of the national economy in the late 1970s and questions about potential buyers being able to obtain mortgages at affordable rates. Although the site was cleared and graded, high interest rates discouraged the sale of lots. The foundation eventually decided to sell the property (with protective covenants) in 1985 to a private developer who chose to build based on the original design. The first six townhouses were offered for sale in 1989 at prices considerably more expensive than original predictions, from $170,000 to $250,000 apiece, reflecting both the costs of development by the 1980s and current market values.[18]

While the intention of the Judith-Chapel Street initiative had been to anchor Wraggborough with the investments of moderate-income home owners, the Home Ownership Project as envisioned by Gregory Paxton targeted both low- and middle-income residents. Unlike the infill venture, the Home Ownership Program focused on the use of historic architecture. Under an agreement with municipal government, Historic Charleston Foundation purchased small landlord-owned buildings, undertook rehabilitation, and then sold to owner-occupants from the community. The foundation characterized the purpose of the Home Ownership Program in one funding request: "to maximize rehabilitation of small deteriorated homes of architectural merit, while minimizing displacement of neighborhood residents. We consider this project a novel approach to residential revitalization which will improve the physical surroundings of the neighborhood while simultaneously increasing neighborhood stability through the concept of home ownership."[19] In order to keep the selling price affordable to neighborhood residents, the foundation frequently took a loss on its investment by selling below market value. Often rehabilitation involved the creation of two units in a structure, one for the owner-occupant and a second that was rented out to assist the property owner make the monthly mortgage payment. Foundation staff worked with buyers to locate appropriate financing, and purchasers were permitted to offer "sweat equity" as part of their down payments. For example, purchasers might undertake interior painting, finishing floors, and landscaping, while the foundation would contract for all exterior rehabilitation, rewiring, modernizing of the kitchen and bathrooms, and upgrading of the heating, air conditioning, and water systems.

Significantly, the criteria for identifying appropriate buyers reflected a commitment to avoiding residential displacement. Priority was given to tenants of the building at the time it was purchased by the foundation, other tenants of the neighborhood, and people from similar nearby neighborhoods, in that order.[20] The goal was to "assist lower income black residents of Wraggborough in remaining in a revitalized neighborhood."[21] The foundation was conscious of both the risks and the promise of the Home Ownership Project. As Frances Edmunds wrote to one Department of the Interior official in December 1977: "We're moving ahead now in our new area rehabilitation project in the slum areas—98% black—with a really compelling program. It is the scariest one we have undertaken to date, but an exceedingly significant one as it combines white housing, black housing, rich housing and low-middle income housing."[22] To cover its bets in Wraggborough, Historic Charleston Foundation had deployed the "three pronged approach" outlined by Gregory Paxton: using its revolving fund to acquire and market the large homes, developing new infill housing for moderate-income families, and implementing the Home Ownership Program to broaden the number of owner-occupants in the neighborhood. As the program expanded, the foundation thought it might have the potential to serve as a national model.

The Home Ownership Program became the foundation's primary initiative in a second uptown neighborhood, Radcliffeborough. While Radcliffeborough had long been identified as a promising area for its rehabilitation work, it was not until 1978 that the foundation undertook a project in the community, purchasing its first houses in May of that year to inaugurate the

Home Ownership Program there. Radcliffeborough in the 1970s was more integrated racially than neighboring Wraggborough and comprised the area directly west of King Street between Vanderhorst and Morris. The area had an active neighborhood association, organized in 1973 to oppose a proposed high-rise apartment building and to obtain historic district designation for Radcliffeborough.[23]

The operation of the Home Ownership Program in Wraggborough and Radcliffeborough depended on the presence of outside funding, usually through urban redevelopment or historic preservation grants from the federal government, as well as the availability of affordable home mortgages. The City of Charleston participated in the foundation's program using federal funds in the form of Community Development Block Grants from the Department of Housing and Urban Development; these monies were used for rehabilitation. The foundation matched these funds with monies from its own revolving fund and with federal grants from the Department of the Interior administered through the state historic preservation office; these funds were used for the purchase of the buildings and for some rehabilitation. By the time Housing and Urban Development funds had been exhausted in the mid 1980s, Historic Charleston Foundation had been able to facilitate the ownership of fourteen houses. The first three purchases had been made in Wraggborough at 36 Mary Street, 1 Judith Street, and 5 Charlotte Street in late 1977 and early 1978. Shortly thereafter, beginning in May 1978, eleven subsequent purchases were made in Radcliffeborough at 138, 140, 142, and 144-D Coming Street; 44, 50, and 68 Warren Street; and 174, 181, 197, and 199 Smith Street. (Vacant parcels were also purchased at 144 A-B-C Coming Street and 38–40 Warren Street.) The last property under the Home Ownership Program, 174 Smith Street, was sold in 1986, and the deal was closed following some delays clearing title to the property and arranging the purchaser's financing.[24]

In summary, Wraggborough and Radcliffeborough were the first two uptown neighborhoods selected by Historic Charleston Foundation for these programs that sought to use preservation to battle urban decay. The initiative had begun in 1972 with the first purchase in Wraggborough through the foundation's revolving fund, and it continued through the sale in 1986 of the last Radcliffeborough property rehabilitated with Housing and Urban Development funds under the Home Ownership Program. The success of these programs was mixed. The Judith-Chapel Street infill project did not live up to the expectations of proponents, and the new townhouses and homes at the

*174 Smith Street, Radcliffeborough*
   The sale of 174 Smith Street in 1986 was the last Radcliffeborough property rehabilitated
   with Housing and Urban Development funds through the foundation's Home Ownership
   Program. Courtesy, HCF.

site have attracted more affluent buyers than anticipated. While the Home Ownership Program proved successful in rehabilitating individual residences, the jury remains out on its catalytic power to stimulate the rejuvenation of entire streets. Taken as a whole, though, these efforts did illustrate a significant new departure for Historic Charleston Foundation in the 1970s and 1980s: a commitment to Charleston neighborhoods previously ignored by preservationists and a willingness to experiment with how best to use historic preservation to meet pressing urban needs. In this regard, the programs announced an important new direction for the preservation community in Charleston and in the country generally.

### East Side and West Side Projects

One attempt to revive the concept of the Home Ownership Project in the late 1980s was the establishment of Charleston Heritage Housing, Inc., which emerged from a planning study undertaken by Historic Charleston Foundation during 1987. The foundation was concerned about the quality of housing in the neighborhoods that stretched up the peninsula beyond Wraggborough and Radcliffeborough, into the Upper East and West Sides. Noting that 44 percent of the housing in these neighborhoods was unsound or deteriorating, the foundation concluded that it was crucial "to rehabilitate and stabilize the existing stock of heritage houses and produce safe, affordable dwellings without displacing the responsible low-to-moderate income tenants."[25] The mechanism for locating the funds to undertake this enormous task was a new nonprofit organization, Charleston Heritage Housing, which was charged with identifying revenue sources from both the public and private sectors in a process called "coalition funding." The organization was designed to be independent of Historic Charleston Foundation, although the latter did provide seed money of fifty thousand dollars and staff support to help get the program under way. An initial project—to create two hundred rental units through a combination of new construction and rehabilitation on the city's West Side—was just getting off the ground in its efforts to identify a sufficient number of appropriate vacant properties, clear titles, and contract with qualified residents by a September 1989 deadline when Hurricane Hugo hit Charleston the same month. The National Housing Partnership, a reluctant partner in Charleston from the beginning, pulled out in the wake of Hugo.[26] A year later Heritage Housing was reorganized as a new entity, Charleston Affordable Housing, which was also independent of Historic

Charleston Foundation, and this incarnation has proved a durable mechanism for providing new and rehabilitated housing for low- and moderate-income citizens, making use of both new infill construction and historic structures.[27]

To support the initial efforts of Charleston Affordable Housing, Historic Charleston Foundation offered four properties it had recently acquired as part of its own area rehabilitation work. In 1987–88 the foundation had begun to target Hampstead, an East Side neighborhood just north of Wraggborough. In what came to be called the Nassau-Columbus Project the foundation sought to rejuvenate its revolving fund, in part through city and federal grant monies, in order to purchase and rehabilitate selected residences and eventually resell them with protective covenants for use as rental housing. A second purpose of this initiative was to experiment with a preservation intern program that would train local high school students and serve as a demonstration of proper restoration methods. Toward these ends the foundation purchased six properties: 14 and 18 Amherst, 70 and 72 Nassau, 93½ Columbus, and 32 Mary Street. In 1991 four of these (18 Amherst, 72 Nassau, 93½ Columbus, and 32 Mary) were sold at a bargain price to Charleston Affordable Housing as a way to underwrite the work of the fledgling independent organization.[28] In the following decade the foundation would work to expand its own efforts to provide affordable historic housing in the uptown boroughs and to enlarge its preservation training program. These ventures—the Neighborhood Impact Initiative and the building crafts training program, both of which focused on Elliottborough—are discussed in the final chapter, which covers foundation activities in the 1990s.

THE NATIONAL REGISTER CONTROVERSY

As the 1980s drew to a close, a controversy erupted in Charleston that offered a sobering snapshot of the relation between historic preservation and the politics of race as they had developed over the last several decades. The dispute involved the potential nomination of Charleston's Upper East Side and West Side to the National Register of Historic Places. Although Historic Charleston Foundation was not a vocal participant in either the nomination process or the subsequent public debate, the organization was nevertheless a presence at least in terms of historical background. The foundation's early activity in Ansonborough in the 1950s and 1960s provided a context for the National Register controversy, and many of its conservation initiatives in uptown Charleston in the 1970s and 1980s would have been viewed from the perspective of the racial divide delineated by the discussion. The controversy illustrated how the enterprise of historic preservation in American cities in the late twentieth century continued to be inseparable from racial perceptions and politics. This insight would need to be heeded by Historic Charleston Foundation and preservation organizations elsewhere in the United States in coming years.

Race and preservation had been closely linked in Charleston, of course, well before the National Register nomination surfaced in the 1980s. The Ansonborough area rehabilitation project in the 1950s and 1960s had dramatized the twin problems of displacement and gentrification, and both carried strong racial overtones, especially for Charleston's African-American community. In the 1970s the architectural inventory undertaken as part of the Feiss-Wright-Anderson historic preservation plan had surveyed all of peninsular Charleston south of the Crosstown Expressway, but commentators pointed out that the predominately African-American neighborhoods had been slighted.[29] Calls for a more thorough inventory of uptown were a chief reason for the resurvey—an initiative supported by Historic Charles-ton Foundation—and it was undertaken by the Geier Brown Renfrow firm for the city in the mid 1980s.

The idea for listing the Upper East Side in the National Register of Historic Places originated in 1982 when a residents' association, the East Side Neighborhood Council, set about studying the possibility with the encouragement of city officials.[30] Listing in the National Register is largely honorific, and unlike properties in a municipally designated historic district under the jurisdiction of the city's Board of Architectural Review, nomination to the National Register places no requirements on private property owners to maintain or restore historic structures. The immediate impetus for considering a National Register nomination, besides fostering civic pride, would have been the opportunity to take advantage of a significant tax credit established in the Economic Recovery Tax Act of 1981 for rehabilitation of commercial property. Under the provisions of this federal legislation owners of income-producing properties listed on the National Register were potentially eligible for a significant tax credit, up to 25 percent of the cost of rehabilitation. In residential areas of uptown Charleston, where as much as half of the housing stock might be in rental units, the door seemed open to an infusion of private capital undertaking significant conservation work, and in fact some tax projects had already begun in the Upper West Side.

When the Geier Brown Renfrow firm completed its survey of the upper boroughs in 1985 and provided the city with its first thorough inventory of the historic architecture of uptown, Mayor Joseph P. Riley Jr. urged that neighborhoods on both the East Side and the West Side be nominated to the National Register. The plan proposed in 1986 called for a National Register district that extended as far north as the Crosstown Expressway and included significant examples of a distinct vernacular architecture associated with the antebellum free black communities that had existed in the area.[31]

In a series of public forums and pronouncements residents articulated a number of concerns about what they thought would be the effects of a National Register listing: investors would flood into neighborhoods, tenants would be displaced during renovations, landlords would raise rents, longtime residents would be forced to move, property values and taxes would rise, property owners would lose rights.[32] Fear of losing one's home was always high on the list of concerns. "It's nice to know that we live in an historic city, but it's even nicer to know that we at least have a place to live in an historic city," one East Side resident told a reporter for the city's African-American newspaper.[33] While preservationists and public officials tried to correct misconceptions about the National Register and the implications of a listing, it was clear that the community response was rooted in an unarguable interpretation of recent local history. Arthur K. Maybank, president of the East Side Neighborhood Council, became one of the most vocal opponents: "Many blacks used to live in Ansonborough, and now very few do. Most were forced out by the rising prices." His conclusion was, "We don't want this to happen again."[34]

Community opposition to the National Register listing eventually caused city government to back off from its support for the idea in June 1988, when both City Council and the Board of Architectural Review voted unanimously against the proposed nomination. One board member explained his vote, noting that he personally favored the proposed listing, "but not over the mandate of the people. We need to support their fears, whether real or imaginary."[35] Despite favoring the listing initially, Mayor Riley explained his change of position: "Citizens in the neighborhood expressed great concern that participation in a National Register district and the tax credit incentives that come with it would artificially inflate land values and cause displacement through land speculation and inflated rents."[36]

But the nomination document took on a life of its own a few months later. A lawyer with clients interested in the tax credit opportunities knew enough about preservation regulations to realize that any citizen could appeal directly to the Keeper of the National Register to have the nomination accepted, despite local objections. The tactic left one avenue open to opponents: acceptance of the nomination could be stopped if a majority of property owners in the affected area voted against listing by submitting notarized letters of objection. Appreciating the political sensitivity of the situation, the mayor facilitated the vote by sending to home owners stamped, addressed envelopes for their letters of opposition, and notaries public knocked on doors volunteering their services. When the January 1989 deadline arrived, the state historic preservation officer announced that the protest had succeeded and the National Register listing would not be approved.[37]

The reopening of the nomination produced another round of commentary in the local press. An editorial in one of the major dailies offered a historical perspective, suggesting that a National Register listing forced on unwilling neighborhoods threatened to "destroy the foundation of community consensus on which the preservation movement in Charleston was built."[38] Many African Americans seemed to find in historic preservation a wider conspiracy of interests to push blacks out of Charleston and bring whites in. "They know as I know that once the Eastside is in that Register, Blacks will soon become a memory around here," one resident asserted.[39] The columnist for the *Charleston Chronicle,* who was an especially fierce critic of the National Register nomination, reminded his readers continually of the historic displacements forced by the building of the municipal auditorium in the 1960s. He held up the modern specter of the new Wraggborough—"Yuppies walking their dogs, polishing their BMW's along Chapel, Charlotte and Judith St."—to warn that "Black People Removal" had become official city policy.[40] Despite the attention given to this point of view, the outcome of the controversy over the National Register nomination actually testified to something quite different: the significant political clout enjoyed by Charleston's African-American community by the 1980s, particularly in issues of urban planning. Whether or not the nomination would have had the effects feared, the larger issue for preservationists was how to broaden their demographic base to reach African-American citizens in meaningful ways. At the time, though, preservationists argued that the National Register was simply a confusing program, that misconceptions had always existed about it, and that they had simply failed to mount a persuasive educational campaign in this case. Preservationists also pointed out that as a conservation strategy, the federal investment tax credits would have been effective in revitalizing the blighted buildings and businesses of upper King Street and that the National Register listing got sidetracked by residential issues. But in general the controversy seemed to suggest that the topic of historic preservation resonated differently on different sides of the American racial divide.

During the 1970s and 1980s Historic Charleston Foundation had made determined efforts to expand its area rehabilitation initiatives into urban neighborhoods previously neglected by the preservation movement. The revitalization experiments in uptown Charleston sometimes met with mixed results, but in the 1990s the foundation would continue its attempts to craft fresh initiatives for using preservation as a way to address challenging social questions. As the foundation started its work in the uptown boroughs during the 1970s and 1980s, it was also beginning to focus on conservation and preservation planning issues beyond the peninsular city, and this is the subject of the next chapter.

## Chapter 8

# A REGIONAL AND ENVIRONMENTAL AGENDA

WHILE MAINTAINING ITS traditional focus on historic preservation in the city of Charleston, Historic Charleston Foundation started to address issues of regional importance in the 1970s. Just as suburban flight from the historic city had stirred earlier efforts to revitalize commercial and residential districts downtown, the pace and scale of metropolitan development in the 1970s and 1980s stimulated awakening interest in regional and environmental affairs. As a consequence, the foundation began to shift its gaze beyond the peninsular city to address planning and conservation issues in the surrounding Lowcountry region. The transportation corridors and housing subdivisions that accommodated population growth provoked debates over construction of the James Island Bridge and development along the Ashley River Road, as well as efforts to rescue such Lowcountry plantation landscapes as Drayton Hall, Snee Farm, and Mulberry Plantation. In expanding its preservation agenda in the 1970s and 1980s to include regional and open-space issues, Historic Charleston Foundation was anticipating national trends to develop linkages between historic preservation and the environmental movement.

### THE JAMES ISLAND BRIDGE

Interest in forging closer links between the peninsular city and its nascent western suburbs had inspired frequent proposals for new bridges across the

Ashley River. Few people questioned the wisdom of supplementing the Ashley River Memorial Bridge, built in 1926, or the adjacent span added in 1961. Instead, the preservation planning issues involved the proper location for an eastern terminus: where in the city would the on- and off-ramps be constructed, and how would the flow of traffic affect downtown? A proposal in 1963 for what became the James Island Bridge envisioned the highway emptying onto Broad Street, a suggestion that ignited protest from those who lived in the nearby neighborhoods south of Broad. Shortly thereafter engineers agreed to move the terminus a couple of blocks north to Beaufain and Wentworth Streets. The planning debate then centered on whether or not it could be pushed even further up the peninsula to the commercial thoroughfare of Calhoun Street.[1]

Historic Charleston Foundation played a leading role in efforts to minimize the James Island Bridge's impact on historic areas. In a formal statement in February 1969 the foundation recognized the utility of the bridge—"it is only by making our 300 year-old city available to 20th century vehicles that we can hope to preserve this American treasure"—but warned of the importance of managing the flow of cars and trucks so that the Charleston portion of the route did not become "a speed corridor to the northern industrial areas and military complexes."[2] To avoid this outcome the foundation urged that residential on-street parking be retained along Beaufain and Wentworth Streets and, more significantly, that Lockwood Boulevard be extended northward through the Ashley River marshes as a direct connection to the industrial areas of the Charleston Neck and the new interstate highway. By this plan the James Island Bridge and the so-called "Lockwood Extension" would accommodate the growing suburban traffic but reduce its impact on downtown by diverting a portion of it completely around the historic city. The foundation was also concerned about the erection of highway infrastructure so close to a historic district. Executive director Frances Edmunds expressed fear about bridge ramps fragmenting the adjacent neighborhood "so [that] it could no longer survive, as an historic residential area of large and small houses."[3]

A February 1971 meeting of the President's Advisory Council on Historic Preservation in Charleston served to highlight some of the issues at stake. Review by the Advisory Council was mandated because properties near the proposed terminus at Beaufain and Wentworth were eligible for listing in the National Register of Historic Places. (The City of Charleston had expanded its Old and Historic Charleston District in 1966 to include most of the city south of Calhoun Street, and the boundaries of the National Register district were expanded to include this same area in 1970 as debate continued on the James Island Bridge.) As a result of its visit, the Advisory Council issued a finding that the proposed bridge did indeed threaten to affect the historic district adversely.[4] Within nine months of the Advisory Council meeting the state highway department had redesigned its plans to propose a bridge that entered Charleston at Calhoun Street. Historic Charleston Foundation applauded the recommendation of Calhoun Street but continued to insist on the necessity of a direct connection between the bridge and the interstate highway near Charleston Neck.[5] Thomas E. Thornhill, the president of the foundation, predicted that there would be serious damage to downtown, "especially those areas known as Radcliffeborough and Harleston Village which are the nearest concentrations of valuable buildings to the bridge terminus," unless the Lockwood Extension were built.[6]

Resolution of the historical issues came in July 1975 in the form of a memorandum of agreement worked out by the Advisory Council on Historic Preservation and signed by the state historic preservation officer, Charleston's mayor, and the Federal Highway Administration. Because Charles E. Lee, the director of the South Carolina Department of Archives and History and the state historic preservation officer, had ruled that building the James Island Bridge would have an adverse effect on properties eligible for the National Register, the parties agreed to a set of conditions that sought to mitigate this impact: traffic would be minimized on Calhoun Street and directed away from the historic district; the final bridge design would be compatible with Charleston's architecture; and the city would have to adopt a historic preservation plan.[7]

In the initial Advisory Council hearings four years earlier, Charles Lee had argued that much of the controversy over the James Island Bridge stemmed from an absence of long-term preservation planning on the city's part. From the outset, Lee maintained, the city ought to have incorporated preservation issues into its own transportation studies. The memorandum of agreement in 1975 sought to rectify this situation. The Advisory Council informed the mayor and City Council that its approval of the James Island Bridge was contingent on municipal adoption of a preservation plan.[8] Despite local grumbling about federal intimidation, two ordinances were adopted: one in June 1975 that doubled the size of the Old and Historic Charleston District and a second in July that made the Feiss-Wright-Anderson preservation plan, with its inventory and system of architectural classification, an official city document. Adoption of the inventory placed historic structures on the entire peninsula as far north as Highway 17 under the regulatory authority of the Board of Architectural Review. One result of the debate over the effects of the James Island Bridge, then, was to force the first systematic attempt at citywide historic preservation planning.[9]

While the memorandum of agreement on the James Island Bridge seemed to bring resolution in the mid 1970s to the controversy about its potential impact on historic properties, the federal assessment of the environmental effects of the project persisted into the early 1980s. Throughout this period Historic Charleston Foundation continued to reiterate its position on the necessity of the Lockwood Extension, but this roadway became somewhat controversial because of its proposed location in the marshlands along the Ashley River. The roadway that was supposed to save historic structures seemed to endanger environmental resources. Ultimately the Lockwood Extension was deleted from the project in 1983 because of its expense and environmental impact.[10] The memorandum of agreement signed in 1975 had specified only that the effect of the traffic was to be minimized; it did not require construction of a direct connection between the James Island Bridge and Interstate 26. Thomas E. Thornhill, who as president of the foundation had worked to devise an acceptable design for the bridge, felt betrayed: "I feel like the agreement has been broken," he told the mayor upon learning the news.[11] Nevertheless the project went forward, with the state highway department beginning its purchases of properties for the Calhoun Street terminus in 1985. Construction began on the first segments in 1986, and the last component of the expressway project, a one-mile connector joining the new James Island Expressway and Highway 61, opened in February 1996.[12] Anticipating that construction of the bridge would create development pressures, in 1990 the city had extended the jurisdiction of its Board of Architectural Review off the peninsula for the first time. The Old City Historic District, with its accompanying controls over height and new construction, was expanded to include Albemarle Point on the west bank of the Ashley River.[13]

The thirty-year-long process of building the James Island Expressway reflected the struggle of an American city seeking to accommodate suburban growth in an era of increasing environmental and preservation concerns. Charleston's preservation community had worked assiduously to fashion a compromise that permitted construction of the bridge while seeking to minimize the most deleterious effects of the highway. Success had been realized in locating the terminus at Calhoun Street and in leveraging municipal adoption of a historic preservation plan, but the effort to divert bridge traffic off the city's surface streets was a failure. Much of the delay for the project as a whole was due to the novelty of the newly instituted collateral process of environmental review and the challenges of securing funding from local and federal governments in the 1980s.[14]

## THE ASHLEY RIVER ROAD

As one of the most picturesque roadways in South Carolina, and perhaps the oldest still in use, the Ashley River Road had attracted preservationist attention in the 1970s and 1980s as suburban development began to take its toll. Authorized by the colonial government in 1690, the historic thoroughfare had linked river-front plantations along the western shore of the Ashley. By the 1970s and 1980s it was a modern, two-lane highway that nevertheless retained considerable historic charm; stately processions of moss-draped live oaks along its edges formed an evocative canopy over the roadway. Highway 61, as it was officially designated, provided tourists access to several plantation houses and gardens open to the public, and it offered the suburban residents of "West Ashley" a convenient, even scenic, commercial and commuter thoroughfare. But as subdivisions, golf courses, and shopping centers extended further and further up the Ashley River Road, residents grew increasingly concerned about traffic congestion, highway safety, and the navigability of the road for emergency vehicles. Proposals to remedy the modern problems of the old highway raised many issues for preservationists, and Historic Charleston Foundation participated in a number of these discussions in the 1970s and 1980s.

One set of solutions came to focus on attempts to manage growth, although planning controls evolved slowly in the unincorporated portions of Charleston County. In the early 1970s the foundation supported an effort to preserve some of the scenic quality of the Ashley River Road by urging changes in county zoning to permit residential but not commercial structures fronting the highway.[15] In general, though, the imposition of significant planning guidelines in the western suburbs, including the areas bordering the Ashley River Road, followed their annexation by the city of Charleston. Interested in following the population and tax base into the suburbs, municipal government had pursued a policy of fairly aggressive annexation in West Ashley beginning in the 1960s.[16] Development pressures and the challenges of

*Ashley River Road, 1938*
    As one of the oldest and most picturesque roadways in South Carolina, the Ashley River
    Road attracted preservationist attention in the 1970s and 1980s as suburban development
    began to take its toll. Courtesy, The Charleston Museum.

traffic congestion on the Ashley River Road reached a head in the 1980s following a controversy over McLaura Hall, a proposed housing subdivision.
From this debate emerged a call from Historic Charleston Foundation, the
Preservation Society of Charleston, the National Trust for Historic Preservation, and others for comprehensive planning of the Ashley River Road, and
city and county governments decided to impose a temporary development
moratorium in order to fashion a formal plan. In the first joint planning
effort by the three government bodies with jurisdiction in the area, the *61
Corridor Growth Management Plan* was adopted in 1986–87 by the City of
Charleston, Charleston County, and Dorchester Country. The plan and its
companion documents presented a set of guidelines on land usage, site planning, preservation of scenic and aesthetic values, and environmental protection, although the recommendations were never given teeth by being
translated into ordinances.[17]

Closely related to these planning questions was a second set of issues
involving environmental concerns, which were often central in discussions of
the Ashley River Road's future. One of the earliest debates concerned the fate
of the trees on the lower stretches of Highway 61; they had begun falling to
the forces of commercialization in the late 1960s. By the late 1970s the state
highway department proposed widening the road to four lanes and the
removal of almost six hundred trees, including some three hundred live oaks,
on the Ashley River Road below Church Creek. Subsequent proposals
reduced the number of affected trees considerably, but the arguments of
opponents remained the same.[18] Historic Charleston Foundation contended
that the centuries-old trees made the Ashley River Road "the most beautiful
and scenic highway in South Carolina" and that cutting them down would
destroy the defining landscape feature of the historic thoroughfare.[19] For some
time a parallel Highway 61 Expressway had been proposed as a way to relieve
congestion without widening the old highway, but construction of this new
route, just a mile or two inland, has encountered environmental objections as
well because its path would imperil freshwater wetlands, although it remains
on the drawing board.[20] Potential developments along the river itself have
been the catalysts for the most recent efforts at environmental management.
Triggered by a proposal from the county parks and recreation commission to
construct two boat ramps, a restaurant, and a parking lot adjacent to historic
Drayton Hall, Historic Charleston Foundation joined with the National
Trust for Historic Preservation and the Middleton Place Foundation to halt

the project. One proactive response has been the fashioning of the Ashley River Special Area Management Plan, jointly funded by the South Carolina Coastal Council and the South Carolina Department of Archives and History. Its adoption in 1992 prohibited private marinas and public boat launches in the Ashley River historic district.[21]

Debates about the future of the Ashley River Road often involved the desire to preserve open space, particularly vistas of the river and historically associated rural areas. To work for such "scenic preservation," as it was initially called, a private, nonprofit organization named the Lowcountry Open Land Trust was founded in 1984 and was then revitalized in 1986 with a grant from Historic Charleston Foundation. The trust sought to protect the views that were "special to the character of the Lowcountry" and "intrinsic to our sense of place," such as scenes of open marsh or a row of oak trees. Admitting that it was not usually possible to save large tracts of land through purchase, the trust hoped "to preserve those roadside glimpses of sudden beauty, which reinforce the quality of our lives."[22] Primarily through conservation easements and quiet efforts to educate private property owners, by the early 1990s the Lowcountry Open Land Trust had protected thousands of acres, much of it marshlands along the Ashley River and vistas from Highway 61.[23] In recent years the scope of the trust's activities has broadened to include the protection of open spaces along the South Carolina coast from Georgetown almost to Beaufort.

Despite this success, the preservation legacy of the 1970s and 1980s was one of both victory and disappointment. On the one hand, preservation issues had often been identified relatively rapidly because a historically rural area of considerable natural beauty had been transformed within a generation into a metropolitan suburb. Preservationists had responded quickly, broadening their own definitions of what constituted a historic resource. Informed by the perspectives of the environmental movement, they spoke in holistic terms about the necessity of conserving landscape features, open space, and historic vistas. On the other hand, preservation of the Ashley River Road involved a number of obstacles, including a host of competing private interests, overlapping government jurisdictions, and the challenges of implementing regional planning. Preservationists found it difficult to fight the incremental loss of character along the Ashley River Road one shopping center at a time.

A useful way to judge the legacy of the 1970s and 1980s is from the hindsight of the following decade. In 1995 the National Trust for Historic

Preservation listed the Ashley River Road as one of the eleven most endangered historic places in the United States. The listing was a warning intended both to underwrite ongoing local efforts and to emphasize to a national audience the trust's newfound concern with "urban sprawl." While citing some recent concerns about boat traffic, docks, and cellular telephone towers, preservationists in the 1990s continued to work on many of the same earlier problems: subdivisions, commercial development, scenic vistas, the route and length of the alternative Highway 61 Expressway, and the adequacy of the current area management plan. Ironically, twenty-five years of preservationist activity may have created a degree of complacence about the Ashley River Road and its plantation landscapes, according to Charles H. P. Duell, who in the early 1970s had been one of the first to speak out for landscape preservation and environmental planning. "I think people have a false illusion that everything is protected out here," he lamented in the 1990s.[24] The Ashley River Road was perhaps unique in having attracted concerted preservationist activity for so long, but it was also typical of an increasingly familiar dilemma in metropolitan areas characterized by growth and prosperity.

## DRAYTON HALL

One plantation house on the Ashley River Road, Drayton Hall, became the focus of a national preservation campaign spearheaded by Historic Charleston Foundation that enabled the National Trust for Historic Preservation to purchase the property in 1974. Historic Charleston Foundation played a pivotal role in negotiating and funding this purchase and continues to participate in the management of Drayton Hall today. Located about ten miles upriver from Charleston, Drayton Hall is generally considered the finest example of Georgian Palladian architecture in the United States. The mansion was built between 1738 and 1742 by John Drayton, a wealthy rice planter and prominent royal official in the colony, and it became the only Ashley River plantation to survive the destruction of the Civil War with its main house intact. The property had remained in the hands of the Drayton family since its construction. After ownership passed to the two nephews of Charlotta Drayton in 1969 Charles Drayton explained, "it became evident that we had to do something to preserve it or it would go." Rising taxes, the costs of maintenance, and the threat of vandalism on the isolated property prompted the Drayton heirs to begin considering ways to preserve the property for public benefit.[25]

When the National Trust for Historic Preservation held its annual meeting in Charleston in 1970, preservationists from all across the country had a chance to become familiar with Drayton Hall through a special tour arranged for conference participants, and this exposure became an important catalyst for its eventual acquisition by the National Trust. Attention was again directed to Drayton Hall at the trust's meeting the following year, when Frances Edmunds was honored with the Louise du Pont Crowninshield Award. In her acceptance speech Historic Charleston Foundation's executive director announced that she would donate the one-thousand-dollar award to the Drayton Hall fund: "My fondest hope is that Drayton Hall can be acquired and restored, with guidance coming from Historic Charleston Foundation, the National Trust, conservation organizations and others [in order] that this splendid, almost untouched Georgian mansion and its surrounding woodlands and marshes will become a public trust, practically funded, preserved, and open to the public, combining the dual and equally important goals of conservation and preservation."[26] Negotiations with the Drayton family reached fruition in January 1973, when Historic Charleston Foundation and the National Trust for Historic Preservation signed a lease-option agreement with Drayton heirs. Under the terms of the agreement Drayton Hall and a surrounding six-hundred-acre parcel were leased for one year, renewable for a second, with an option to purchase. The lease allowed the foundation and the trust time to explore financing and restoration alternatives that would make the historic site "available to the public as a part of our national heritage."[27]

Over the next year and a half Historic Charleston Foundation and the National Trust investigated ways to purchase both the house and its immediate environs, on the assumption that the historic setting was as important to preserve as the architectural monument itself. The formula that was eventually devised involved an unusual cooperative arrangement with the state parks system whereby both the private, nonprofit National Trust and the State of South Carolina undertook the joint purchase of the property. In July 1974

Overleaf

*Dedication of Drayton Hall (1738–1742) as a property of the National Trust for Historic Preservation, 1975*

Historic Charleston Foundation played a pivotal role in negotiating and fund-raising for the acquisition of Drayton Hall by the National Trust for Historic Preservation in 1974, and it continues to participate in the management of Drayton Hall today. Courtesy, HCF.

the National Trust exercised its option to buy the house and 610 acres for $680,900, and a year later it sold 485 acres of the surrounding woodlands and marshes to the state.[28]

To make possible this purchase, Historic Charleston Foundation inaugurated a formal fund-raising campaign early in 1974 seeking to raise $300,000, to be matched by a similar campaign by the National Trust. The governor declared a "Drayton Hall Week" in mid April, and the foundation opened the mansion for tours and the grounds for picnicking to anyone willing to donate ten tax-deductible dollars to its fund-raising campaign.[29] Drayton family descendants throughout the United States were canvassed through a letter-writing campaign that appealed to their "love for this plantation" and its significance in the history of South Carolina.[30] The foundation also approached potential contributors with a lavishly illustrated booklet that emphasized Drayton Hall's majestic facades, the elegant symmetry of its interior woodwork, and the stunning river-front location. The booklet concluded with the hope that historic preservationists could join with conservationists and ecologists to make Drayton Hall "the center of a conservation area for the protection of the river and the road, as they too are endangered."[31] A wide range of individuals contributed to the campaign, and a sizable gift of $50,000 came from the Richardson Foundation of New York, which had previously helped Historic Charleston Foundation purchase the Nathaniel Russell House and establish its revolving fund in the 1950s.[32]

The management structure for Drayton Hall reflected the process by which the property had been acquired and the unusual private-public partnership employed. Under the terms of the cooperative agreement between the National Trust and the State of South Carolina, a Drayton Hall Council was established "to coordinate and advise" on the operation of the site as a "unified" park in dual ownership. As initially constituted, the council was composed of two representatives each from the National Trust for Historic Preservation (which owned the house and an adjacent 125 acres), the State of South Carolina (which, through two purchases, owned a surrounding parcel of 555 acres), and Historic Charleston Foundation (which had been instrumental in negotiating and funding the purchase from the Drayton heirs), and one ex officio member designated by the Drayton family. Historic Charleston Foundation continues to play a role in the management of Drayton Hall; today the Drayton Hall Council consists of thirteen members: three representatives from each of the three organizations, three representatives of the community at large, and a member of the Drayton family. Throughout the late 1970s the architectural, historical, archaeological, and environmental importance of the property prompted the commissioning of a series of consulting reports designed to assess the history of alterations to the mansion, Drayton family history, the evolution of the historic landscape, and modern maintenance issues for the historic structure.[33]

One of the earliest management debates concerned what preservation philosophy ought to be implemented: should Drayton Hall be stabilized in its current condition or should it be restored to its appearance in an earlier era? Drayton Hall was remarkable in the American context for having remained in the same family for seven generations, but it was even more astounding that so few structural changes had been made to the main house in the 230 or so years it had been in private ownership. An indication of how little tinkering and remodeling had been undertaken by the family is suggested by the fact that the mansion lacked electricity, gas, and plumbing; some rooms had only two coats of paint, the original from the 1740s and a second from the 1880s. The professional architects brought in by the National Trust in 1975 were clearly moved by the evidence of architectural continuity: "Its survival in an almost untouched state through earthquake, war, affluence, and poverty was extraordinary, and [this fact] puts a heavy responsibility on the National Trust to preserve both its clear architectural values and the even more unusual purity of its condition. . . . Any changes of any kind would inevitably obscure rather than clarify its worth as architecture."[34] Their conclusion was that "the only proper approach to the preservation of Drayton Hall is one of the sensitive, intelligent stabilization of the house as it now exists." Other well-meaning preservationists had different ideas. They preferred a more traditional museum solution: restoration of the interior and decoration of the rooms, in order to portray to visitors what the house might have looked like when it was inhabited. Although the house was virtually empty when the National Trust took title, the whereabouts of a considerable amount of Drayton furniture was known, and family pieces could be assembled to furnish rooms. The philosophy of stabilization eventually prevailed, along with a complementary interpretive approach whereby visitors tour the unfurnished and unrepaired house with guides who speak about the value of preserving rather than restoring Drayton Hall in order to retain the patina of time.[35]

Despite the strong feeling of timelessness evoked in most visitors by the unique environment of Drayton Hall, the property is not without alterations. Wealth from the post–Civil War phosphate industry had allowed the family to add a number of Victorian architectural and landscape features, for example. As further research by the National Trust began to reveal the nature and extent of these historic modifications, another management debate arose over how significant the nineteenth-century changes were in relation to what was unquestionably an eighteenth-century architectural treasure. Should the Victorian changes be removed to return the site to its colonial appearance? Should the later alterations be retained—and interpreted to the public—as illustrative of the changing fortunes of the Drayton family? Should the no-restoration policy be modified into a more flexible "selective restoration" philosophy? In the early 1980s issues such as these became so intractable that a task force was brought to Charleston to offer its independent recommendations. The final report urged that all that has survived at Drayton be respected.[36]

In the 1990s management issues at Drayton Hall have focused on the linkage between preservation and environmental concerns. The connection between the two at Drayton Hall was not new, of course, having been predicted by Frances Edmunds in her 1971 Crowninshield address when she spoke about the dual challenge of "conservation and preservation" at the six-hundred-acre site. Perhaps the most recent example of this linkage has been the effort to protect the historic vista across the Ashley River at Drayton. These "view-sheds," as they have become known, are considered as much a part of the historic setting of Ashley River plantations as their drives, ornamental plantings, and marshes. By the 1990s housing developments, cellular phone towers, and boat docks and wakes had become flash points of contention for preservationists battling the forces of urban sprawl. The view at Drayton Hall won a degree of protection in the mid 1990s, though, when the National Trust was able to purchase land on the opposite shore to prevent further metropolitan encroachment.[37]

### SNEE FARM

Historic Charleston Foundation played an important role in preserving for public use another historic Lowcountry plantation in the 1980s. As a member of a coalition calling itself the Friends of Historic Snee Farm, the foundation joined with other preservationists to help purchase a property associated with Charles Pinckney (1757–1824), a South Carolina governor, diplomat, and delegate to the Constitutional Convention of 1787. After acquiring the land, the Friends conveyed Snee Farm to the National Park Service, which opened it as the Charles Pinckney National Historic Site in 1995. It is one of the newest additions to the national park system and consists of a twenty-eight acre remnant of the former plantation and a modest two-story house that recent research suggests was actually built in the 1820s, after Pinckney had sold Snee Farm. Today archaeological work focuses on understanding the historic plantation landscape and slave life at the site.[38]

The Friends of Historic Snee Farm was formed in 1987 to respond to the threat of a housing development at Snee Farm, which was located in the growing suburban community of Mount Pleasant, a few minutes from Charleston across the Cooper River. The developer's plans called for construction of forty-one homes on the parcel, arrayed around the historic house; the subdivision as a whole was to be called Pinckney Hall. The house itself was to be left standing, in the hope that a potential purchaser might restore it for modern use. Even though Snee Farm had been designated a National Historic Landmark in the 1970s, this honorific title offered no protection against private development. Beginning in August 1987 an ad hoc group of preservation and conservation organizations—consisting of Historic Charleston Foundation, the Preservation Society of Charleston, the National Trust for Historic Preservation, the Rebecca Motte chapter of the Daughters of the American Revolution, the Friends of the Old Exchange, the Christ Church Parish Preservation Society, the South Carolina Historical Society, the Lowcountry Open Land Trust, and the Sierra Club—started talking about how to rescue the property.[39] The nonprofit Friends of Historic Snee Farm, Inc., emerged from these discussions; it was chartered to raise funds to preserve the Pinckney property through purchase. Relatively early in the deliberations the National Park Service was identified as a potential long-term proprietor, largely because of the national importance of the site for its connection to one of the framers of the Constitution. The Friends hoped to make a donation of Snee Farm to the federal government.[40]

As press reports focused attention on the Pinckney house during the fall of 1987—frequently capitalizing on the irony that the home of a framer of the Constitution, and an official National Historic Landmark, could face such a threat during the nation's bicentennial celebration of the Constitution—developers eventually expressed a willingness to sell the entire parcel to preservationists for $2 million.[41] In December 1987 the Friends of Historic Snee Farm exercised an option to purchase the property for the asking price, and the group inaugurated a high-profile campaign to raise $2 million and obtain congressional authorization for a new national park. With grants from several public agencies, as well as corporate and individual donations, the Friends were able to assemble an acceptable financial package and bank loan, and they formally closed on the purchase in July 1988. Exploration of imaginative financing strategies and general fund-raising continued throughout 1988 and 1989, but ultimately the campaign fell some $700,000 short of the goal.[42]

The South Carolina congressional delegation was extremely supportive of the idea of a national park at Snee Farm, and its influence proved decisive in acquiring the site for public benefit. In September 1988 Congress passed legislation authorizing establishment of the Charles Pinckney National Historic Site with a threefold purpose: interpreting the life of Charles Pinckney, preserving and interpreting his home, and presenting the history of the United States as a young nation.[43] From congressional testimony, it was clear that the latter mandate was intended to encourage the National Park Service to interpret Pinckney in the context of his times and to discuss "the role that the institution of slavery played in our Nation's early history and the slaves' role at the Snee farm plantation."[44] As the private fund-raising effort seemed to stall during 1989, the South Carolina delegation devised a solution by which the federal government agreed to purchase the property from the Friends of Historic Snee Farm for the balance of the outstanding mortgage, $705,000. A formal celebration in May 1990 marked the ceremonial conveyance of Snee Farm to the National Park Service. Five years later the Charles Pinckney National Historic Site opened to the public.[45]

The campaign to rescue Snee Farm that began as a citizen effort late in 1987 had achieved considerable success within a relatively short period of time, especially in view of the decision to use the expensive strategy of preservation through purchase. Even more remarkable was that the Friends of Historic Snee Farm had been able to persuade the federal government to establish a national park in an era when budgets were tightening and government was being downsized. This record of success reflected, in part, the credentials and prominence of the volunteer membership of the nonprofit Friends organization. It also reflected the patriotic appeal of the cause: an opportunity to save the last unprotected home of a framer of the Constitution. Although the citizen campaign had focused public interest on a mid-eighteenth-century plantation house where Charles Pinckney had lived and where he had entertained

President George Washington in 1791, further research raised doubts about its actual association with Pinckney. In the summer of 1990, shortly after Snee Farm passed into public ownership, a team from the Historic American Buildings Survey was brought in to study and document the house, through funding provided by the Friends of Historic Snee Farm. To the consternation of everyone involved, the research suggested that the current building was constructed after Charles Pinckney had sold the property in 1817. Evidence that the extant structure had been built sometime in the 1820s was first surmised by the presence of manufactured nails in the construction and subsequently confirmed by a thorough analysis of the building.[46]

The outcome of the Snee Farm story, though, has not diminished the ability of the National Park Service to discuss the role of Charles Pinckney in the public life of South Carolina or his contributions to the drafting of the Constitution at the Philadelphia convention of 1787. The Snee Farm house is now interpreted as a well-preserved example of an early Lowcountry cottage, and its rooms are filled with exhibits that highlight Pinckney and his world. The Charles Pinckney National Historic Site may turn out to be particularly exciting from an archaeological standpoint. The location of the remains of Pinckney's house is now known, and archaeological research promises important new information on the material culture of plantation slavery and the Africans who lived and labored at Snee Farm.[47]

## MULBERRY PLANTATION

The purchase of Mulberry Plantation by Historic Charleston Foundation in 1987 represented a far-flung fire-fighting effort in Berkeley County, some forty miles outside the city. The crisis that precipitated this rescue conservation was a pending foreclosure sale on the historic property and the threat of subsequent development. The property itself consisted of an architecturally unique plantation house built about 1711 and eight hundred acres situated on a bluff overlooking the Cooper River, near the community of Moncks Corner. The two-story main house had a striking exterior appearance with small single-story rooms, each topped with an unusual bell-shaped roof, placed in all four corners. The house was considered the third oldest in South Carolina, after Middleburg and Medway plantations, and had been designated a National Historic Landmark in 1962. Although Historic Charleston Foundation already had an easement on the exterior of the house, the rest of the property was unprotected.[48]

Historic Charleston purchased the house and its furnishings, outbuildings, and surrounding acreage for $2,865,000 in July 1987, with assistance
from a loan arranged through the National Trust for Historic Preservation
with the cooperation of the current owner and help from the former owner.
The foundation promptly began a search to identify a sympathetic buyer willing to donate a set of conservation easements that would prevent the property from being developed or subdivided. Just over a year later the foundation
resold the house and land for $2,550,000 to a New York investment banker
and his wife, who consented to a set of easements on the interior of the main
house, gardens, and entrance road. In spite of the fact that Historic
Charleston Foundation took a loss on the sale, the foundation's executive
director, who had owned the property between 1946 and 1952, expressed satisfaction with the transaction.[49] "We have achieved our preservation goals,"
Lawrence Walker announced. "The property is in private hands and will be
protected from development and can enter its 278th year of existence
unharmed and secure for the future."[50]

One final way to gauge the extent of the foundation's involvement in historic preservation in the Lowcountry region was its growing list of easements
for properties located outside the peninsular city. The foundation had established its easements program in 1982, and the donation of a facade easement
on the main house at Mulberry Plantation in 1984 (three years before the
foundation purchased the property) was its first outside the Old and Historic
Charleston District.[51] The Mulberry donation was followed by easements at
the William Seabrook House on James Island (1985), the Frank Lloyd
Wright–designed Auldbrass Plantation in Yemassee (1986), Millbrook Plantation in Georgetown County (1986), the residence at 116 Marion Street in
Summerville (1987), Medway Plantation near Goose Creek (1991), the residence at 429 Whilden Street in Mount Pleasant (1995), and Chicora Wood
Plantation on the Pee Dee River near Plantersville (1996).[52]

In the 1970s and 1980s Historic Charleston Foundation had embraced
a new regional and environmental agenda for itself, focusing on preservation
issues in the Lowcountry as a whole. Often the foundation's involvement in
these regional issues reflected a crisis-management approach to preservation,
as in the successful rescue efforts at Mulberry Plantation, Snee Farm, and
Drayton Hall. At other times the foundation had been able to take a more
proactive approach to preservation, as in its decades-long assessment of the
impact of the James Island Bridge and its support for growth management

along the Ashley River Road. Because they were propelled by metropolitan expansion, many of these regional issues linked historic preservation with questions of environmental conservation. In discussions of saving the characteristic landscape features of historic roadways, retaining plantation houses in their rural contexts, and maintaining open space and scenic vistas, preserving culture seemed inseparable from conserving nature. In the 1990s Historic Charleston Foundation would continue to explore the interconnections between the preservation and environmental movements.

# Chapter 9

# FINANCING PRESERVATION

IN THE DECADES after its founding in 1947 Historic Charleston Foundation undertook an impressive array of preservation projects: pioneering in area rehabilitation, implementing wide-ranging planning initiatives, experimenting with innovative conservation strategies, and defining a broadened social relevance for historic preservation. These diverse ventures enjoyed considerable local success and attracted significant national attention. The ability of the foundation to undertake so much so effectively can be attributed to several factors, including talented leadership and staff (and the growth of the latter from a single paid director to today's sizable professional staff), the benefits of access to sources of political and social power, creative but pragmatic approaches to issues, and the uniqueness of the local environment. As much as anything, though, the achievements of Historic Charleston Foundation reflected its capacity to fund preservation ventures. While many private, nonprofit organizations struggle simply to stay afloat, Historic Charleston Foundation has been able to both sustain itself and finance an ambitious preservation agenda in Charleston and the Lowcountry.

Since the beginning the foundation has looked to a number of different types of financial support: private benefactors, a revolving fund, public and private grants, targeted appeals on behalf of specific projects, and revenue generated by the operation of museums, annual house and garden tours, and a historic reproductions program. Most recently, the foundation has embarked on a capital campaign aimed at creating a stable endowment and replenishing its long-established revolving fund. In all of these fund-raising endeavors Historic Charleston Foundation has been able to attract sympathetic and generous support from Charlestonians and from a national constituency.[1]

Private philanthropy has provided an important source of financial support for Historic Charleston Foundation from the beginning. Prior to incorporation of the foundation, Robert Whitelaw's Carolina Art Association had benefited from the generosity of Dr. and Mrs. William Emerson of Boston, who had supported publication of *Plantations of the Carolina Low Country* (1938) and preservation projects in Charleston as early as the 1920s. Henry Smith Richardson of New York played a pivotal role during the 1950s in the purchase of the Nathaniel Russell House and the subsequent successful establishment of the revolving fund, and the Richardson Foundation also made a substantial contribution toward the purchase of Drayton Hall in the 1970s. Remarkable assistance has come from Mr. and Mrs. Charles Henry Woodward of Philadelphia, who were usually the "anonymous donors" left unidentified in the newspaper stories about the Ansonborough area project in the 1950s and 1960s. To underwrite the Ansonborough enterprise the Woodwards purchased and donated properties on East Bay Street, often making additional funds available for rehabilitation. The Woodwards' support of Historic Charleston Foundation continued in the 1970s and 1980s with their donation of the Isaac Jenkins Mikell House and assistance with the purchase of the property at 108 Meeting Street that became the Frances R. Edmunds Center for Historic Preservation. Their gifts also made possible the purchase and donation of Snee Farm to the National Park Service, land acquisition for what became the city's Cooper River Waterfront Park, and the disaster relief fund established in the wake of Hurricane Hugo.[2] Here, too, they often chose to work anonymously. H. Smith Richardson and the Woodwards were just two examples of the many private benefactors who chose to support Historic Charleston Foundation over the years by donating real property, stocks and bonds, furniture, and other gifts.

The revolving fund, established in 1957 to undertake area rehabilitation projects, has been a significant force for historic preservation in both Charleston and the surrounding Lowcountry. The foundation made use of the revolving fund initially in Ansonborough and subsequently in some of the uptown boroughs; it has also been used to provide funds for rescue conservation, as in the salvage of the William Gibbes House and Mulberry Plantation. Despite the name (and initial expectations), a revolving fund does not revolve indefinitely like some sort of perpetual motion machine. Most revolving funds deplete themselves eventually, as properties are sold below cost. Consequently they require an influx of funds from time to time. The capital campaign announced in 1992 was designed, in part, to rebuild the revolving fund in order to continue area rehabilitation projects and fire-fighting efforts.

Grant monies were essential to the operation of the Carolina Art Association—particularly from the Carnegie Corporation and the Rockefeller Foundation—in the years before it established Historic Charleston Foundation, and they continued to be an important funding mechanism for foundation activities. In the mid 1960s the foundation hired a staff planner to identify federal urban renewal programs appropriate to its work (the Woodwards offered to pay the salary for several years). A grant from the nonprofit America the Beautiful Fund helped underwrite the Broad Street Beautification Plan of the late 1960s. The foundation first approached municipal government in the mid 1970s for grants in support of its uptown initiatives, and federal urban redevelopment grants and historic preservation funds were used to implement the foundation's low-income home ownership program in Wraggborough and Radcliffeborough in the late 1970s. Private grants have enabled the foundation to resurrect the program in the 1990s. A grant from the Getty Foundation has made possible the recent historical, architectural, and archaeological research at the Nathaniel Russell House.

Fund-raising on behalf of specific preservation projects has proved quite successful over the decades. As early as the 1950s targeted appeals helped purchase the Nathaniel Russell House and establish the revolving fund, even before Ansonborough was identified as the initial focus. The campaign in the 1970s to acquire Drayton Hall for the National Trust for Historic Preservation was unprecedented in its effectiveness in tapping a national audience in a relatively short time. An appeal to preserve a site associated with one of South Carolina's delegates to the Constitutional Convention made possible the purchase and donation of Snee Farm to the National Park Service in the late 1980s.

Revenue from the operation of three distinct programs—museums, the spring house and garden tours, and historic reproductions—has been a crucial source of funding for the foundation's preservation projects. Historic Charleston Foundation has operated a total of four  museums over the years, three at present. The Nathaniel Russell House opened for public tours in 1956, and its admission fees continue to generate revenue for the foundation today. The Russell House has been an important source of income because there was no mortgage to pay off, chiefly due to the generosity of the Richard-son and Avalon Foundations, which made possible the acquisition and initial renovation of the mansion. Between 1973 and 1989 the foundation operated the Edmondston-Alston House as a museum in a revenue-sharing arrange-ment with its owners; it continues today under the management of the Mid-dleton Place Foundation. In the 1990s the foundation acquired the Aiken-Rhett House from the Charleston Museum, reopening it to the pub-lic in 1996. Through a long-term lease the foundation has recently restored and reopened the Powder Magazine as a museum of early Charleston history.[3]

Two of the foundation's most successful revenue-generating programs warrant extended discussion in their own right: the annual tour of homes, first offered in 1948, and Historic Charleston Reproductions, established in 1972. Together both have contributed mightily to the financial muscle and general effectiveness of Historic Charleston Foundation. Each has also shaped public perceptions of the foundation in important ways, and in this sense both are educational and public relations programs as much as sources of revenue.

### THE ANNUAL SPRING TOURS

Today the Festival of Houses and Gardens is one of the most well-known public programs organized by Historic Charleston Foundation. The popu-larity of the annual springtime tour of historic homes and gardens has risen progressively and dramatically over the years. Much of the appeal lies in the lure of getting "inside" to see how Charlestonians actually live in their mag-nificent old houses. The festival has given considerable visibility to Historic Charleston Foundation and performed a significant educational function in introducing Charleston's architecture and decorative arts to visitors and resi-dents alike. Revenue from the festival now accounts for over 25 percent of the foundation's yearly budget.[4]

Because the idea of house tours had been discussed by members of the Carolina Art Association's Civic Services Committee as a way to provide income for the new organization, tours were one of the first programs devel-oped by the foundation after its incorporation in 1947. The Civic Services Committee had begun discussing plans for tours in 1945 and 1946, follow-ing a suggestion by Kenneth Chorley of Colonial Williamsburg that visitors "share the expense of maintaining Charleston for future generations" through their purchase of admission tickets to historic buildings.[5] Dorothy Haskell Porcher Legge visited Natchez, Mississippi, to learn how public tours of pri-

vate homes in that historic community were being organized by the local garden club. She returned with advice on the logistics and economics of implementing the idea in Charleston, and the foundation's first tour took place the
following year.[6]

During the first season of tours, as in subsequent years, the public was
invited to visit private homes under closely supervised conditions. For the
1948 tours the foundation recruited twenty to thirty young women to serve
as hostesses. At each house on the tour one hostess would greet visitors at the
front door, punch tickets, distribute a flyer on the house, and guide guests to
an assembly room. At regular intervals visitors would be shown the house by
a second hostess, who would explain tour rules (no smoking or photography,
for instance), narrate the history of the dwelling, and describe significant furnishings. From the outset tour organizers decided that hostesses should not
be residents of the homes they showed; this would rescue guests from listen-
ing to lengthy family anecdotes and spare homeowners from overhearing
unkind judgments about their taste. Prior to the tours hostesses were given
background information on local history and instructed on the subtleties of
moving people along and handling troublesome visitors.[7]

The foundation's publicity for the inaugural season of 1948 was probably
the first marketing of Charleston tours to a national audience. Advertising
through travel agencies and with rail, air, and bus lines attracted over three
thousand people from thirty-eight states in March and April. A typical tour
included three houses and a walk through the rehabilitated Dock Street Theatre, where most of the tours began. A total of twenty-three homes were on
display over a five-week period for the 1948 tour, among them some of the
most outstanding examples of Charleston's eighteenth- and nineteenth-century architecture and many that were associated with the most illustrious
names in the city's history. Not all were private homes; two were historic house
museums operated by the Charleston Museum. Tickets were sold in the lobby
of Dock Street Theatre for two dollars, a significant sum considering that a
good hotel room cost six to ten dollars.[8] Unfortunately the 1948 season did
not live up to financial expectations. The president of the foundation, though,
saw the long-term promise of the spring tours: "Through the Tours we have
gained considerable national and local publicity. . . . The fact that the Tours
did not entirely pay for themselves should not concern us unduly, as publicity
for the foundation and Charleston has been gained which in value far exceeds
the deficit. In addition the experience gained points the way for future opera-

*Hostesses for the 1948 house tours*

The house tours were one of the first programs developed by Historic Charleston Foundation. They became one of its best-known public programs and an important source of revenue for the nonprofit organization. Pictured here are Mrs. Thomas Waring Jr. and Henry P. Staats at the Dock Street Theatre, instructing the volunteer hostesses for the inaugural 1948 season. Frances R. Edmunds is seated in the front row, second from the right; she was hired at the conclusion of the season to run the tours. Courtesy, *Charleston Evening Post,* 10 March 1948.

tion and future profit. I consider the deficit as an investment in the future."[9] In anticipation of a more remunerative second season, the foundation created a staff position of tours director and hired Frances R. Edmunds to fill it. She had volunteered as a hostess during the just-completed spring season and was at the time a thirty-one-year-old mother of three married to attorney S. Henry Edmunds. In 1954 she began supplementing her salary as tours director by working as a real estate agent, experience that would prove useful as her involvement with the foundation deepened and she assumed a leadership role in the Ansonborough area rehabilitation project.[10]

Over the next couple of years Frances Edmunds organized a far-flung advertising campaign on behalf of the tour program. Through her efforts articles appeared in over one hundred newspapers across the country, and numerous magazines ran feature stories on the tours. In the year 1950 alone sixty-five thousand brochures were distributed locally or mailed to travel agencies, hotels, and assorted carriers. Promotion also involved experimenting with a "progressive" house and garden tour that began in Charleston in March under the auspices of the foundation and then moved northward into Virginia and Maryland in April, sponsored by garden clubs in those states. One indication of the success of this concerted effort was that in the early 1950s the recently opened offices for the tours, at 94 Church Street, received about thirty-five letters a day seeking information.[11]

The continuing publicity emphasized both the charms of Charleston and the work of Historic Charleston Foundation. An article in *Antiques* magazine featuring the tours reminded readers of the unique appeal of a place where people "live with antiques which have not been collected but have been inherited from the ancestors who acquired them when they were new."[12] Writing for the *New York Times,* one Charlestonian sought to promote the tours by capitalizing on the potential mystique of a city where private homes were "for years shuttered against the outside world and seen only by friends and relatives of the owners."[13] The publicity emphasized the worthiness of the preservation cause, not just the layers of history to be found in an ancient city. Typical was the local newspaper story that explained that the tours were highly educational and that the funds raised from ticket sales were intended to help the foundation "preserve and use" Charleston's buildings "not by making them museums" but as "homes or places of business, properly restored."[14] In both the content of the advertising campaign and its national distribution, Frances Edmunds and Historic Charleston Foundation were promoting what would come to be called "heritage tourism" in a later decade.

In their early years the tours did not generate enormous revenue for the foundation, and organizers worked diligently to concoct a winning formula by raising (and lowering) ticket prices, adjusting the days and times of tours, and refining the number and variety of properties on display. Sometimes the foundation chose to use as an incentive for ticket sales its own ongoing preservation projects. The Nathaniel Russell House was added to the ninth annual tour in March 1956 a year after its purchase, and tours in the 1960s often featured homes in Ansonborough. In the first nineteen seasons of the tour program, from 1948 through 1966, the annual number of patrons averaged about twenty-four hundred and varied between fifteen hundred and thirty-six hundred. During that time gross receipts fluctuated

*House tour, late 1940s*
   A docent describes the furnishings in the drawing room of the William Gibbes House during one of the first Historic Charleston Foundation tours of private homes. Courtesy, HCF.

erratically between roughly $5,600 and $12,800 per tour season and averaged about $8,500.[15]

   The year 1967 represented a significant turning point in the history of the spring tours, as suggested by the fact that revenues almost doubled within a single year, from $9,637 in 1966 to $18,415 in 1967. The remarkable growth and consequent profitability of the tour program that began in the late 1960s resulted from a foundation commitment to revamping the program and the advice of a professional consultant brought to Charleston from New York. Among the most persuasive of the consultant's findings was the recommendation to conceptualize the spring tour as a "festival" and include Charleston's enchanting, but frequently hidden, gardens. The suggestion had special appeal because March and April were the optimal months for enjoying the azaleas, wisteria, and dogwoods of the southern spring. Under the leadership of Alicia Rhett Walker Rudolf, director of tours from 1965 until her untimely death in a horseback-riding accident in 1977, the foundation expanded the program from the fifteen to twenty houses opened to the public on early tours to an extravaganza of fifty to one hundred properties that included gardens, churches, and houses. In 1969 the tours attracted more than five thousand patrons for the first time, and by 1976 the number first surpassed ten thousand.[16] In 1977 revenues exceeded $100,000 per year. Receipts for the Festival of Houses and Gardens topped $200,000 in 1987 and $300,000 for the first time in 1994.[17]

The tours are as successful as they have ever been, and this achievement reflects the considerable logistical talent of the Division of Tours and Special Programs. Today almost fourteen thousand patrons visit well over one hundred properties opened for public view during the month-long festival. Recently various special events have been added to the festival schedule, such as plantation oyster roasts, garden symposia, and behind-the-scenes tours with specialists. Organizing these events and the tours requires a massive volunteer effort on the part of seven hundred people, the consent of a hundred or so owners, and a high degree of professional coordination from foundation staff, who must equip docents with accurate information about everything from the history of Charleston and its architectural traditions to garden design and plant identification.[18]

The success of the foundation's tours has brought its own set of problems, beyond the logistical challenges. Inspired by the foundation's example, other nonprofit groups have organized their own tours, and there has long been concern that home owners will eventually decline to open their houses and gardens, no matter how worthy the causes, because of the imposition they represent and a fear that thieves can use a public tour to "case the joint." Tours like these are completely dependent upon the goodwill of property owners, who are not financially compensated for their generosity.[19] Such concerns have been voiced for over twenty years, though, and for the moment the Festival of Houses and Gardens is enjoying good success. The tours offer both visitors and residents a glimpse of life behind the front doors and garden walls of Charleston, as they educate the public about Historic Charleston Foundation and make possible its other preservation work.

### HISTORIC CHARLESTON REPRODUCTIONS

Like the house and garden tours, the reproductions program is one of the single most important ways that people learn about Historic Charleston Foundation. Over the years it has directed significant attention to the cultural heritage of Charleston and helped to promote the city as a tourist destination. Compared with the spring tours, it is a comparatively recent part of the organization, established in 1972, but it has become enormously effective in generating revenue for the foundation's direct preservation activities. The program arranges for the manufacture and marketing of reproductions and adaptations of the elegant furnishings associated with eighteenth- and nineteenth-century Charleston homes. At present the product line includes furniture, porcelain and brass, mirrors, wallpaper, fabrics, and needlework. Their sale accounts for over 40 percent of the current foundation budget.[20]

The idea of manufacturing a line of Charleston reproductions was suggested to the foundation by two people, Richard H. Jenrette and Alison B. Harwood. Jenrette was a New York investment banker and a friend of preservation in Charleston who had recently reconstructed the old Mills House hotel and reopened it as the Mills Hyatt House; he was looking for ways to bring attention to Charleston. Harwood was a senior editor at *Vogue* magazine with useful and important connections to manufacturers, advertisers, and major American stores. Jenrette and Harwood had initially approached the Charleston Museum, which had unveiled a line of reproduction fabrics in the 1960s, but they found Historic Charleston Foundation and its president, Thomas E. Thornhill, more receptive to the idea. The foundation thought the spring tours might cease to be a steady source of income at some point, and a reproductions program seemed to be a way to diversify the stream of revenue.[21]

The reproductions program was modeled on a similar venture at Colonial Williamsburg that helped support its museum operations in Virginia. Under the plan endorsed in September 1972 the foundation would "license" (or lend its name) to a line of home furnishings inspired by antiques in private or museum collections. These pieces might be replicas of antiques or adaptations designed for modern purposes. The foundation would receive a royalty on every sale, and if an object came from a museum collection, that institution would receive a share of the royalty too.[22] Individuals who loaned pieces from their own collections donated their share of royalties, and they generally preferred anonymity. As a result these contributions in support of Historic Charleston Foundation have gone largely unrecognized.

The first product line of Historic Charleston Reproductions was unveiled at a wholesale market convened at the Mills Hyatt House in October 1973, and the merchandise reached retailers the following year. Consumers enjoyed a wide selection of adaptations and reproductions of furniture, chandeliers and sconces, mirrors, lamps and vases, china and crystal, silver and brass pieces, and fabrics and wallpaper, among other items. Soon after the introduction of the line, in 1976, Alison Harwood took early retirement from *Vogue* and moved to Charleston to direct the program for the foundation. From the beginning the program emphasized faithfulness of reproduction and high quality in manufacture. Among the earliest manufacturers licensed to use Historic Charleston Foundation's name were Baker Furniture and Mottahedeh porcelain, which continue as licensees today.[23] Under Harwood, advertising for the program stressed that buying the reproductions furthered preservation in Charleston, and recent catalogs continue to announce at the bottom of every page, "Your Purchase Helps Save Historic Charleston."[24]

Much of the success of the program can be attributed to the long and rich decorative arts history on which modern artisans draw. The Reproductions Division can take advantage of a cultural tradition extending for almost two centuries, from the 1670s to the 1860s. However, not all reproductions were taken from pieces originally made in Charleston. Some were inspired by objects made elsewhere that had long been found in the homes of the prosperous port city. As the 1992 catalog explained, the reproductions were inspired by "fashionable furnishings made by master craftsmen in Charleston or imported from England, Europe, and the Orient in the eighteenth and nineteenth centuries."[25] Today the program works with over thirty national manufacturers, and the product line includes some six hundred pieces sold primarily in showrooms and retail outlets. The Reproductions Division currently manages a licensing and royalties program with an international scope, and in Charleston it operates two retail stores. Historic Charleston Reproductions' shop has been located at 105 Broad Street since 1974, and a small book and gift store greets visitors at the Frances R. Edmunds Center for Historic Preservation at 108 Meeting Street.

In sum, the Festival of Houses and Gardens and the reproductions program remain primary sources of revenue for Historic Charleston Foundation, and they play influential educational and public relations roles as well. In the 1980s and 1990s, though, the foundation embarked on a new funding initiative: to build an endowment that would "ensure a long-term, stable source of operating income" for its future.[26] The foundation had established an endowment for the first time in 1986 by liquidating the historic properties it still owned on East Bay Street at the northeastern corner of Ansonborough.

*Historic Charleston Reproductions*

The first line of products from the reproductions program was unveiled in 1973. Historic Charleston Foundation licensed a line of home furnishings inspired by antiques in private or museum collections; these were replicas of antiques or adaptations for modern purposes. This Baker Furniture Company advertisement, photographed in Charleston in 1985, shows Historic Charleston Collection furniture, with porcelain and brass by Mottahedeh. The advertisement drew record response for Baker and ran in shelter publications for more than five years. Courtesy, HCF.

The sale of these properties, which it had held for almost thirty years following their donation to the foundation by Mr. and Mrs. Charles Henry Woodward, netted some $900,000. By 1991 the young endowment had doubled to $1.8 million, and to build it further the foundation embarked on an ambitious capital campaign in June 1992.[27] The Heritage Campaign intended to raise $4 million, of which $1.5 million was to go to the endowment, $1 million to the revolving fund, and $1.5 million to finance a museum-quality restoration of the Nathaniel Russell House. The Heritage Campaign represented an important new venture for the foundation as it entered the decade of the 1990s, the subject of the final chapter.

Chapter 10

# CONTINUITIES AND
# NEW DIRECTIONS

THIS FINAL CHAPTER places some of the current activities of Historic Charleston Foundation into historical perspective through an examination of how its preservation projects in the 1990s reflected both continuities with past work and new directions for the organization. In the 1990s the foundation sought to combine a commitment to a proven institutional agenda with initiatives designed to extend its effectiveness in fresh ways. The foundation continued to play a wide-ranging role in preservation planning, participating in efforts to take a proactive approach to urban growth by encouraging downtown revitalization and acting as preservation advocate, as in the Charleston County Courthouse project. Conservation programs ranged from the restoration of the colonial-era Powder Magazine to the rehabilitation of historic buildings in uptown for low-income housing through the Neighborhood Impact Initiative. The latter strategy reflected a continuation of the foundation's pioneering effort to broaden the social agenda of the preservation movement to address needs in the African-American community. The commitment to an expanded regional and environmental focus was reaffirmed most clearly in the 1990s by the acquisition of McLeod Plantation on James Island.

Other ventures represented new departures for Historic Charleston Foundation. Some of these were direct responses to the impact of Hurricane Hugo, which slammed into the South Carolina coast at Charleston in September 1989. The inauguration of the building crafts training program and an increasingly significant role in providing technical assistance to public agencies and private individuals were two important ways that the foundation grappled with the recovery effort and its aftermath. In the 1990s the foundation also began to take the lead in the preservation and interpretation of African-American heritage in Charleston. The acquisition of the Aiken-Rhett House announced a clear commitment to using historic architecture to educate the public about African-American life in Charleston, a subject long neglected in local museums and interpretive efforts. In moving in these directions, Historic Charleston Foundation was continuing its pioneering role within the national preservation movement. The embrace of new institutional directions represented, in itself, a form of continuity for an organization that has sought to take an innovative approach to preservation issues from the beginning.

This chapter will look first at some of the projects and programs that linked foundation activity in the 1990s with earlier work in preservation planning, conservation, and regional issues. Attention will then turn to some of the foundation's important new initiatives.

## THE CHARLESTON COUNTY COURTHOUSE

In the 1990s, as in previous decades, Historic Charleston Foundation participated in a variety of preservation planning and advocacy efforts designed to enhance the quality of urban life. Among the most significant of these undertakings was its contribution to the debate about the future of the Charleston County Courthouse. The foundation played a major role in persuading county government to undertake an extensive restoration of this historic building, despite the expense of the project and the smaller courthouse that would result. Restoring the county courthouse was important to the foundation for two reasons. It would return a landmark building to its former glory, and it would keep courtrooms and law offices downtown, underwriting the current economic viability of Broad Street and preserving a historic use for the area known as the Four Corners of Law. In this sense the foundation's interest in the Charleston County Courthouse represented a proactive form of preservation planning, not simply the restoration of an individual building.

During the 1980s the county had discussed plans to rehabilitate the aging courthouse, but the issue took on new meaning after September 1989, when Hurricane Hugo inflicted severe damage to the structure. As a result, all judicial operations had to be removed to a converted warehouse in North Charleston. The misfortune created an opportunity to consider a more extensive restoration of the courthouse, which had occupied the northwest corner of the intersection of Broad and Meeting Streets for over two hundred years, since its construction in the 1790s on the site of the former colonial capitol. Local lore suggested that the courthouse incorporated the walls of the old capitol, which had burned in 1788, and this possibility gave the building an even finer pedigree.[1]

How to repair and restore the courthouse inspired a lively philosophical and political debate in the early 1990s. Consulting architects for Charleston County recommended that the courthouse be restored to its appearance between 1886 and 1941. The building had been badly damaged during an earlier natural disaster, the Charleston earthquake of 1886, and repairs then had modified the original design through the addition of rusticated stonework on the first-story exterior and the removal of chimneys, a slate roof, and belt courses. Major additions to the rear of the courthouse had doubled the building's size by 1941. The county's restoration plan, then, called for retaining and repairing these nineteenth- and early-twentieth-century changes, as part of the living history of the building; only the remodeling of the 1960s would be removed. The county's plans were opposed by a coalition of preservationists calling themselves the Friends of the Courthouse, and this group urged that the building be restored to its appearance in 1792, the date of construction. The Friends argued that the original design was of paramount historical significance and that subsequent changes to the building had been shoddily done and, in any event, were not historically significant. County architects responded that there was not sufficient documentation for a restoration of the original design.[2]

Resolution of the debate turned in large part on the quality of the architectural and historical evidence that might permit the earlier restoration, and in March 1991 county council bowed to entreaties from the Friends of the Courthouse to postpone a final decision on the nature of the restoration until a thorough study of the courthouse could be completed. Historic Charleston Foundation played an important role in undertaking this study, under the supervision of Jonathan H. Poston, the director of preservation programs for the foundation and also vice-chair of Friends of the Courthouse. The foundation partially funded the study, provided technical assistance, and arranged consulting visits by architectural historians and preservation professionals from Colonial Williamsburg and Mary Washington College during the summer of 1991.[3]

The investigative field work revealed that not only had the county courthouse indeed been built on the site of the former colonial capitol, but the courthouse was actually the capitol itself, in slightly modified form. Apparently the fire of 1788 had only gutted the building, leaving walls and exterior openings intact. When the capitol was rebuilt as a courthouse (the state capital had since been moved from Charleston to Columbia), a third story was added. The research had succeeded in discovering new information about the eighteenth-century design, and even more surprising, it had uncovered an enormously significant early history for the extant structure. The building had taken on transcendent, statewide significance as the last seat of colonial government in South Carolina. The final report on the research called for restoration of the exterior to its 1788–92 appearance, restoration of the original interior floor plan, and removal or rebuilding of the 1941 wing.[4]

In 1993 county council agreed to restore the facades of the courthouse to their eighteenth-century appearance, to remove the twentieth-century additions, and to restore interior floor plans on the first and much of the second floors to reflect their 1792 appearance. Insufficient evidence existed to guide a historically accurate restoration of room interiors. Because this restoration plan involved the removal of the courthouse additions, construction of a new county judicial center was necessary to compensate for the loss of almost half of the courtroom and office space. This proposed complex was to be built in the interior of the block surrounding the old courthouse, and its design eventually elicited a debate of its own, focused primarily on the relocation and demolition of two structures affected by the new construction.[5] The plan adopted for the restoration of the Charleston County Courthouse required the demolition of substantial portions of the historic building and a significant new construction project on an adjacent site with its own impact on historic resources. Some Charlestonians questioned the wisdom of demolishing any structures, especially to make room for a sizable new building in the historic district, and design of the new judicial center inspired a fresh round of debate about height, mass, and the historical sensitivity of new construction. As discussion proceeded in 1996 and 1997, Historic Charleston Foundation staked out a position of firm support. While it urged an "architecturally quiet" building and offered its own set of suggestions on design, screening, and access, the foundation consistently argued that its over-

*Charleston County Courthouse*

Historic Charleston Foundation was instrumental in pressing for restoration of the exterior of the Charleston County Courthouse to its 1788–1792 appearance, which required removal of the wing built in 1941. Courtesy, County of Charleston.

riding concern was "ensuring the viability, vitality, and character of Broad Street."[6] For the foundation, the issue involved a planning choice about downtown revitalization. Pointing to "the shattered wrecks of cities" that had forgotten that their health depended on "maintaining a mix of activities, public and private, corporate and civic, at their centers," the president of the foundation in 1996 urged citizens to understand that "keeping law at the Four Corners is essential."[7]

### The Powder Magazine

One of the most significant examples of the foundation's conservation work in the 1990s involved the Powder Magazine, a National Historic Landmark considered to be the oldest extant secular building in the Carolinas and an important reminder of the role of the Lords Proprietors in establishing the colony and city. Under an arrangement with the National Society of Colonial Dames in the State of South Carolina, which had purchased the structure in 1902 in one of Charleston's first preservation projects, Historic Charleston Foundation agreed to research and fund a restoration of the Powder Magazine.[8]

Construction of a storehouse for gunpowder had been authorized as part of the defenses for Charles Towne in 1703 by the colonial assembly, and the brick magazine was completed on the northern wall of the fortified city by 1713. As it lost its military utility by the early nineteenth century, the storage facility came to be used successively as a livery stable, a printing shop, and a wine cellar, and the structure was modified to accommodate these changing uses. To save the building from demolition, in 1902 the Colonial Dames purchased the former Powder Magazine. They used it for their own meetings and operated it as a museum until 1993, when the necessity of stabilizing the decaying structure could no longer be avoided. The Colonial Dames turned to Historic Charleston Foundation, which agreed to lease the building for up to forty years, undertake the repairs and restoration, and as a way to offset some of these expenses take on the operation of the Powder Magazine as a museum.[9]

As it turned out, the restoration effort necessitated so much structural work on the Powder Magazine that it might more accurately be termed a reconstruction. Extensive archaeological and architectural research revealed the poor quality of the initial building design, which the passage of time and subsequent repairs had only exacerbated. "When we've taken layers off, we've begun to confront the building's flaws," the foundation's executive director explained in 1996. "It's sort of like an architectural Pandora's Box."[10] While research into the history and condition of the building did permit thorough repairs (and some historically sensitive redesign) that included stabilizing the foundation and walls and replacing the roof, it did not furnish sufficient information on which to base an accurate eighteenth-century restoration. As a result the Powder Magazine was returned to its mid-nineteenth-century appearance, a period for which visual evidence confirmed the current window and door arrangement.[11]

To interpret the significance of the Powder Magazine to the public, the foundation installed a sophisticated, interactive set of museum exhibits within the small interior space. Through sound and light shows, visual imagery, display of excavated objects, and text panels the exhibits sought to give visitors an understanding of the first decades of life in colonial Charles Towne. The restored Powder Magazine and its new museum opened to the public in June 1997.

### THE NEIGHBORHOOD IMPACT INITIATIVE

The Powder Magazine project represented an important example of the conservation work of Historic Charleston Foundation, but conservation in the 1990s encompassed more than just unique and architecturally significant properties. As in previous decades, the foundation continued to be vitally interested in strategies that sought to join historic preservation with issues of urban decay and social justice, and this was nowhere more apparent than in the Neighborhood Impact Initiative established by Jonathan H. Poston, the foundation's director of preservation programs. This conservation program was a direct descendant in the foundation's venerable lineage of area rehabilitation projects extending back to Ansonborough in the 1950s and 1960s and to Wraggborough and Radcliffeborough in the 1970s and 1980s. As in the Ansonborough project, the Neighborhood Impact Initiative relied for financing on private donations and the foundation's revolving fund. As with the Wraggborough and Radcliffeborough ventures, its geographic focus was to be the antebellum neighborhoods on the Upper East and West Sides of the city.

Like a multibladed Swiss army knife, the Neighborhood Impact Initiative was designed as a single tool with many purposes. First, it sought to rehabilitate individual houses in the uptown boroughs, where over one thousand historic buildings were in need of major work.[12] Second, it was intended to encourage home ownership for low- and moderate-income people. Third, by selling homes to people with connections to a neighborhood, it attempted to discourage gentrification. And fourth, through rehabilitation and sales to appropriate buyers, it was supposed to have a ripple effect, encouraging similar repairs and improvements and, in time, stabilizing whole neighborhoods.[13] All of these multiple purposes were familiar goals that the foundation had tried to implement in Wraggborough and Radcliffeborough in the 1970s and 1980s. In the 1990s the foundation coupled the Neighborhood Impact Initiative with a new venture, the building crafts training program, which was intended both to undertake architectural rehabilitation and to provide jobs and craft training for inner-city youth.[14]

The first uptown district targeted by the Neighborhood Impact Initiative was Elliottborough, an area on the west side of the city just above Radcliffeborough that was chosen by the preservation staff after several years of study. A middle- and working-class neighborhood in the nineteenth century, Elliottborough had been transformed in the late twentieth century by the construction of the Crosstown Expressway on its northern periphery, suburban flight, and disinvestment. In the 1990s residents were struggling with crime and safety issues, as well as streets lined with dilapidated and abandoned buildings. Through matching grants from banks and donations from private sources, Historic Charleston Foundation was able to begin the process of buying and rehabilitating houses in Elliottborough in the early 1990s.[15]

The first house completed through the Neighborhood Impact Initiative was the property at 33 Bogard Street. The frame single house, built in the 1850s, had been converted to a multifamily duplex and eventually abandoned prior to its purchase by Historic Charleston Foundation. With financial support from the South Carolina National Bank and the Merck Family Fund, the foundation acquired the property and contracted out the electrical and plumbing work. Using a remodeling design prepared by a professional architect (which could be applied to similar single houses in the area in the future), a cadre from the foundation's building crafts program then undertook most of the carpentry, converting the structure into a single family residence with three bedrooms and two and a half baths. The house was sold to a young woman who had grown up in the neighborhood, and she undertook painting and some other repairs to help with the purchase price. An open house to mark the completion of the project was held in June 1995.[16] One of the foundation trustees viewed the rehabilitation of 33 Bogard Street as "a testament to the opportunities and the benefits of preservation to low-income and African-American communities."[17] The local newspaper took notice of

*33 Bogard Street*

Historic Charleston Foundation joined its building crafts training program with the Neighborhood Impact Initiative in 1994 to undertake its first project in Elliottborough: the rehabilitation of the frame single house at 33 Bogard Street. Courtesy, HCF.

*McLeod Plantation*

    McLeod Plantation (three photographs) is a remarkable remnant of a sea island cotton plantation set now among the burgeoning suburbs of James Island. How it will be preserved—and financed—remains an open question for Historic Charleston Foundation. Courtesy, HCF.

33 Bogard in an editorial that applauded the Neighborhood Impact Initiative in general: "Through this program, the Historic Charleston Foundation mends not only the material fabric of our neighborhoods—the wood and brick—but also seeks to preserve the human element by offering a vehicle for community pride and individual hope. In an age of large-scale suburban growth, projects like this that promote the vitality of our inner-city are an essential and welcome element of modern preservation."[18] The work in Elliottborough continued in the 1990s, reaffirming the foundation's pioneering commitment in the 1970s to use historic buildings to provide affordable housing in uptown Charleston.[19]

## McLeod Plantation

The acquisition of the McLeod Plantation demonstrated the continuing importance of a regional and environmental agenda for Historic Charleston Foundation. The fifty-acre property was a remarkable remnant of a sea island cotton plantation, isolated among the burgeoning suburbs of James Island. The foundation decided in the 1990s to preserve the site because of its significance to Lowcountry and African-American history and its importance as open space within the metropolis. But what form this preservation should take and how it will be financed are less clear as the decade draws to a close.

Historic Charleston Foundation became concerned about the future of McLeod Plantation through the initiative of Jonathan Poston, who raised the issue of its long-term preservation with the organization's Area Projects Committee and eventually with a representative for the McLeod family. One result of these discussions was that the foundation inherited a partial, one-third interest in the property upon the death of William E. McLeod in January 1990 at the age of 104. Through McLeod's will and those of two sisters who had predeceased him, two-thirds of the property was to be divided among a considerable number of churches, charities, and nonprofit organizations, complicating the task of preserving the plantation as had been McLeod's intention. The foundation began a set of negotiations with the other beneficiaries of the will, commissioned a land-use study of the entire parcel, and in 1993 arranged to purchase the outstanding interests of all the other parties for approximately $1,138,000.[20]

As a working cotton plantation, the McLeod property extended over a thousand acres at one point, but today the parcel consists of about fifty acres bounded most visibly by the busy commercial thoroughfare and shopping centers of Folly Road. It includes a plantation house built in the 1850s and various domestic and agricultural outbuildings. Perhaps the most striking architectural feature of the site is the street of frame slave cabins, which has been characterized by the state historic preservation officer as "one of the most intact in the state and perhaps in the nation."[21] Extant landscape features include oak avenues leading to the main house and lining the slave street, a large open field, a centuries-old live oak, and an adjacent slave cemetery.

The history associated with this plantation landscape vividly illustrates the transition of African Americans from slavery to freedom. The most noticeable structures at McLeod today represent the material culture of a slave-based agricultural economy. Archaeological field work suggests Native American occupation of the site and an agricultural history extending back to at least the seventeenth century, but it is the antebellum buildings and their tangible connection to the production of sea island cotton that dominate the scene. The story of the military and political forces that transformed the Old South can also be found at McLeod. Both Confederate and Union troops occupied the site during the Civil War; skirmishes took place nearby, and the main house served for a time as a Confederate field hospital. The role of McLeod in Reconstruction South Carolina may provide its most unique and powerful historical association. During Reconstruction the Freedmen's Bureau appropriated the main house at McLeod as its headquarters on James Island, and thousands of emancipated men and women camped in the nearby fields while the federal government worked to assist them.[22]

While possible future educational roles for the site remain under discussion, Historic Charleston Foundation has already taken steps to use McLeod to support the preservation of the most well-known African craft tradition of the Lowcountry, the making of sweetgrass baskets. In collaboration with horticultural experts at Clemson University, the Mount Pleasant Sweetgrass Basketmakers Association planted two thousand sweetgrass seedlings in the fields at McLeod in the spring of 1993, and plantings continue. Basket makers had always depended upon harvests of grass from the wild, but the plant has become a threatened species in recent years, as coastal development in South Carolina has taken its toll on native habitats. In this way reviving productive use of the land at McLeod has addressed a contemporary environmental issue and encouraged survival of an important cultural tradition.[23]

Since acquiring the site in the early 1990s, Historic Charleston Foundation has wrestled with the question of how best to preserve the house, outbuildings, and rural setting of McLeod Plantation in the long term. At one end of the spectrum of choices is the time-tested approach taken by the foundation with another Lowcountry plantation, Mulberry, where the house and adjacent acreage were sold to a sympathetic private purchaser who donated a set of conservation easements protecting the property in perpetuity. At the other end of the spectrum is a less traditional approach for the foundation: development and operation of an outdoor museum at the site, in recognition of its educational potential for Lowcountry and African-American history. In addition to being costly, such a venture would represent a major departure from the foundation's original institutional mission to eschew museums and focus on area rehabilitation.

But in the 1990s Historic Charleston Foundation revealed that it was willing to embark on new directions, both in the interpretation of African-American heritage and in direct assistance to the youth of Charleston's modern African-American community. As its work in preservation planning and conservation continued in Charleston and the surrounding region through projects such as the county courthouse restoration, the reconstruction of the Powder Magazine, the Elliottborough rehabilitation initiative, and its studies at McLeod Plantation, the foundation was also beginning to explore new roles for itself.

Hurricane Hugo passed over Charleston on the night of 21 September 1989 causing extensive and severe damage to the city's historic architecture. During the storm winds gusted to 135 miles an hour, toppling trees and ripping off the roofs, decorative ironwork, and other architectural elements of Charleston buildings. Torrential rains followed for several days, pouring through once-secure roofs, while tidal flooding in the low-lying city filled streets at the tip of the peninsula with waist-deep water. Interior walls, plaster ceilings, woodwork, and furnishings all suffered enormous water damage. "We moved all our furniture to the second floor," one home owner recalled, "but then a tree fell through the roof and everything got soaked anyway."[24] Within the historic city fifty buildings collapsed and almost two hundred more suffered severe damage. By one estimate, 80 percent of all structures had some degree of storm-related roof damage.[25] In the recovery from Hugo, Historic Charleston Foundation joined with other preservation organizations and the city to play a major role in emergency relief and assistance. In the long term the storm also prompted the foundation to begin development of a systematic program of technical assistance in anticipation of similar natural disasters.

In the immediate aftermath the foundation turned its Frances R. Edmunds Center for Historic Preservation, opened only a few years previously at 108 Meeting Street, into a command post for coordinating relief programs in conjunction with municipal agencies and the preservation community as a whole. Anticipating a torrent of out-of-town building contractors descending on the city (and worried about unscrupulous operators), Mayor Joseph P. Riley Jr. asked the foundation to set up a process to register and screen contractors. Volunteer crews were organized to scavenge salvageable building components among the street debris, in advance of zealous clean-up crews, that could be warehoused until needed for repairs. Through its network of professional contacts the foundation arranged to bring in preservation architects, civil engineers, building technicians, roofing specialists, and historic preservation officials from across the country to offer advice on repairs and restoration. Students in university preservation programs in South Carolina and along the East Coast from Vermont to Florida traveled to Charleston to assess and photograph buildings and storm damage, under the direction of the foundation. Public workshops were conducted on such topics as controlling moisture damage, drying out masonry, and properly repairing roofs.[26]

One of the most challenging issues for the preservation community in the aftermath of the hurricane concerned the standards to which property owners were going to be held in making their storm-related repairs. Because municipal ordinance required the approval of the Board of Architectural Review for exterior alterations visible from a public right-of-way, in the historic district many of the repairs and most of the roof work came under BAR jurisdiction. To ensure that the BAR continued to have this police power even during the difficult months of recovery, Historic Charleston Foundation was able to intercede with the Federal Emergency Management Agency to keep it from suspending enforcement of the city's preservation ordinances. In a difficult and controversial decision the Board of Architectural Review decided that storm damage should be repaired using original, historic materials in order to preserve architectural integrity. Insurance adjusters had initially wanted to replace historic roofing materials (such as slate, standing-seam metal, and clay tile) with less expensive modern substitutes, but because of the firm position of the BAR in this matter, insurance companies eventually agreed to higher reimbursements to help cover the added costs for home owners. Nevertheless, the financial impact of these mandated repairs was acute for many residents.[27]

Historic Charleston Foundation joined with other preservation organizations to coordinate a national fund-raising campaign to establish a disaster relief fund designed, in part, to minimize the impact of these requirements on low-income and uninsured property owners. Administered in conjunction with the Preservation Society of Charleston and the Charleston Museum, the disaster fund was also intended to stabilize endangered properties, to set up a conservation laboratory for damaged artifacts and works of art, and to fund survey and documentation efforts. Within a year the campaign had raised almost one-half million dollars.[28]

For the long term the foundation sought to apply the lessons of Hurricane Hugo in a more sustained manner through development of a systematic program of technical assistance. Even before Hugo the foundation had undertaken projects to equip home owners with the knowledge to maintain historic buildings, through organization of seminars on historic paint colors, stone conservation, and historic gardens, among other topics. The opening of the Edmunds Center at 108 Meeting Street in 1986 had represented an attempt to establish a clearinghouse for preservation information and a site for educational forums, as well as a visitor center and gift shop. Hugo was the catalyst, though, for accelerating these efforts. Since 1990 the foundation has provided funding to bring teams from the National Park Service's Historic American Buildings Survey (HABS) and the Historic American Engineering Record (HAER) to Charleston to document historic architecture through measured drawings and photogrammetry. In the event of future natural disasters buildings could be restored or even reconstructed based on this archival record housed in the Library of Congress. The foundation has also taken the lead in disaster management planning, as well as in studies of how to retrofit historic masonry buildings to withstand future wind, water, and earthquake damage.[29]

### The Building Crafts Training Program

One of the most innovative forms of technical assistance developed by Historic Charleston Foundation in response to Hugo was the building crafts training program. "After Hurricane Hugo, the city of Charleston didn't have sufficient craftsmen to do the repairs that were necessary," conservation projects coordinator M. E. Van Dyke explained in 1995. "The foundation felt the craftsmen capable of this work were nearing retirement, and we didn't have a new crop of craftsmen to take their place."[30] Training a new generation in preservation craftsmanship was the rationale for creating the program, and this has remained its primary purpose through the 1990s. As it has evolved, though, the program has come to serve two additional functions: providing job training for inner-city youth and supplying the skilled labor for the foundation to undertake its area rehabilitation project in Elliottborough through the Neighborhood Impact Initiative. For all three reasons the building crafts training program has brought Historic Charleston Foundation national attention for an imaginative venture that combines a revival of craftsmanship with urban concerns about social justice.

The foundation had given some thought to the shrinking reservoir of craft skills in Charleston even before Hurricane Hugo highlighted the issue. As early as the spring of 1987 the foundation had initiated a pilot program in historic masonry at Burke High School that enabled two students who were enrolled in the masonry vocational curriculum to serve as paid interns for local contractors. The experiment was expanded during the following school year to include seventeen high school students in a two-year program designed to provide hands-on experience working on historic properties. Simultaneously with this local initiative the foundation had begun to explore an international collaboration with Les Campagnons du Devoir, a venerable French crafts guild, to establish an exchange of craftsmen and apprentices between France and Charleston that would involve training of ironworkers, stoneworkers, plasterers, and woodworkers. Eventually two French roofers and an upholsterer came to Charleston.[31]

The Historic Preservation Building Crafts Training Program, as it was called, built upon these earlier efforts when it was established in 1992 with a seventy-eight-thousand-dollar grant from the Charleston County Private Industry Council and the Charleston County Employment Training Administration. Twenty-seven local high school students enrolled in a ten-week summer program. The historic masonry curriculum was based at the old Bennett Rice Mill, which by 1992 was simply a brick facade propped up by steel supports, although it boasted some of the city's finest early brickwork. The instructor was Frank "Rip" Bennett, a seventy-one-year-old master mason with five decades of experience laying brick. The preservation carpentry curriculum used as its outdoor laboratory a fire-damaged house owned by the foundation at 32 Mary Street, where students repaired the piazzas as part of a project to rehabilitate the Greek Revival structure into low-income rental housing.[32] One seventeen-year-old girl explained her inspiration to enroll in the program: "It seems like not too many people in South Carolina know how to do historical work. From watching my grandfather do it, it seemed like something good to look into."[33]

Craft training has continued in subsequent years following a format similar to the one successfully pioneered in 1992. The program expanded its target audience during the summer of 1993 to include underprivileged youth throughout Charleston County, recruiting vocational students and dropouts aged fourteen to twenty-one, as well as high school students. Participants were hired at minimum wage to work thirty-five hours a week while learning either masonry or carpentry. The Bennett Rice Mill continued as the site for instruction in masonry, and there students were taught to replicate historic finishing techniques. McLeod Plantation, just recently acquired by the foundation, provided the carpentry classroom where participants were introduced to the basics of wood conservation, repair of roofing systems, and strategies for identifying and saving historic building materials. Under the supervision

of Benjamin Wilson, a graduate of Boston's highly regarded North Bennett
Street School, carpentry students undertook work at the McLeod slave cabins removing modern siding, asphalt shingles, and plywood sheathing and
replacing them with materials similar to the original.[34] "It's a great opportunity for the kids and myself," Wilson observed during the 1993 program at
McLeod. "One student didn't know how to hammer a nail and now he is the
last student off the roof."[35]

In an experiment whose success is not yet clear, Historic Charleston
Foundation joined the building crafts training program with the Neighborhood Impact Initiative in 1994 to undertake its first project in Elliottborough, the rehabilitation of the frame single house at 33 Bogard Street. The
carpentry to convert the abandoned building into a comfortable three-bedroom home was performed by Ben Wilson and a crew of five young men.
"Most of them didn't have high school diplomas. They had police records and
children," Wilson explained at the open house marking completion of the
project. "If we can turn one or two kids on to doing quality restoration, then
we're doing well. This could be one of their last chances," he noted, emphasizing an important social purpose of the crafts training program.[36]

The building crafts training program has become an essential component of the area rehabilitation project currently under way in Elliottborough.
Since completing the house at 33 Bogard Street in 1995, Historic Charleston
Foundation has moved on to tackle other properties in the neighborhood, at
25 Sires Street and 258 Ashley Avenue, among others.[37] While area rehabilitation has long been a focus of the foundation's approach to historic preservation, its coupling with the crafts training program represents an important
new dimension with national implications. In seeking to awaken an interest
in historic building skills among a new generation, the foundation has created a modest jobs program that provides temporary work to disadvantaged
youth while offering training for life-long employment in a community
whose own collective future is tied to the prospects of its inner-city neighborhoods in more ways than one.

## AFRICAN-AMERICAN HERITAGE PRESERVATION

Implementation of the building crafts training program was just one new
direction for Historic Charleston Foundation in the 1990s that illustrated a
willingness to explore fresh ventures for promoting education and historic
preservation. The acquisition of the Aiken-Rhett House represented another

new initiative with an important educational dimension. While the purchase of this grand mansion showed a renewal of interest in historic house museums that recalled the rescue of the Nathaniel Russell House in the 1950s, the foundation had quite a different priority in mind at Aiken-Rhett: a commitment to preserve and interpret African-American heritage in Charleston. The foundation purchased the Aiken-Rhett House from the Charleston Museum, which had owned the property at 48 Elizabeth Street since 1975 and operated it as one of its historic house museums beginning in 1979, along with the nearby Joseph Manigault House and the Heyward-Washington House on Church Street. Despite plans to restore Aiken-Rhett to its former glory, when it was the home of antebellum governor and congressman William Aiken Jr., the Charleston Museum never had the funds for the ambitious task. In time the mansion became too costly for the museum to maintain, and it was closed to the public at the end of 1993. Historic Charleston Foundation agreed to purchase Aiken-Rhett for six hundred thousand dollars in 1995, and the doors were reopened to the public in June 1996.[38]

For the foundation the appeal of the Aiken-Rhett House was its unrestored, even unaltered, condition and the possibilities that its remarkable architectural integrity held out for understanding life on a domestic urban complex of the antebellum era. Unlike rooms in most grand Charleston homes today, those of this mansion were largely unmodernized, and many showed exposed plaster, worn paint, and missing wallpaper. Aiken-Rhett had last been decorated in the 1850s, and the tattered historic fabric created a powerfully evocative atmosphere for visitors. Even more unusual, and possibly unique, were the dependencies in the block-long lot at the rear of the mansion. Slave quarters, kitchens, a carriage house, stables, animal sheds, privies, and an open work yard survived intact, protected by a high brick wall and never converted into apartments or garden.[39] Dr. Carter L. Hudgins, executive director of the foundation, explained the educational promise of this unusual collection of antebellum buildings: "The house holds the potential to interpret for the public not only the life and times of one of Charleston's most important merchant-entrepreneurs but the untold story of life within the walls of a Charleston estate. Nowhere else in Charleston is the potential to interpret urban slavery stronger."[40]

Under the management of Historic Charleston Foundation the workyard buildings and more of the house have been opened for public inspection, and consequently the meaning of the site has become more inclusive.

*Aiken-Rhett House*
    The complex of domestic structures
at the Aiken-Rhett House museum,
now operated by Historic Charleston Foundation, offers a unique setting for telling the story of urban
slavery. Courtesy, HCF.

The basement of the main house has been configured as a visitor reception area, and tours focus first on work and labor at the house and then on the living areas of the mansion. To help the public understand why there are no plans to restore or furnish Aiken-Rhett, visitors are encouraged "to marvel at what survives from the nineteenth century rather than search for what is missing." In addition the slave quarters are now open to the public. Visitors are instructed that "few house museums provide better insight into an urban residential complex on the eve of the Civil War and fewer have the ability and resources to interpret both life in the big house and the African-American experience in an urban context."[41]

The purchase of the Aiken-Rhett House in 1995 represented a major financial commitment on the part of the foundation to use Charleston's architecture for teaching African-American history. The foundation's support of African-American heritage preservation has continued in other ways as well, most notably through its participation in efforts to establish a museum of African-American history in South Carolina. One of the many possibilities currently under discussion is a "scattered site" museum that would take advantage of the rich array of historic places in South Carolina associated with African-American life and culture.[42] Not only is Historic Charleston Foundation in the position to contribute its professional expertise in the planning phases of this project, but it is also presently the steward for a number of historic properties with important links to African-American history. The Aiken-Rhett House tells the story of urban slavery, and McLeod Plantation speaks to rural slavery on a cotton plantation. The foundation is in the process of reinterpreting the Nathaniel Russell House to include the Africans who lived and labored there, and research has recently revealed that one of the Russell slaves was the blacksmith who made the pikes to be used in the abortive Denmark Vesey slave uprising of 1822. The reinterpretation of the Russell House holds possibilities for viewing slavery from the perspective of resistance and survival. Reconstruction has long been neglected in museums and historical exhibits in South Carolina, and the Freedmen's Bureau connection with McLeod Plantation offers a promising lens for examining the aims and legacy of that postwar experiment in biracial government and social reform.

❦

The far-flung preservation challenges confronting Historic Charleston Foundation by the 1990s had grown well beyond the expectations of the

*Marking the 50th anniversary*
Frances R. Edmunds is recognized at Historic Charleston Foundation's 50th anniversary celebration in April 1997, with Richard H. Jenrette, Joseph H. McGee, and Mayor Joseph P. Riley Jr. Courtesy, HCF.

Charlestonians who founded the organization in the 1940s. Its founders had envisioned it as an agency for promoting area-wide rehabilitation by targeting neighborhoods and districts rather than rescuing individual buildings, and despite the acquisition of historic properties such as the Aiken-Rhett House, McLeod Plantation, and the Nathaniel Russell House, area rehabilitation remained central to the foundation's mission. Few of its founders, though, could have anticipated how the organization would broaden the idea so successfully or that their small, local organization would achieve national influence. The founders had pondered issues of growth and planning, but none foresaw the pace of metropolitan development that accelerated pressures on historic architecture in the peninsular city. Nor could they imagine the resulting need to address environmental issues of the region as a whole. Within the old city itself the foundation's activities expanded to encompass the concerns of diverse groups of citizens in uptown neighborhoods. There it experimented with preservation as a tool to tackle difficult issues of affordable housing, urban decay, and jobs training, deepening the social relevance of the preservation agenda. In spite of the nature and breadth of the challenges by the 1990s, the founders would still discern the core purpose they had defined with the assistance of civic planner Frederick Law Olmsted Jr. in the 1940s: to encourage practical preservation in "a living, growing city." This perspective had been articulated by Olmsted in his consultant's report to the Carolina Art Association as it formulated the strategy that would establish the foundation in 1947. The philosophy continues to animate Historic Charleston Foundation today as it seeks to weave change into the historic city through proactive planning and by capitalizing on the vitality of the private sector. Because of its early embrace of this approach the foundation has pioneered in shaping the current view of historic preservation as a form of planning concerned with the quality of modern life.

The role of the foundation in broadening the concept of preservation and its national impact were acknowledged throughout the celebrations that marked its fiftieth anniversary year in 1997. The public events organized by a group of trustees, former officers, and staff members celebrated the achievements of the first half-century while also asking what the future might look like. An oyster roast at McLeod Plantation marked the beginning of the celebration. A series of lectures followed, one on the history of the foundation delivered by Joseph H. McGee (who had been involved with the work of Historic Charleston Foundation since the 1960s, when as a young attorney he had helped the organization revise the city's historic preservation ordinance). A tourism forum, co-sponsored with the Preservation Society of Charleston, the College of Charleston, and municipal government, initiated a discussion that would lead to significant changes in the city's tourism management policies. Tours of rehabilitation projects brought new attention to the plight of failing historic neighborhoods and to the impact of poorly managed suburban growth on the settings of historic plantations and rural communities near Charleston. Toward the end of the anniversary year Paul Goldberger, architecture critic for *The New Yorker*, gave an address on the opportunities for the American preservation movement to inspire successful urban design and to revive commercial districts and neighborhoods.

A symposium held in conjunction with a gala celebration at Drayton Hall in April 1997 presented the community with a provocative discussion of the legacy of the foundation and the future of the city. Working with the staff and a trustee committee, former president Joseph McGee assembled a distinguished panel of national preservation leaders to ponder the role that heritage preservation should play in coming years, both in Charleston and throughout the country. Panelists brought to their talks experience gained in a variety of preservation endeavors. Richard H. Jenrette, trustee of the National Trust for Historic Preservation and then chairman of the Equitable Company, had long been active in Charleston's preservation efforts, having led the campaign to rehabilitate the Mills House hotel in the 1960s. Among other ventures, he had restored and furnished the Roper House, one of the most significant of the city's grand residences. Jenrette joined Richard Moe, president of the National Trust for Historic Preservation; Roger Kennedy, then director of the National Park Service; and Joseph P. Riley Jr., mayor of Charleston for more than two decades and principal architect of the city's late twentieth-century renaissance. With them on the stage of the Sottile Theater at the College of Charleston was Judge Alexander Sanders Jr., the college president, who moderated a discussion that served to remind the audience of eight hundred that historic preservation has been, and will remain, a dynamic endeavor with multiple points of view.

That night panelists debated how, by the 1990s, the enterprise of historic preservation defined its mission. Richard Jenrette asserted that preservation's crowning achievements were the restoration of houses that epitomized the best in American architectural design. Historic places like Monticello, Jenrette argued, connected the nation to the lives of its great leaders, and they had the power to inspire the construction of new places of lasting beauty. The evening's other panelists agreed that the preservation of distinctive residences had shaped the beginnings of the preservation movement. Collectively, though, their remarks emphasized the new directions followed in recent decades, especially the broadening of historic preservation to take account of the health of America's cities and towns. Richard Moe contended that revitalizing downtowns should be the primary task of preservationists. Pointing to the National Trust's long-standing Main Street program and its recent initiatives targeting suburban sprawl, Moe stressed the importance of preserving historic buildings by managing communities in sustainable ways. Roger Kennedy applauded the successes of the preservation movement in giving citizens a sense of connectedness with their surroundings. But he suggested that the real purpose of preservation was to recall through historic places how the American nation had emerged and the events that shaped the country's character and identity. Mayor Riley recounted the numerous public benefits that resulted when cities pay close attention to quality architectural design in the public realm. Reiterating an opinion expressed by other speakers that night, Riley maintained that preservation was the most significant development in urban planning in the twentieth century.

The speakers that spring evening offered diverse views on where the preservation movement should focus future efforts—restoring great houses, teaching history, inspiring architectural and urban design, promoting economic development, planning sustainable communities—and their remarks illustrated how capacious the goals of the movement had become, especially in the city of Charleston. Forged in the early twentieth century by concerns over the loss of landmark buildings, Charleston's preservation movement by the 1990s encompassed wide-ranging efforts to ensure that suburban sprawl did not undermine either the vitality of the city's historic commercial district or the unique sense of place in the South Carolina Lowcountry. Rooted in a nostalgic impulse to preserve the most beautiful buildings in the old city, the movement had come to see its central task as effective community planning that would join aesthetics with economics, architecture with social justice, private energy with public purpose, urban neighborhood with ecological region, the inheritance of the past with the promise of change.

# Appendix 1

# HISTORIC PRESERVATION IN CHARLESTON
## *A Time Line of Significant Twentieth-Century Events*

1902      Powder Magazine (79 Cumberland Street) is preserved through purchase by the National Society of Colonial Dames in the State of South Carolina.

1911      Susan Pringle Frost buys her first property in the slums of eastern Tradd Street, beginning her decades-long private campaign to stabilize and rehabilitate the Tradd Street–Bedon's Alley–East Bay Street area.

1913      To preserve the Old Exchange Building (122 East Bay Street), Congress authorizes its transfer to the Daughters of the American Revolution.

1914      *Twenty Drawings of the Pringle House* is published by Alice Ravenel Huger Smith.

1916      The National Park Service is established within the U.S. Department of the Interior.

1917      *The Dwelling Houses of Charleston, South Carolina* is published by Alice Ravenel Huger Smith and Daniel Elliott Huger Smith.

Apr. 1920      The Society for the Preservation of Old Dwellings is established.

May 1920      Joseph Manigault House (350 Meeting Street) is preserved through purchase by the Society for the Preservation of Old Dwellings.

| | |
|---|---|
| Mar. 1922 | Mr. and Mrs. Ernest Pringle Jr. assume the debt on the Joseph Manigault House from the Society for the Preservation of Old Dwellings. |
| Dec. 1923– Dec 1931 | Thomas Porcher Stoney serves as mayor. |
| Mar. 1924 | The state of South Carolina passes enabling legislation (Act 642) permitting cities to adopt zoning laws. |
| Nov. 1924 | The American Wing of the Metropolitan Museum of Art in New York City opens, attracting attention to historic house interiors. |
| Dec. 1924 | Charleston Chamber of Commerce urges City Council to implement a system of planning and zoning. |
| May 1926 | Ashley River Memorial Bridge opens. |
| 1926 | In *Euclid* v. *Ambler* the U.S. Supreme Court affirms the validity of zoning as a proper use of the municipal police power. |
| 1926 | Restoration begins at Williamsburg, Virginia, supported by John D. Rockefeller Jr. |
| 1927 | *Charleston, South Carolina* by Albert Simons and Samuel Lapham Jr. is published by the American Institute of Architects. |
| 1928 | Mansion House hotel (71 Broad Street) is dismantled. |
| 1928 | Joseph Manigault House opens briefly as Charleston's first historic house museum. |
| 1929 | Heyward-Washington House (87 Church Street) is purchased by Charleston Museum; mortgage is liquidated in 1953. |
| Apr. 1929 | A temporary City Planning and Zoning Commission is established by City Council. |
| Aug. 1929 | Grace Memorial Bridge over the Cooper River is dedicated. |
| Oct. 1929 | A Special Committee on Zoning is established by City Council to draft a zoning ordinance; it produces a temporary ordinance ratified in August 1930 and recommends hiring a professional firm. |

Oct. 1930     A permanent City Planning and Zoning Commission is established.

Oct. 1930     Morris Knowles firm of Pittsburgh is hired by City Council to develop a comprehensive zoning ordinance and recommendations for a city plan.

1931     Heyward-Washington House opens as a house museum.

1931     Rehabilitation begins on Rainbow Row (79–107 East Bay Street) through private initiative.

Oct. 1931     Zoning Ordinance is ratified by City Council, designating an Old and Historic Charleston District and setting up a Board of Architectural Review (BAR).

Dec. 1931–     Burnet Rhett Maybank serves as mayor.
Dec. 1938

Apr. 1932     American Institute of Architects urges museums to avoid use of historic interiors in exhibits.

1932–53     Robert N. S. Whitelaw serves as director of the Carolina Art Association.

1933     Joseph Manigault House is donated to the Charleston Museum after its purchase at auction by Harriett Pollitzer, Princess Pignatelli.

Dec. 1933     Historic American Buildings Survey is established by National Park Service.

1935     Historic Sites and Buildings Act is passed by U.S. Congress.

1936     Rehabilitation of kitchen building and courtyard on Cabbage Row at the William Hendricks Tenements (83–85 Church Street) inspires renovation of other former dependencies into substantial residences.

1937     Reconstructed Dock Street Theatre (135 Church Street) opens, under management of the Carolina Art Association until 1950, on the former site of Planter's Hotel.

1938     *Plantations of the Carolina Low Country* is published by the Carolina Art Association.

| | |
|---|---|
| Sept. 1938 | Hurricane and tornadoes hit Charleston; federal funds assist with restoration. |
| Dec. 1938–June 1944 | Henry Whilden Lockwood serves as mayor. |
| 1939 | *Prints and Impressions of Charleston* is published by Elizabeth O'Neill Verner. |
| Dec. 1939 | Robert N. S. Whitelaw organizes an ad hoc committee of the Carolina Art Association to promote historic preservation and community planning; it is subsequently expanded and named the Charleston Regional Planning Committee in early 1940 and the Charleston Civic Services Committee in January 1942; it establishes Historic Charleston Foundation in 1947. |
| 1939–41 | Robert Mills Manor public housing project is built with New Deal funding; some historic structures on the site are preserved. |
| Jan. 1940 | Frederick Law Olmsted Jr. visits Charleston to consult for the Carolina Art Association. |
| Feb.–Mar. 1940 | Frederick Law Olmsted Jr. gives preliminary advice on an architectural survey and city planning. |
| 1940–41 | An architectural survey is conducted by the Carolina Art Association. |
| Mar.–Apr. 1942 | "This Is Charleston" exhibit is organized by Carolina Art Association at Gibbes Art Gallery. |
| June 1944–Dec. 1947 | E. Edward Wehman Jr. serves as mayor. |
| Dec. 1944 | *This Is Charleston* is published by the Carolina Art Association. |
| Apr. 1945 | Kenneth Chorley is invited by Carolina Art Association to deliver address on "The Challenge to Charleston" recommending creation of a nonprofit foundation. |
| Apr.1947 | Historic Charleston Foundation (HCF) is incorporated. |
| Dec. 1947–Dec. 1959 | William McGillivray Morrison serves as mayor. |

Mar. 1948    First annual spring tour of historic houses is organized by HCF.

June 1948    Frances R. Edmunds hired by HCF as director of the spring tour of historic houses; she serves subsequently as executive secretary, director, and ultimately executive director of HCF until her retirement in 1985.

June 1949    Tour headquarters, and later HCF offices, are established at 94 Church Street.

Oct. 1949    National Trust for Historic Preservation is chartered by U.S. Congress.

June 1952    Bennett Rice Mill on the Cooper River waterfront is threatened with demolition, following its condemnation as a fire hazard.

1952    Joint project between HCF and the Rebecca Motte chapter of the Daughters of the American Revolution to restore the west pediment of the Old Exchange Building.

1952–53    Charleston Orphan House (160 Calhoun Street) and Chapel (13 Vanderhorst Street) demolished.

1953    Mortgage on Heyward-Washington House, operated by Charleston Museum, is paid off by HCF.

Mar. 1955    Nathaniel Russell House (51 Meeting Street) is purchased by HCF; offices are relocated there.

Mar. 1956    Nathaniel Russell House opens to the public as a museum.

1956    Society for the Preservation of Old Dwellings is reorganized as Preservation Society of Charleston; *Preservation Progress* begins publication.

Feb. 1957    Revolving fund for area rehabilitation is established by HCF.

Oct. 1958    Bennett Rice Mill is jointly leased by HCF and the Preservation Society of Charleston for five years.

Dec. 1958    Gadsden House (329 East Bay) is donated to HCF by Woodwards; this and subsequent acquisitions on East Bay Street are sold in 1986 to provide the nucleus for HCF endowment.

Feb. 1959       Ansonborough is selected as the first area rehabilitation project of HCF; purchases begin at the intersection of Society and Anson Streets.

July 1959       Public announcement is made of the first revolving fund purchases in Ansonborough.

Nov. 1959       First modification of the 1931 zoning ordinance is made: BAR is given power to delay demolition and review exterior alteration of pre-1860 buildings within city limits.

Dec. 1959–      J. Palmer Gaillard Jr. serves as mayor.
Aug. 1975

Apr. 1960       Charleston Hotel (200 Meeting Street) is demolished.

July 1960       Primerose House (332 East Bay) is donated by the Woodwards to HCF; it is sold in 1986 to establish an endowment fund.

Sept. 1960      Bennett Rice Mill is largely destroyed by Hurricane Donna.

Jan. 1961       Eastbound span is added adjacent to Ashley River Memorial Bridge.

May 1961        First public tour of Ansonborough properties is conducted.

Mar. 1962       Isaac Jenkins Mikell House (94 Rutledge Avenue) is purchased by the Woodwards; it is donated to HCF in 1978.

July 1962       Presqu'ile (2 Amherst Street) is purchased by HCF; it is sold in 1973.

Oct. 1962       Stephen Shrewsbury House (311 East Bay) is purchased by HCF.

1962            Andrew Moffett House (328 East Bay) is acquired by HCF with assistance from the Woodwards; it is sold in 1986 to establish an endowment fund.

1962–64         "Three Sisters" is demolished at 37–39–41 Calhoun Street; popular outcry facilitates subsequent revision of the zoning ordinance.

1964–65         "Landmarks in Use" tours are inaugurated by HCF to illustrate adaptive use.

Mar. 1965       William Blake House (321 East Bay) is donated to HCF.

| 1965 | Faber House (631 East Bay) is purchased by HCF. |
|------|--------|

May 1966     44 Charlotte Street is donated to HCF.

Aug. 1966     Significant revision is made to 1931 zoning ordinance: BAR is given power to deny demolitions, major expansion of Old and Historic Charleston District, among other changes.

Oct. 1966     National Historic Preservation Act is passed by U.S. Congress.

1966     Second span is added adjacent to Cooper River's Grace Memorial Bridge.

1966–67     Four houses from auditorium site are relocated by HCF.

Mar. 1967     HCF adds gardens and churches to its spring tour of historic houses.

1967     Crosstown Expressway (Highway 17) is constructed.

1967     State responsibilities for historic preservation under the National Historic Preservation Act of 1966 are assumed in South Carolina by the Department of Archives and History; the State Historic Preservation Office (SHPO) is officially created in 1973.

Apr. 1968     Plans are announced by Richard H. Jenrette, with encouragement and investment of HCF, to raze the St. John Hotel (115 Meeting Street) and reconstruct it as the Mills House in an effort to foster downtown revitalization.

1968     Broad Street Beautification Project is established.

1968     Municipal auditorium is completed; it is subsequently named the Gaillard Auditorium.

1969     National Environmental Policy Act is passed by U.S. Congress.

Oct. 1970     Mills Hyatt House opens on site of St. John Hotel.

Nov. 1970     National Trust for Historic Preservation holds annual meeting in Charleston.

1970–72     Arch Building (85 Calhoun Street) is restored by HCF and federal grants.

Feb. 1971        Advisory Council on Historic Preservation meets in Charleston to review the proposed James Island Bridge; it finds the current proposal would adversely affect the historic district.

Oct. 1971        Frances R. Edmunds receives Louise du Pont Crowninshield Award from the National Trust for Historic Preservation at its annual meeting in San Diego.

Nov. 1971        State highway department consents to a Calhoun Street terminus for the James Island Bridge.

Sept. 1972       Purchase of 6 Judith Street inaugurates first concerted HCF effort in Wraggborough.

Sept. 1972       Historic Charleston Reproductions program is established; the collection is available in retail shops in 1974.

Jan. 1973        HCF and National Trust for Historic Preservation sign a lease with option to purchase Drayton Hall on the Ashley River Road.

Apr. 1973        Old City Historic District is established to include area south of Line Street.

July 1973        Height ordinance is proposed by HCF to control new construction.

1973–89          Edmondston-Alston House (21 East Battery) is operated by HCF as a museum.

June 1974        Feiss-Wright-Anderson historic preservation plan is presented to the city; it includes inventory and classification scheme for historic architecture south of the Crosstown Expressway and is adopted by City Council in 1975.

July 1974        National Trust for Historic Preservation purchases Drayton Hall with the assistance of HCF.

Nov. 1974        Historic Charleston Reproductions opens its showroom at 105 Broad Street.

1974             Nathaniel Russell House is designated a National Historic Landmark.

Feb. 1975        Consultant Ann Satterthwaite conducts organizational review: *Historic Charleston Foundation: Its Past, Present and Future;* the report leads eventually to the expansion and increased professionalism of HCF staff.

June–July 1975  Major expansion is made to the Old and Historic Charleston District through inclusion of most of the area below Calhoun Street and some areas above it; authority of BAR is enhanced south of Crosstown Expressway by adoption of 1974 inventory and classification scheme for historic buildings.

July 1975       Advisory Council on Historic Preservation completes a memorandum of agreement on the James Island Bridge after requiring the city to adopt a historic preservation plan, among other provisions.

Aug.–Dec. 1975 Arthur B. Schirmer Jr. serves as interim mayor.

Dec. 1975–      Joseph P. Riley Jr. serves as mayor.

May 1976        Drayton Hall is designated a National Historic Landmark.

1976            Tax Reform Act of 1976 establishes tax incentives for rehabilitation of income-producing historic structures.

1976–86         Heyday of investment tax credit projects in U.S.

Mar. 1977       *Charleston Commercial Revitalization Program* is presented by Barton-Aschman Associates of Washington, D.C., recommending construction of a hotel-convention complex.

Apr. 1977       Annual revenue for HCF's Festival of Houses and Gardens exceeds $100,000.

May 1977        36 Mary Street is purchased by HCF, its first property in Wraggborough under the Home Ownership Program; the program operates until 1986.

May 1977        Annual Spoleto Festival USA is held in Charleston for the first time as a result of efforts of HCF and others.

July 1977       Mayor Riley announces that a hotel-convention complex will be built by Theodore Gould and his Holywell Corporation.

Sept. 1977      Southern Regional Office of the National Trust for Historic Preservation officially opens in Charleston in the William Aiken House (456 King Street).

Oct. 1977      Theodore Gould releases his plans for a hotel-convention complex on the block bounded by King, Market, Meeting, and Hasell Streets.

Dec. 1977      In a statement of nonopposition, HCF raises questions about the proposed hotel-convention complex.

1977      Planning begins for the Judith-Chapel Street infill project in Wraggborough; the first townhouses are completed in 1989.

Jan. 1978      Save Historic Charleston Fund is formed to oppose the hotel-convention complex.

Feb. 1978      *Tourism Impact and Management Study* for Charleston County is released by Barton-Aschman Associates of Washington, D.C., recommending establishment of a visitor center.

May 1978      Citizens committee appointed by Mayor Riley questions the need for a convention center and describes the proposed hotel as too tall and too massive for the site.

May 1978      HCF purchases its first properties in Radcliffeborough under the Home Ownership Program.

Aug. 1978      Environmental impact statement on proposed hotel-convention complex is released.

Aug. 1978      State supreme court rules invalid the city's contract with the developer of the hotel-convention complex.

Oct. 1978      Downtown Residents for Charleston Center is formed to support the hotel-convention complex.

Dec. 1978      Height ordinance is adopted by City Council.

Jan. 1979      HCF gives conditional endorsement to the hotel-convention complex at the Charleston meeting of the Advisory Council on Historic Preservation.

Feb. 1979      Architects brought to Charleston by HCF suggest design changes for the hotel-convention complex.

Feb. 1979      Public hearing on environmental impact statement for the hotel-convention complex takes place.

| | |
|---|---|
| Mar. 1979 | Battle for control of the Preservation Society of Charleston erupts over the issue of the hotel-convention complex. |
| July 1979 | Memorandum of agreement on the hotel-convention complex is formally ratified by the Advisory Council on Historic Preservation. |
| Sept. 1979 | Frances R. Edmunds is appointed to the Advisory Council on Historic Preservation by President Carter. |
| Sept. 1979 | Supplement to the final environmental impact statement for the hotel-convention complex is released. |
| 1979 | Charleston Museum moves into a new building on Meeting Street across from the Joseph Manigault House. |
| 1979–93 | Aiken-Rhett House (48 Elizabeth Street) is operated as a house museum by Charleston Museum. |
| June 1980 | King Street Facade Program is implemented by the city. |
| Dec. 1980 | Federal lawsuit fails to stop hotel-convention complex. |
| Sept. 1981 | HCF hires its first full-time, professionally trained curator at the Nathaniel Russell House. |
| 1981 | Economic Recovery Tax Act increases tax incentives for private rehabilitation of income-producing historic structures. |
| Oct. 1982 | Conservation easement program is established by HCF. |
| Jan. 1983 | Financing collapses for the Gould proposal for the hotel-convention complex. |
| Mar. 1983 | Restoration is done by HCF of the graveyard at the Circular Congregational Church (150 Meeting Street), the oldest graveyard in Charleston, dating from the 1680s. |
| May 1983 | Plans for a less massive, eight-story hotel-convention complex are released by new developers, A. Albert Taubman and Rainbow Square; John Carl Warnecke is selected as architect. |

Aug. 1983        Sale of the site and plans for the hotel-convention complex to new developers are completed.

Sept. 1983       Lockwood Boulevard Extension is dropped from the James Island Expressway project due to financial and environmental concerns.

Fall 1983        Quarterly newsletter of Historic Charleston Reproductions, *Charleston,* begins publication.

Nov. 1983        A twelve-mile section of the Ashley River Road is listed in the National Register of Historic Places.

Nov. 1983        Second supplement to the final environmental impact statement for the hotel-convention complex is released.

Dec. 1983        Advisory Council on Historic Preservation convenes public meeting in Charleston to hear testimony on the proposed Federal Courthouse Annex.

May 1984         HCF takes option to purchase the William Gibbes House (64 South Battery); it is sold in 1986 to a private buyer.

1984             Full-time historic preservation officer is hired by the city.

Oct. 1984        Mayor Riley announces plans for a marine science museum; a site for the South Carolina Aquarium is eventually selected at the eastern end of Calhoun Street on the Cooper River.

Dec. 1984        BAR gives "interim final approval" for construction to begin on hotel-convention complex.

1984–85          Architectural survey is conducted by Geier Brown Renfrow Architects of buildings not inventoried in 1974, including those more than fifty years old, some as far north as the Crosstown Expressway.

Jan. 1985        Ground breaking on the hotel-convention complex.

1985             BAR is given power to forbid demolition or relocation of any building over seventy-five years old south of Mount Pleasant Street.

July 1985        Frances R. Edmunds retires as executive director of HCF after an association of thirty-eight years.

| Aug. 1985–<br>June 1987 | R. Angus Murdoch serves as executive director of HCF. |
|---|---|
| May 1986 | Frances R. Edmunds Center for Historic Preservation is dedicated at 108 Meeting Street. |
| Sept. 1986 | Charleston Place opens. |
| Oct.1986 | HCF grant revitalizes the scenic preservation work of the Lowcountry Open Land Trust. |
| 1986 | HCF properties on East Bay Street are sold to create nucleus of its endowment. |
| 1986 | Tax Reform Act of 1986 reduces private incentives to rehabilitate historic structures. |
| 1986–87 | *61 Corridor Growth Management Plan* is adopted by City of Charleston, Charleston County, and Dorchester County. |
| Apr. 1987 | Annual revenue for HCF's Festival of Houses and Gardens exceeds $200,000. |
| July 1987–<br>Dec. 1993 | Lawrence A. Walker serves as executive director of HCF. |
| July 1987 | Mulberry Plantation on the Cooper River in Berkeley County is purchased by HCF; it is sold in August 1988. |
| 1987 | City adopts expansion of Old and Historic Charleston District regulations to the 1984–85 survey area. BAR is given review powers over new construction in the Old City Historic District, an area extending as far north as the Crosstown Expressway. |
| Fall 1987 | Friends of Historic Snee Farm is established to purchase home associated with Charles Pinckney in Mount Pleasant. |
| Fall 1987 | Charleston Heritage Housing, Inc. is established with HCF assistance to provide affordable housing in uptown boroughs. |
| Dec. 1987 | Friends of Historic Snee Farm exercise option to purchase Snee Farm for $2 million, halting development at the site. |

| June 1988 | Mayor and city government bow to neighborhood sentiment and decide to oppose nomination of East Side and West Side to the National Register of Historic Places. |
|---|---|
| Nov. 1988 | Federal Courthouse Annex is dedicated. |
| July 1988 | Friends of Historic Snee Farm purchase Snee Farm. |
| Sept. 1988 | Congress authorizes establishment of Charles Pinckney National Historic Site at Snee Farm. |
| Jan. 1989 | Notarized letters of opposition from property owners prevent East Side and West Side from being listed in the National Register of Historic Places. |
| Jan. 1989 | *Calhoun Street Corridor Study* is adopted conceptually by City Council. |
| Sept. 1989 | Hurricane Hugo hits Charleston. |
| Oct. 1989 | Preservation disaster fund is established by HCF and other organizations. |
| Jan. 1990 | City extends the Old City Historic District (and the accompanying height and new construction controls) off the peninsula for the first time, to Albemarle Point on the west bank of the Ashley River; BAR expands to three full-time staff. |
| Jan. 1990 | Partial interest in McLeod Plantation on James Island is inherited by HCF. |
| Mar. 1990 | Consultant Gretchen Klimoski facilitates strategic planning retreat for HCF, producing *Historic Charleston Foundation Planning Retreat Report.* |
| May 1990 | Snee Farm is conveyed by Friends of Historic Snee Farm to the National Park Service. |
| May 1990 | Cooper River Waterfront Park is dedicated. |
| Oct. 1990 | National Trust for Historic Preservation holds annual meeting in Charleston. |
| 1990 | Charleston Heritage Housing is reorganized as Charleston Affordable Housing. |
| May 1991 | Visitors Reception and Transportation Center opens. |

| | |
|---|---|
| Sept. 1991 | Consultant Charles Bentz recommends strategy for $4 million fund-raising campaign in *Historic Charleston Foundation Marketing/Feasibility Study Report.* |
| Sept. 1991 | *Charleston 2000* plan adopted by city. |
| Oct. 1991 | Mayor Joseph P. Riley Jr. receives National Preservation Honor Award from the National Trust for Historic Preservation. |
| Fall 1991 | Consultant Letitia Galbraith compiles *Heritage Education Feasibility Study* for HCF. |
| 1992 | Building crafts training program is established by HCF. |
| Spring 1992 | HCF relocates its offices from the Nathaniel Russell House to leased quarters at 11 Fulton Street; the Russell House can now be managed in its entirety as a historic house museum. |
| June 1992 | Heritage Campaign is launched by HCF to raise $4 million. |
| Nov. 1992 | HCF organizes a reunion of descendants of Nathaniel Russell. |
| 1992 | Ashley River Special Area Management Plan is adopted. |
| May 1993 | Restoration begins on Charleston County Courthouse with demolition of twentieth-century additions. |
| 1993 | Full title to McLeod Plantation is acquired by HCF. |
| June 1993 | Sweetgrass seedlings are first planted at McLeod Plantation. |
| 1993 | Colonial Dames lease the Powder Magazine to HCF for restoration. |
| Jan. 1994– | Dr. Carter L. Hudgins serves as executive director of HCF. |
| Jan. 1994 | Frances R. Edmunds is first recipient of the Frances R. Edmunds Award for Historic Preservation from HCF. |
| Apr. 1994 | *Tourism Management Plan* is adopted by the city. |
| Apr. 1994 | Annual revenue for HCF's Festival of Houses and Gardens exceeds $300,000. |

Fall 1994     Quarterly newsletter of HCF, *Historic Charleston,* begins publication.

Jan. 1995     Mr. and Mrs. Charles Henry Woodward receive the Frances R. Edmunds Award for Historic Preservation from HCF; the award to Mr. Woodward is presented posthumously.

May 1995     Charles Pinckney National Historic Site opens to the public.

June 1995     First property under the Neighborhood Impact Initiative is rehabilitated at 33 Bogard Street in Elliottborough.

July 1995     National Trust for Historic Preservation identifies the Ashley River Historic District as one of the country's eleven most endangered historic places.

Dec. 1995     Aiken-Rhett House is purchased from Charleston Museum by HCF.

Feb. 1996     Charleston Place purchases the Riviera Theater (227 King Street) for adaptive use as conference space, shops, and offices.

June 1996     Aiken-Rhett House reopens under HCF management.

Oct. 1996     HCF relocates its offices to the recently purchased Missroon House on Charleston Harbor at 40 East Bay Street.

Apr. 1997     HCF celebrates its 50th anniversary.

June 1997     The restored Powder Magazine reopens as a museum under HCF management.

Oct. 1997     Trustees Award for Organizational Excellence is presented to HCF by the National Trust for Historic Preservation at its annual meeting in Santa Fe.

# Appendix 2

# OFFICERS OF HISTORIC CHARLESTON FOUNDATION SINCE 1947*

| PRESIDENTS | TERM OF SERVICE |
|---|---|
| C. Bissell Jenkins Jr. | 1947–1951 |
| Samuel G. Stoney | 1951–1955 |
| Ben Scott Whaley | 1955–1969 |
| Thomas C. Stevenson Jr. | 1969–1972 |
| Thomas E. Thornhill | 1972–1975 |
| Benjamin A. Hagood | 1975–1977 |
| Joseph H. McGee | 1977–1980 |
| Sidney W. Stubbs Jr. | 1980–1983 |
| John McCrady Jr. | 1983–1986 |
| Lawrence A. Walker | 1986–1988 |
| Richard W. Salmons | 1988–1990 |
| Bachman S. Smith III | 1990–1992 |
| Dr. Thomas A. Palmer | 1992–1994 |
| John H. Warren III | 1994–1996 |
| J. Rutledge Young Jr. | 1996–1998 |
| Jane P. Hanahan | 1998– |

* This list was assembled from information provided by Historic Charleston Foundation.

| Vice Presidents | Term of Service |
|---|---|
| Ben Scott Whaley | 1947–1955 |
| Berkeley Grimball | 1955–1957 |
| Samuel G. Stoney | 1957–1967 |
| Thomas C. Stevenson Jr. | 1967–1969 |
| Peter Manigault | 1969–1972 |
| Rufus C. Barkley Jr. | 1972–1974 |
| Benjamin A. Hagood | 1974–1975 |
| Joseph H. McGee | 1975–1977 |
| Robert M. Hollings | 1977–1979 |
| Sidney W. Stubbs Jr. | 1979–1980 |
| John McCrady Jr. | 1980–1983 |
| Lawrence A. Walker | 1983–1986 |
| Richard W. Salmons | 1986–1988 |
| Bachman S. Smith III | 1988–1990 |
| Thomas A. Palmer | 1990–1992 |
| John H. Warren III | 1992–1994 |
| J. Rutledge Young Jr. | 1994–1996 |
| Jane P. Hanahan | 1996–1998 |
| Harold R. Pratt-Thomas Jr. | 1998– |

| Secretaries | Term of Service |
|---|---|
| E. Gaillard Dotterer | 1947–1951 |
| Frances R. Edmunds | 1951–1986 |
| Douglas C. Plate | 1986–1987 |
| Jane P. Hanahan | 1987–1990 |
| Amelia P. Cathcart | 1990–1996 |
| Dorothy B. Kerrison | 1996–1998 |
| Katharine S. Robinson | 1998– |

| TREASURERS | TERM OF SERVICE |
|---|---|
| C. Lester Cannon | 1947–1967 |
| Thomas E. Thornhill | 1967–1972 |
| I. Mayo Read Jr. | 1972–1975 |
| Charles H. P. Duell | 1975–1983 |
| Douglas C. Plate | 1983–1989 |
| Richard B. Grimball | 1989–1990 |
| Richard W. Salmons | 1990–1991 |
| J. Rutledge Young Jr. | 1991–1994 |
| David Maybank Jr. | 1994–1996 |
| Harold R. Pratt-Thomas Jr. | 1996–1998 |
| John F. Maybank | 1998– |

Appendix 3

# Trustees of Historic Charleston Foundation Since 1947*

| Name of Trustee | Term of Service |
| --- | --- |
| Rt. Rev. C. FitzSimons Allison | 1985–1993 |
| W. E. Applegate III | 1998– |
| Dianne Phillips Avlon | 1992– |
| Edward R. Ball | 1974–1983 |
| Rufus C. Barkley Jr. | 1969–1982 |
| Thomas R. Bennett | 1965–1973 |
| C. Harrington Bissell | 1988–1994 |
| Loutrel W. Briggs | 1947–1969 |
| Honorary Trustee, 1970 | |
| Frank W. Brumley | 1998– |
| E. Milby Burton | 1947–1963 |
| W. Harold Butt | 1963–1972 |
| C. Lester Cannon | 1947–1972 |
| T. Heyward Carter Jr. | 1997– |
| Amelia P. Cathcart | 1981–1988, 1989–1998 |
| Richard E. Coen | 1980–1986, 1988–1997 |
| J. Walker Coleman Jr. | 1984–1993 |
| Steade R. Craigo | 1973–1975 |
| Alston Deas | 1947–1948 |
| Herbert A. DeCosta Jr. | 1992– |

* This list was assembled from information provided by Historic Charleston Foundation.

| Name of Trustee | Term of Service |
|---|---|
| John Henry Dick | 1964–1967 |
| E. Gaillard Dotterer | 1947–1960 |
| Charles H. P. Duell | 1971–1983, 1984–1993 |
| Frances R. Edmunds | 1954–1983 |
| Lifetime Trustee, 1986 | |
| Mrs. James B. Edwards | 1979–1988, 1989–1998 |
| Mrs. John Ashby Farrow | 1950–1961 |
| Mrs. John P. Frost | 1952–1979 |
| Leonard C. Fulghum Jr. | 1985–1992 |
| J. Palmer Gaillard Jr. | 1979–1988 |
| Mrs. Coming Ball Gibbes | 1952–1971 |
| Berkeley Grimball | 1955–1957 |
| Henry E. Grimball | 1983–1992 |
| Richard B. Grimball | 1969–1972, 1988–1997 |
| Theodore B. Guérard | 1988–1997 |
| Mrs. Theodore B. Guérard | 1969–1979 |
| Benjamin A. Hagood | 1959–1981, 1982–1985 |
| James M. Hagood | 1993– |
| Jane P. Hanahan | 1978–1989, 1992– |
| Alison B. Harwood | 1983–1992 |
| Ralph M. Hendricks Jr. | 1979–1988 |
| Robert M. Hollings | 1969–1981 |
| John E. Huguley | 1976–1985, 1990– |
| Thomas A. Hutcheson | 1981–1988 |
| Richard W. Hutson Jr. | 1996– |
| W. Elliott Hutson | 1977–1985, 1987–1996 |
| J. Addison Ingle Jr. | 1970–1982, 1990–1999 |
| C. Bissell Jenkins Jr. | 1947–1970 |
| Honorary Trustee, 1970 | |
| Richard H. Jenrette | 1971–1973 |
| George A. Z. Johnson Jr. | 1972–1981 |
| Mrs. Percy Gamble Kammerer | 1947–1964 |
| Dorothy B. Kerrison | 1980–1989, 1990–1999 |
| John W. Kessler | 1981–1985 |
| Benjamin R. Kittredge Jr. | 1948–1967 |
| Edward Kronsberg | 1965–1978 |
| Hugh C. Lane | 1964–1980 |
| Hugh C. Lane Jr. | 1983–1986 |
| Douglas B. Lee | 1995– |
| Lionel K. Legge | 1947–1952 |

| NAME OF TRUSTEE | TERM OF SERVICE |
|---|---|
| Mrs. Charles Woodward<br>  Honorary Trustee, 1983<br>  Lifetime Trustee, 1987 | 1959–1983 |
| Elizabeth Jenkins Young<br>  Lifetime Trustee, 1990 | 1956–1981, 1984–1990 |
| J. Rutledge Young Jr. | 1990–1999 |

# Appendix 4

# Staff of Historic Charleston Foundation Since 1947*

| Name of Staff Member | Term of Service |
|---|---|
| Peggy Allen<br>Secretary, Preservation Division | 1987–1988 |
| Jane Ball<br>Historic Houses Administrator,<br>Tours Director, Volunteer Coordinator | 1982–1991 |
| Jacqueline Bennett<br>Ticket Office Administrator | 1984–1996 |
| Rae Ann Blyth<br>Secretary, Preservation Division | 1989–1994 |
| Debbie Bordeau<br>Heritage Fund Coordinator | 1995–present |
| Sherri Bottoms<br>Office Manager | 1994–present |

* This list was assembled from information provided by Historic Charleston Foundation.

| NAME OF STAFF MEMBER | TERM OF SERVICE |
|---|---|
| Carroll Ann Bowers<br>Marketing Coordinator | 1991–present |
| Ashley Brant<br>Sales Manager | 1996–present |
| Miriam Brown<br>Secretary, Reproductions Division | 1991–1994 |
| Lee Buckley<br>Secretary, Reproductions Division | 1981–1983 |
| Gene Carpenter<br>Merchandise Manager | 1996–1999 |
| Julie Carpenter<br>Edmondston-Alston House Administrator | 1975–1977 |
| Annette Chamberlain<br>Receptionist-Secretary, Tours Assistant | 1986–present |
| Michelle Clum<br>Secretary, Preservation Division | 1994–1995 |
| Jane Stoney Cook<br>Secretary, Reproductions Division | 1978–1981 |
| Carolina Coon<br>Sales Assistant, Reproductions Shop | 1974–1978 |
| Jo Alexander Cox<br>Manager, Reproductions Shop | 1974 |
| Jane Craver<br>Sales Assistant, Reproductions Shop | 1974–1983 |
| Jim Crow<br>Manager, Foundation Properties and<br>Easements | 1996–present |

| NAME OF STAFF MEMBER | TERM OF SERVICE |
|---|---|
| Frances R. Edmunds<br>Tours Director, Russell House Manager,<br>Executive Secretary, Executive Director | 1948–1985 |
| Polly Eells<br>Ticket Office, Preservation Shop Manager | 1981–1983 |
| Mary Louise Gadsden<br>Volunteer Coordinator | 1983–1986 |
| Henrietta Gaillard<br>Volunteer Coordinator | 1986–1989 |
| Jeanie Gornto<br>Secretary, Reproductions Division | 1988–1991 |
| Pat Groves<br>Secretary, Preservation Division | 1987–1989 |
| Betty T. Guerard<br>Executive Secretary | 1988–present |
| Polly Butler Hamilton<br>Secretary, Reproductions Division | 1983–1988 |
| Leigh Handal<br>Director, Educational Programs and Tours | 1998–present |
| Alison B. Harwood<br>Reproductions Director | 1974–1983 |
| Kitty Holt<br>Russell House Administrator | 1977–1979 |
| Sean Houlihan<br>Coordinator, Neighborhood<br>Impact Initiative | 1995–present |
| Carter L. Hudgins<br>Executive Director | 1994–present |

| Name of Staff Member | Term of Service |
|---|---|
| Frances Hutson<br>Manager, Reproductions Shop | 1981–1996 |
| Louise Jardine<br>Weekend Administrator, Russell House | 1983–present |
| W. Jackson Kirby<br>Accountant, Business Manager | 1984–1994 |
| Jane Kreitzer<br>Product Development Coordinator | 1996–1998 |
| Scott Lane<br>Director of Development | 1995–present |
| Jackie Laro<br>Accountant | 1996–1998 |
| Robert A. Leath<br>Assistant Curator | 1991–1999 |
| Alice Levkoff<br>Administrator, Edmondston-Alston House | 1974–1982 |
| Lee Manigault<br>Volunteer Coordinator | 1995–1997 |
| Renee Marshall<br>Collections Manager | 1991–present |
| Peter J. McCahill<br>Administrative Assistant,<br>Urban Renewal Specialist | 1966–1968 |
| Sarah Pat McKenzie<br>Volunteer Coordinator | 1976–1980 |
| Doris Meadowcroft<br>Russell House Administrator,<br>Curator of Education | 1955–1984 |

| NAME OF STAFF MEMBER | TERM OF SERVICE |
|---|---|
| Judy Middleton<br>Russell House Administrator | 1979–present |
| Betsy Minor<br>Ticket Office Staff | 1972–1990 |
| Betsy Momeier<br>Ticket Office Manager | 1975–1984 |
| Therese Munroe<br>Secretary, Preservation Division | 1996–present |
| R. Angus Murdoch<br>Executive Director | 1985–1987 |
| Carol Myatt<br>Receptionist | 1982–1988 |
| Ellen Myerson<br>Preservation Assistant | 1980–1982 |
| Louis Nelson<br>Preservation Assistant | 1990–1994 |
| Jason Neville<br>Building Conservator | 1995–present |
| Minh Van Nguyen<br>Maintenance Coordinator | 1979–present |
| Vinh Nguyen<br>Maintenance | 1989–present |
| Thomas A. Palmer<br>Interim Executive Director | 1993–1994 |
| Melissa Paulsen<br>Product Development Manager | 1998–present |

| NAME OF STAFF MEMBER | TERM OF SERVICE |
|---|---|
| Gregory B. Paxton<br>Preservation Administrator | 1977–1981 |
| Cornelia H. Pelzer<br>Reproductions Shop Manager;<br>Director, Reproductions Division | 1974–present |
| Dat Van Phan<br>Maintenance | 1987–present |
| Jonathan H. Poston<br>Director, Preservation Division | 1982–present |
| Sally Rains<br>Bookkeeper, Executive Secretary | 1977–1984 |
| John Repik<br>Maintenance | 1997–present |
| Jane Riley<br>Volunteer Coordinator | 1991–1993 |
| Michael Robertson<br>Preservation and Development Assistant | 1993–1994 |
| Katharine Robinson<br>Tours Director | 1986–1993 |
| Alicia Rhett Walker Rudolf<br>Tours Director, Assistant to Director | 1965–1977 |
| Jan Russell<br>Volunteer Coordinator | 1982–1983 |
| Katherine Saunders<br>Preservation Programs Coordinator | 1996–present |
| J. Thomas Savage Jr.<br>Museum Curator | 1981–1998 |

| NAME OF STAFF MEMBER | TERM OF SERVICE |
|---|---|
| Fanio Spanos<br>Volunteer Coordinator | 1997–present |
| Rebecca Taber<br>Curator of Education and Interpretation | 1998–present |
| M. E. Van Dyke<br>Conservation Programs Coordinator | 1987–1995 |
| Kristy Varn<br>Director of Finance and Administration | 1994–present |
| Lawrence A. Walker<br>Interim Executive Director,<br>Executive Director | 1987–1993 |
| Adelaide Waller<br>Russell House Administrator | 1977 |
| Mary Pope Waring<br>Tours and Special Events Director | 1993–1997 |
| Patti Whitelaw<br>Decorative Arts Consultant | 1976–1993 |
| Candy Wilkin<br>Receptionist | 1979–1981 |
| Benjamin Wilson<br>Crafts Training Coordinator | 1993–1996 |
| Nancy Wood<br>Executive Secretary | 1984–1988 |
| Connie Wyrick<br>Tours Director, Corporate Development<br>and Public Relations | 1980–1994 |

# Appendix 5

# COVENANTS HELD BY HISTORIC CHARLESTON FOUNDATION AS OF 1997*

PROPERTY ADDRESS

5 Alexander Street
2 Amherst Street
14 Amherst Street
18 Amherst Street
27 Anson Street
34 Anson Street
42 Anson Street
48–50 Anson Street
53 Anson Street
60 Anson Street
63 Anson Street
64–66 Anson Street
69–71 Anson Street
72 Anson Street
73 Anson Street
73 Anson Street, Unit X
73 Anson Street, Unit Y
73 Anson Street, Unit Z
74 Anson Street
75 Anson Street

PROPERTY ADDRESS

82 Anson Street
2 Ashe Street
289–291 East Bay Street
311 East Bay Street
321 East Bay Street
328 East Bay Street
329 East Bay Street
332 East Bay Street
635 East Bay Street
33 Bogard Street
57 Cannon Street
36 Chapel Street
40 Chapel Street
5 Charlotte Street
44 Charlotte Street, Unit A
44 Charlotte Street, Unit B
44 Charlotte Street, Unit C
44 Charlotte Street, Unit D
102 Church Street
93 Columbus Street

* This list was assembled from information provided by Jonathan H. Poston.

PROPERTY ADDRESS

138 Coming Street
140 Coming Street
142 Coming Street
144 Coming Street
144½ Coming Street
8 George Street
9 George Street
11 George Street
45 Hasell Street
66 Hasell Street
1 Judith Street
6 Judith Street
9 Judith Street
11 Judith Street
13 Judith Street
39 Laurens Street
41 Laurens Street
42 Laurens Street
43 Laurens Street
45 Laurens Street
48 Laurens Street
49 Laurens Street
61 Laurens Street
5 Maiden Lane
32 Mary Street
36 Mary Street
58 Meeting Street
54 Montagu Street
72 Nassau Street
6–8 Queen Street
94 Rutledge Avenue
185 Rutledge Avenue
174 Smith Street
181 Smith Street
197 Smith Street
199 Smith Street
32 Society Street
40 Society Street
42 Society Street

PROPERTY ADDRESS

44 Society Street
55 Society Street, Unit A
55 Society Street, Unit B
55 Society Street, Unit C
55 Society Street, Unit D
56 Society Street
59 Society Street
66 Society Street
36–38–40 Warren Street
44 Warren Street
50 Warren Street
64 Warren Street
68 Warren Street
84–92 Warren Street
8 Wentworth Street
10 Wentworth Street
11 Wentworth Street
12 Wentworth Street
13 Wentworth Street
15 Wentworth Street
18 Wentworth Street
22–24 Wentworth Street
23 Wentworth Street
30 Wentworth Street
32 Wentworth Street
7 Wraggborough Lane
17 Wraggborough Lane
19 Wraggborough Lane
21 Wraggborough Lane
23 Wraggborough Lane
25 Wraggborough Lane
27 Wraggborough Lane
Lot 6–8 Wraggborough Square
7 Wraggborough Square
Lot 10 Wraggborough Square
12 Wraggborough Square
Lot 15 Wraggborough Square
Lot 16 Wraggborough Square

# Appendix 6

# EASEMENTS HELD BY HISTORIC
# CHARLESTON FOUNDATION AS OF 1997*

| PROPERTY | DATE OF EASEMENT |
|----------|------------------|
| 6–16 North Adger's Wharf | 1986 |
| 15 North Adger's Wharf | 1983 |
| 72 Anson Street | 1986 |
| 16 Atlantic Street | 1983 |
| Auldbrass Plantation, Yemassee | 1986 |
| 47 South Battery | 1997 |
| 58 South Battery | 1984 |
| 64 South Battery | 1986 |
| 45 East Bay Street, Unit A | 1986 |
| 45 East Bay Street, Unit B | 1986 |
| 45 East Bay Street, Unit C | 1986 |
| 45 East Bay Street, Unit D | 1986 |
| 45 East Bay Street, Unit E | 1986 |
| 57 East Bay Street | 1997 |
| 83 East Bay Street | 1983 |
| 167–169 East Bay Street | 1984 |
| 234 East Bay Street | 1984 |
| 241–243 East Bay Street | 1985 |
| 3 Broad Street | 1983 |
| 11 Broad Street | 1985 |

* This list was assembled from information provided by Jonathan H. Poston.

| PROPERTY | DATE OF EASEMENT |
|---|---|
| 15 Broad Street | 1983 |
| 17 Broad Street | 1987 |
| 62 Broad Street | 1987 |
| 85–87 Broad Street | 1997 |
| 89 Broad Street | 1983 |
| 89 Broad Street (interior) | 1997 |
| 91 Broad Street | 1997 |
| 138 Broad Street, Unit A | 1984 |
| 138 Broad Street, Unit B | 1984 |
| 138 Broad Street, Unit C | 1984 |
| 138 Broad Street, Unit D | 1984 |
| 161 Broad Street | 1984 |
| 174 Broad Street | 1984 |
| 179 Broad Street | 1988 |
| 99 Bull Street | 1985 |
| 99 Bull Street | 1985 |
| 99 Bull Street | 1985 |
| 99 Bull Street | 1985 |
| Chicora Wood Plantation, Plantersville | 1996 |
| 26 Church Street | 1984 |
| 39 Church Street | 1992 |
| 55 Church Street | 1995 |
| 60 Church Street | 1996 |
| 90 Church Street | 1982 |
| 94 Church Street | 1982 |
| 116 Church Street | 1995 |
| 131 Church Street | 1984 |
| 134 Church Street | 1984 |
| 141 Church Street | 1982 |
| 171 Church Street | 1984 |
| 171 Church Street | 1984 |
| 171 Church Street | 1984 |
| 171 Church Street | 1984 |
| 171 Church Street | 1984 |
| 171 Church Street | 1984 |
| 171 Church Street | 1984 |
| 171 Church Street | 1984 |
| 171 Church Street | 1984 |
| 171 Church Street | 1984 |
| 171 Church Street | 1984 |

*Appendix 6*

| Property | Date of Easement |
|---|---|
| 171 Church Street | 1984 |
| 171 Church Street | 1984 |
| 171 Church Street | 1984 |
| 171 Church Street | 1984 |
| 171 Church Street | 1984 |
| 5 Gibbes Street | 1986 |
| 35 Hasell Street, Unit A | 1985 |
| 35½ Hasell Street, Unit C | 1985 |
| 41 King Street | 1983 |
| 77 King Street | 1983 |
| 79 King Street | 1986 |
| 80 King Street | 1983 |
| 192–198 King Street | 1983 |
| 218 King Street | 1979 |
| 363 King Street | 1982 |
| 8–10 Lamboll Street | 1987 |
| 21 Lamboll Street | 1986 |
| 25 Lamboll Street | 1995 |
| 57 Laurens Street | 1983 |
| 4 Legare Street | 1984 |
| 6 Legare Street | 1996 |
| 14 Legare Street | 1991 |
| 15 Legare Street | 1984 |
| 16 Legare Street | 1984 |
| 35 Legare Street | 1984 |
| 9 Limehouse Street | 1982 |
| 116 Marion Street, Summerville | 1987 |
| 112 North Market Street | 1982 |
| Medway Plantation, Goose Creek | 1991 |
| 2 Meeting Street | 1983 |
| 8 Meeting Street | 1984 |
| 12 Meeting Street | 1984 |
| 23 Meeting Street | 1983 |
| 35 Meeting Street | 1986 |
| 52 Meeting Street | 1994 |
| 54 Meeting Street | 1992 |
| 172 Meeting Street | 1983 |
| 173 Meeting Street | 1988 |
| 309–313 Meeting Street | 1985 |
| Millbrook Plantation, Georgetown County | 1986 |

| PROPERTY | DATE OF EASEMENT |
| --- | --- |
| 25 Montagu Street | 1987 |
| 25 Montagu Street | 1987 |
| 25 Montagu Street | 1987 |
| 25 Montagu Street | 1987 |
| Mulberry Plantation, Berkeley County | 1984 |
| 52 Murray Boulevard | 1993 |
| 62 Murray Boulevard | 1984 |
| 82 Pitt Street | 1984 |
| 30 Rutledge Boulevard | 1996 |
| 154 Smith Street | 1990 |
| 33 Society Street | 1983 |
| 5 St. Michael's Alley | 1991 |
| 114 St. Philips Street | 1984 |
| 11½ State Street | 1983 |
| 41 State Street | 1982 |
| 52–54 State Street | 1984 |
| 1 Tradd Street | 1984 |
| 58 Tradd Street | 1983 |
| 60 Tradd Street | 1989 |
| 92 Tradd Street | 1992 |
| 103 Tradd Street | 1983 |
| 106 Tradd Street | 1984 |
| 108 Tradd Street | 1983 |
| 111 Tradd Street | 1984 |
| 122 Tradd Street | 1983 |
| 125 Tradd Street | 1996 |
| 126 Tradd Street | 1982 |
| 127 Tradd Street | 1997 |
| 129 Tradd Street | 1996 |
| 160–162 Tradd Street | 1984 |
| 174 Tradd Street, Unit 1 | 1983 |
| 174 Tradd Street, Unit 2 | 1983 |
| 174 Tradd Street, Unit 3 | 1983 |
| 25 Warren Street | 1984 |
| 11 Water Street | 1997 |
| 5 Wentworth Street | 1987 |
| 20 Wentworth Street | 1994 |
| 429 Whilden Street, Mount Pleasant | 1995 |
| William Seabrook House, James Island | 1985 |

# NOTES

## CHAPTER 1. ANCESTRAL ARCHITECTURE

1. Martha Zierden, "Charleston's Powder Magazine as a Symbol of Cultural Change" (paper presented at the Southeastern Archaeological Conference, Birmingham, Alabama, 1996); Laurence Vail Coleman, *Historic House Museums* (Washington, D.C.: American Association of Museums, 1933), 152. As part of a strategy to stabilize and restore the structure, the Colonial Dames leased the Powder Magazine to Historic Charleston Foundation in the 1990s, a subject that is discussed in chapter 10.

2. On the acquisition and subsequent use of the Old Exchange Building, see Jana Lynn Trapolino, "The South Carolina Daughters of the American Revolution and Historic Preservation" (M.A. thesis, University of South Carolina, 1995), 78–84.

3. These collectors included museums in Minneapolis and St. Louis, as well as individuals such as Francis P. Garvan of New York, who made significant donations of his collections to the new American Wing of the Metropolitan Museum of Art. Perhaps the most well-known loss was the dismantling of the Mansion House (71 Broad Street) in 1928.

4. Albert Simons to Mrs. William Emerson, 28 April 1928; Schuyler L. Parsons to [William Adams Delano], 18 October 1930. Unless otherwise indicated, correspondence cited in this chapter is located at the South Carolina Historical Society (SCHS) in the Albert Simons Papers.

5. Albert Simons to Leicester B. Holland, 9 November 1931.

6. Jonathan H. Poston, *The Buildings of Charleston: A Guide to the City's Architecture* (Columbia: University of South Carolina Press, 1997), 26, 612–13.

7. When the group reorganized itself in 1956, it changed the name to the Preservation Society of Charleston, to suggest the breadth of the institutional agenda as it actually developed after 1920.

8. For a biography of Frost as well as an informative history of the early preservation movement in Charleston, see Sidney R. Bland, *Preserving Charleston's Past, Shaping Its Future: The Life and Times of Susan Pringle Frost*, 2nd ed. (Columbia: University of South Carolina Press, 1999). For a recent general history of the Preservation Society, see the narrative by Robert P. Stockton and the chronology compiled by Trina South and Ward Reynolds in *Preservation Progress* 38 (Spring 1995): 4–11; 38 (Summer 1995): 11–24; 38 (Winter 1996): 3–20.

See also Michael Kevin Fenton, "'Why Not Leave Our Canvas Unmarred?': A History of the Preservation Society of Charleston, 1920–1990" (M.A. thesis, University of South Carolina, 1990); and William Henry Hanckel, "The Preservation Movement in Charleston, 1920–1962" (M.A. thesis, University of South Carolina, 1962).

9. Harriett Pollitzer, the Princess Pignatelli, was the anonymous benefactor.

10. Bland, *Preserving Charleston's Past,* 64–83; Poston, *Buildings of Charleston,* 612–13; Charles B. Hosmer Jr., *Preservation Comes of Age: From Williamsburg to the National Trust, 1926–1946,* 2 vols. (Charlottesville: University of Virginia Press, 1981), I: 236–38, 242–50.

11. For a recent assessment, see Louise Anderson Allen, "Laura Bragg: A New Woman Practicing Progressive Social Reform as a Museum Administrator and Educator" (Ph.D. diss., University of South Carolina, 1997).

12. Albert Simons to Mills B. Lane, 11 May 1928.

13. Albert Simons to Mr. Rivers, 8 May 1928.

14. Simons to Emerson, 28 April 1928.

15. In a similar vein, Susan Pringle Frost undertook her own private campaign to salvage architectural remnants, filling storerooms at the Miles Brewton House with her acquisitions. Curiously, histories of the Charleston Museum do not seem to recognize the important preservation role that the museum has played as an architectural repository. See, for example, Caroline M. Borowsky, "The Charleston Museum, 1773–1963," *Museum News* (February 1963): 11–21.

16. Bland, *Preserving Charleston's Past,* 73–74; Poston, *Buildings of Charleston,* 77–79; Hosmer, *Preservation Comes of Age,* I: 242–50; *Charleston News and Courier,* 18 May 1929; Albert Simons to Mrs. Victor Morawetz, 2 February 1931; Thomas R. Waring to Mrs. William Emerson, 9 October 1931.

17. The members of the blue ribbon committee included Franklin O. Adams, Leicester B. Holland, Fiske Kimball, Alfred L. Kocher, Robert D. Kohn, Everett V. Meeks, and Horace Peaslee representing the AIA; and Mrs. Cesare Andreini, Alston Deas, Julian Mitchell, Harrison Randolph, Albert Simons, and Thomas R. Waring from Charleston.

18. Mrs. William Emerson to Albert Simons, 23 April 1928, 3 May 1928; [Robert D. Kohn] to Franklin O. Adams, et al., 9 December 1930; Albert Simons to Mrs. William Emerson, 2 February 1931, 28 September 1931; Albert Simons to Alfred Huger, 7 March 1931; Albert Simons to Thomas R. Waring, 2 April 1931; Albert Simons to George W. Bacon, 15 April 1931; *Charleston News and Courier,* 10 April 1932; Hosmer, *Preservation Comes of Age,* I: 245–50.

19. Some commentators trace the origins of historic preservation in Charleston to the nineteenth century, pointing to decisions to restore damaged buildings to their earlier appearance rather than rebuild in the current architectural idiom. Robert P. Stockton makes this case in "Charleston's Preservation Ethic," *Preservation Progress,* special edition (Spring 1993): 11–12, and in "The Preservation of Charleston: The Origin of a Tradition," *Preservation Progress* 38 (Spring 1995): 4–7.

20. Bland, *Preserving Charleston's Past,* 46–63; Poston, *Buildings of Charleston,* 51, 52, 54, 76, 79–80, 99, 100–2, 104–5, 138, 193–94. See also Robert P. Stockton, "The Evolution of Rainbow Row" (M.A. thesis, University of South Carolina, 1979).

21. Frederick Law Olmsted Jr., "Central Considerations" (unpag. typescript report to the Carolina Art Association, located in the Olmsted Associates Records, Job File 2326 [microfilm edition] at the Library of Congress, Washington, D.C., and in the Albert Simons Papers at the South Carolina Historical Society). Olmsted visited Charleston in January 1940 to consult for the Carolina Art Association, and his recommendations were formative in the establishment of Historic Charleston Foundation in 1947, as discussed in chapter 2.

22. Because the historic appearance of the theater is not known, the "reconstruction" is entirely hypothetical.

23. Poston, *Buildings of Charleston*, 179–80, 345, 351–52, 392–93, 439–40; Bland, *Preserving Charleston's Past*, 71; Hosmer, *Preservation Comes of Age*, I: 250–54.

24. City Council of Charleston, *Proceedings*, Regular Meeting of 13 October 1931, 697–711. See also Stephen Neal Dennis, "'The Genius of the Place': Charleston Discovers How to Protect 'The Circumstances and the Locality,'" *Preservation Progress*, special edition (Spring 1993): 21.

25. Thomas P. Stoney to John I. Cosgrove, 27 May 1925, and John I. Cosgrove to Thomas P. Stoney, 29 May 1925, file 30-25-5, SCHS; A. J. Tamsberg to Albert Simons, 22 April 1957. In *Euclid* v. *Ambler* (1926), the United States Supreme Court affirmed the validity of zoning as a proper use of the municipal police power.

26. Alston Deas continued to play an important role as a member of the first Board of Architectural Review and as author of *The Early Ironwork of Charleston* (Columbia, S. C.: Bostick & Thornley, 1941), a study of the city's decorative wrought iron.

27. Tamsberg to Simons, 22 April 1957; Hosmer, *Preservation Comes of Age*, I: 238–40. The first members of the permanent City Planning and Zoning Commission established in October 1930 were M. B. Barkley, Louis Y. Dawson Jr., Alston Deas, J. Ross Hanahan, Burnet R. Maybank, Cotesworth P. Means, James O'Hear, Albert Simons, and Walter B. Wilbur.

28. Albert Simons to Mrs. Victor Morawetz, 2 February 1931.

29. Morris Knowles, Inc., *Report of the City Planning and Zoning Commission upon a Program for the Development of a City Plan with Specific Studies of Certain Features Thereof* (2 July 1931), 34, located in the Olmsted Associates Records, Job File 2326 (microfilm edition), Library of Congress.

30. Morris Knowles, *Report of the City Planning and Zoning Commission*, 17.

31. Debbi Rhoad, "The Board of Architectural Review in Charleston, 1931–1993," *Preservation Progress*, special edition (Spring 1993): 13–18; Civic Services Committee, *This Is Charleston* (Charleston: Carolina Art Association, 1944), 134–36. The first members of the BAR, who assumed their duties in November 1931, were Alston Deas, Albert Simons, E. D. Clement, Stephen F. Shackelford, and Thomas R. Waring, who served as chairman.

32. Quoted in Dennis, "'The Genius of the Place,'" *Preservation Progress*, special edition (Spring 1993): 21.

33. Albert Simons, quoted by Hosmer, *Preservation Comes of Age*, I: 241.

34. Albert Simons to Delos H. Smith, 10 December 1946; Albert Simons to Leicester B. Holland, 18 March 1932.

35. Rhoad, "The Board of Architectural Review in Charleston, 1931–1993," *Preservation Progress*, special edition (Spring 1993): 13–18; Hosmer, *Preservation Comes of Age*, I: 238–42. Only a portion of Broad Street itself was included in the original district.

36. In response, the Standard Oil Company sought to make amends by employing Albert Simons to design a "colonial revival" filling station on the site, using brick, columns, and balusters salvaged from the Gabriel Manigault House, which was then being demolished at 279 Meeting Street. The gas station closed in 1981, and Historic Charleston Foundation acquired it, converting it into the Frances R. Edmunds Center for Historic Preservation, which was dedicated in 1986. This unusual monument to the early preservation movement in Charleston is located at 108 Meeting Street. See Poston, *Buildings of Charleston*, 188.

37. The first revisions to the zoning ordinance, in 1959 and 1966, are discussed in chapter 5.

38. Jacob H. Morrison, *Historic Preservation Law* (New Orleans: Pelican Publishing Company, 1957), 80–85, rev. ed. (1965), 129–86; Hosmer, *Preservation Comes of Age*, I: 231–77; Civic

Services Committee, *This Is Charleston*, rev. ed. (Charleston: Carolina Art Association, 1976), 134–36; Dennis, "'The Genius of the Place,'" *Preservation Progress*, special edition (Spring 1993): 22.

39. On early Charleston architecture, see Poston, *Buildings of Charleston*; James R. Cothran, *Gardens of Historic Charleston* (Columbia: University of South Carolina Press, 1995); Kenneth Severens, *Charleston Antebellum Architecture and Civic Destiny* (Knoxville: University of Tennessee Press, 1988); Beatrice St. Julien Ravenel, *Architects of Charleston* (Charleston: Carolina Art Association, 1945), as well as earlier "classics," including Alice Ravenel Huger Smith, *Twenty Drawings of the Pringle House, on King Street, Charleston, S. C.* ([Charleston]: n.p., ca. 1914); Alice Ravenel Huger Smith and Daniel Elliott Huger Smith, *The Dwelling Houses of Charleston, South Carolina* (Philadelphia: J. B. Lippincott Company, 1917); Albert Simons and Samuel Lapham Jr., eds., *Charleston, South Carolina* (New York: American Institute of Architects,1927); and Samuel Gaillard Stoney, *Plantations of the Carolina Low Country* (Charleston, S. C.: Carolina Art Association,1938).

40. Robert P. Stockton has questioned the "preservation through poverty" thesis by pointing to evidence of commercial, residential, and industrial expansion in the decades after the Civil War; see his paper "Charleston: The Preservation of a City" in C. Edward Kaylor Jr., ed., *A Consideration of Growth in the Trident Area: From the Academy to the Marketplace* (Charleston: South Carolina Committee for the Humanities, 1982), 13–31.

41. Beatrice St. Julien Ravenel, "The Restoration of the Manigault House," *Journal of the American Society of Architectural Historians* 2 (October 1942): 30–32.

42. Don H. Doyle argues that the early preservation movement in Charleston reflected the backward-looking conservatism of the city's upper class and its fascination with genealogy, custom, and family heirlooms; see Doyle, *New Men, New Cities, New South: Atlanta, Nashville, Charleston, Mobile, 1860–1910* (Chapel Hill: University of North Carolina Press, 1990), 159–88, 226–45.

43. DuBose Heyward, *Porgy* (New York: George H. Doran Company, 1925), 11.

44. The Charleston Renaissance is receiving growing study, particularly through the work of Martha R. Severens. See, for example, her *The Charleston Renaissance* (Spartanburg, S.C.: Saraland Press, 1998); *Alice Ravenel Huger Smith: An Artist, a Place, and a Time* (Charleston: Carolina Art Association, 1993); and "Pride of Place and Artistic Renewal," *Preservation Progress*, special edition (Spring 1993): 4–7. See also Michael C. Scardaville, "Elizabeth O'Neill Verner: The Artist as Preservationist," in Lynn Robertson Myers, ed., *Mirror of Time: Elizabeth O'Neill Verner's Charleston* (Columbia: McKissick Museum of the University of South Carolina, 1983), 17–25, and Scardaville's "The Selling of Historic Charleston," *Preservation Progress* 30 (March 1986): 1, 6–11; Boyd Saunders and Ann McAden, *Alfred Hutty and the Charleston Renaissance* (Orangeburg, S.C.: Sandlapper Publishing Company, 1990); Pamme Lynn Eades, "Alice Ravenel Huger Smith and the Development of Charleston Regionalism" (M.A. thesis, University of South Carolina, 1994); Marjorie Elizabeth Peale, "Charleston as a Literary Center, 1920–1933" (M.A. thesis, Duke University, 1941). For a recent, general study of regionalism, see Robert L. Dorman, *Revolt of the Provinces: The Regionalist Movement in America, 1920–1945* (Chapel Hill: University of North Carolina Press, 1993). For a useful case study see Robin Elisabeth Datel, "Southern Regionalism and Historic Preservation in Charleston, South Carolina, 1920–1940," *Journal of Historical Geography* 16 (April 1990): 197–215.

45. Albert Simons (1890–1980) was arguably the most important figure in the early preservation movement whose role continued into the postwar years. He was a preservation archi-

tect, urban planner, and civic leader; a founding trustee of Historic Charleston Foundation, serving until 1962; and a member of the Board of Architectural Review from its establishment until his resignation in 1975. To date, though, he has not been the subject of a book-length biography despite the richness of the Albert Simons collection at the South Carolina Historical Society. The College of Charleston also has a small collection on Simons. For a sampling of information on Simons, see "Architects in Profile: Albert Simons," *Preservation Progress* 8 (March 1963): 4–5; *Charleston News and Courier,* 16 June 1975; Kenneth Severens, "Toward Preservation Before 1931: The Early Career of Albert Simons," *Preservation Progress,* special edition (Spring 1993): 8–10.

## CHAPTER 2. THE FOUNDING AND FIRST YEARS OF
## HISTORIC CHARLESTON FOUNDATION

1. Harold A. Mouzon, "The Carolina Art Association: Its First Hundred Years," *South Carolina Historical Magazine* 59 (July 1958): 125–38. For an overview of the role of Robert N. S. Whitelaw (1905–74), see Hosmer, *Preservation Comes of Age,* I: 254–73; *Charleston Evening Post,* 22 April 1974.
2. *Charleston News and Courier,* 10 December 1939.
3. Robert Whitelaw to Frederick Law Olmsted Jr., 11 December 1939. Unless otherwise indicated, unpublished material cited in this chapter is located at the South Carolina Historical Society (SCHS) in the Albert Simons Papers.
4. Minutes of the Ad Hoc Committee, 22 January 1940. Rittenberg had long worked on behalf of municipal reform; see his article "The Business Men and the Clean-up Campaign," *The American City* 16 (March 1917): 285–87.
5. Robert Whitelaw to Frederick Law Olmsted Jr., 20 December 1939.
6. Whitelaw to Olmsted, 11 December 1939.
7. Due to illness, Olmsted was slow in completing his report; typescript sections dribbled in through February and March 1940, and these fragments apparently comprised the extent of the planner's formal recommendations. Olmsted's views can also be discerned through the minutes of a concluding meeting in Charleston on 22 January 1940 between Olmsted and the full committee. The unpaginated fragments can be found in the Olmsted Associates Records, Job File 2326 (microfilm edition), at the Library of Congress, Washington, D.C., and in the Albert Simons Papers at the South Carolina Historical Society.
8. By contrast, his father had a far less positive impression of Charleston when he visited in the 1850s. Olmsted Senior found it a "metropolitan and convenient" town skeptical of modernity and seemingly "in a state of siege or revolution" as a result of frequent militia parades, the constant activity at the state military school, and the presence of armed police patrols. He spent most of his visit to South Carolina visiting plantations outside the city. For his observations on South Carolina in the 1850s, see Frederick Law Olmsted, *A Journey in the Seaboard Slave States with Remarks on their Economy* (New York: Negro Universities Press, 1968), 377–523. The description of Charleston appears on page 404. The work was originally published in 1856.
9. "Central Considerations," Olmsted Report. The italics are Olmsted's.
10. "Central Considerations," Olmsted Report; Minutes of the Ad Hoc Committee, 22 January 1940; Albert Simons to Robert D. Kohn, 8 February 1940.
11. Frederick Law Olmsted Jr. to Robert Whitelaw, 6 April 1940.
12. Minutes of the Ad Hoc Committee, 22 January 1940.

13. Minutes of the Ad Hoc Committee, 22 January 1940; Simons to Kohn, 8 February 1940.
14. "Certain Financial Factors," Olmsted Report.
15. "Certain Financial Factors," Olmsted Report.
16. Simons to Kohn, 8 February 1940.
17. Minutes of the Ad Hoc Committee, 22 January 1940. Olmsted seems to have borrowed the concept and term "revolving fund" from a suggestion by Sidney J. Rittenberg, but Olmsted was the first to use the term in a public report. While Susan Pringle Frost deserves credit for her courageous preliminary attempts at area rehabilitation, her campaign was an individual effort that was personally financed and not really an example of the revolving fund mechanism as it was developed by Historic Charleston Foundation in the 1950s.
18. Minutes of the Ad Hoc Committee, 22 January 1940. Historic Charleston Foundation launched its easements program in 1982, a subject discussed in chapter 7.
19. "Other Lines of Investigation," Olmsted Report.
20. Minutes of the Ad Hoc Committee, 22 January 1940.
21. Robert D. Kohn to Albert Simons, 1 February 1940.
22. "Inventory," Olmsted Report.
23. Robert Whitelaw to Charleston Regional Planning Committee, 1 March 1940, 1 November 1940; Robert Whitelaw to Frederick Law Olmsted Jr., 11 November 1940; Helen McCormack to Albert Simons, 4 March 1941; Albert Simons to Helen McCormack, 11 March 1941; Albert Simons to Robert Whitelaw, 13 May 1941; Helen G. McCormack, "An Architectural Inventory for Charleston," *Journal of the American Society of Architectural Historians* 1 (July–October 1941): 21–23; Civic Services Committee, *This Is Charleston;* Hosmer, *Preservation Comes of Age,* I: 254–68.
24. These are the figures as published in the first edition of *This Is Charleston* in 1944; contemporaneous reports give a slightly different accounting.
25. Helen G. McCormack, "This Is Charleston," *Journal of the American Society of Architectural Historians* 2 (January 1942): 37; *Charleston News and Courier,* 27 March 1942.
26. The full title was *This Is Charleston: A Survey of the Architectural Heritage of a Unique American City Undertaken by the Charleston Civic Services Committee.*
27. The most recent issue is the 1990 reprint of the 1976 edition.
28. As part of the process of applying for grant assistance from the Carnegie Corporation to undertake the architectural survey, Robert Whitelaw had bestowed the name "Charleston Regional Planning Committee" on the ad hoc group, and this was its working title for two years, from early 1940 to early 1942.
29. Request to the Rockefeller Foundation, 11 February 1942; Frederick Bigger to Albert Simons, 30 May 1942; Albert Simons to Frederick Bigger, 4 June 1942; Robert Whitelaw to Henry W. Lockwood, 2 January 1943; Minutes of the Civic Services Committee, 4 December 1943, 12 December 1944; Robert Whitelaw to George W. Simons Jr., 9 February 1944; Robert Whitelaw to Samuel G. Stoney, 21 March 1945.
30. On how parking lots could be a form of slum clearance, see two articles by the Florida consultant George W. Simons Jr. on "Off-Street Parking" in the Carolina Art Association's magazine *This November* (1944) and *This April* (1945).
31. Minutes of the Civic Services Committee, 3 November 1944, 17 April 1945, 4 January 1946; Homer M. Pace, Preface, in *Charleston Grows: An Economic, Social and Cultural Portrait of an Old Community in the New South* (Charleston: Carolina Art Association, 1949).
32. Kenneth Chorley, *The Challenge to Charleston* (Charleston: Carolina Art Association, 1945); Minutes of the Civic Services Committee, 16 March 1945.

33. The four men who filed for incorporation on 25 April 1947 were C. Bissell Jenkins Jr., Homer M. Pace, Ben Scott Whaley, and Robert N. S. Whitelaw. The quotation is from the charter of incorporation.
34. Robert Whitelaw to the Civic Services Committee, 12 December 1946.
35. Minutes of the Civic Services Committee, 19 December 1946.
36. Carolina Art Association, *The Living Arts* 1 (February 1947): 10; and *The Living Arts* 1 (March 1947): 15.
37. Whitelaw to Civic Services Committee, 12 December 1946.
38. Minutes of the Civic Services Committee, 6 November 1946, 19 December 1946; Proposed Constitution for the Historic Charleston Trust.
39. The current by-laws establish the number of trustees between twenty and thirty, with staggered three-year terms, and trustees may serve up to three successive three-year terms before rotating off the board for a year. For the original set of by-laws, see the Minutes of Historic Charleston Foundation, 15 May 1947, hereafter cited as HCF Minutes. Beyond the early years these records are housed at the foundation's offices.
40. *Baldwin's and Southern's Charleston, South Carolina Directory* (Charleston: Baldwin Directory Company, 1948), 184, 237, 335, 368, 414–15, 444; *Charleston News and Courier*, 22 September 1987; Emily Whaley with William Baldwin, *Mrs. Whaley and Her Charleston Garden* (Chapel Hill: Algonquin Books, 1997), 161–70.
41. Carolina Art Association, *The Living Arts* 1 (March 1947): 10.
42. HCF Minutes, 24 July 1947.
43. The history of the house tours is discussed in chapter 9.
44. Headquarters for the house tours, and eventually the foundation offices, were established at 94 Church Street in June 1949.
45. Robert Whitelaw to C. Bissell Jenkins Jr., 7 October 1947.
46. HCF Minutes, 25 February 1952, 22 May 1952, 19 June 1953; Annual Report of the Tour Director, 1953.
47. HCF Minutes, 19 May 1948, 17 October 1951, 23 June 1953.
48. HCF Minutes, 19 November 1953; *Charleston News and Courier*, 17 December 1953.
49. HCF Minutes, 10 June 1954.
50. The 1959 revisions are discussed in chapter 5 within the context of the sweeping 1966 changes. Through the 1950s foundation trustees such as Albert Simons continued their efforts to monitor the state of community planning in Charleston, especially the adequacy of the municipal zoning ordinance.
51. The Society for the Preservation of Old Dwellings established in 1920 by Susan Pringle Frost and others had reorganized itself and changed its name in 1956 to the Preservation Society of Charleston.
52. HCF Minutes, 17 June 1952, 19 November 1953, 10 June 1954; *Charleston News and Courier*, 10 June 1952, 9 May 1958, 29 July 1958, 22 August 1958, 11 September 1958, 1 October 1958, 18 November 1958; *Charleston Evening Post*, 8 May 1958, 12 September 1958, 20 September 1958, 7 January 1959, 20 August 1962; *Charleston Post and Courier*, 28 July 1996.
53. The building crafts training program is discussed in chapter 10.

## Chapter 3. The Nathaniel Russell House

1. See the previous discussion in chapter 2.
2. HCF Minutes, 8 March 1948. In his recent study of Charleston architecture, Jonathan Poston calls this property the Theodore Gaillard (Gaillard-Bennett) House; see Poston, *Build-*

*ings of Charleston,* 539. Unless otherwise indicated, unpublished material cited in this and subsequent chapters is located in the files of Historic Charleston Foundation.

3. Orlando Ridout V and Willie Graham, *An Architectural and Historical Analysis of the Nathaniel Russell House, Charleston, South Carolina* (Prepared for Historic Charleston Foundation, December 1996), 5–28.

4. Poston, *Buildings of Charleston,* 262.

5. Ridout and Graham, *Architectural and Historical Analysis,* 29–64.

6. HCF Minutes, 8 February 1955; undated real estate offering for the Nathaniel Russell House in scrapbooks presented to Frances R. Edmunds at her retirement.

7. *Charleston News and Courier,* 12 February 1955, 13 February 1955; HCF Minutes, 18 February 1955.

8. Consistent with his wishes, Richardson was not identified publicly until January 1957, when he made his first visit to the Nathaniel Russell House. See *Charleston News and Courier,* 3 January 1957.

9. The foundation raised a total of $33,498.85 in its public campaign. Because the real estate agent and attorneys donated their services, the actual price eventually paid by Historic Charleston Foundation was $61,750.

10. *Charleston News and Courier,* 1 March 1955, 4 March 1955; *Charleston Evening Post,* 2 March 1955; Albert Simons to Mrs. Victor Morawetz, 17 February 1955, 14 March 1955, Simons Papers, SCHS; Albert Simons to Marshall Field III, 1 March 1955, Simons Papers, SCHS; HCF Minutes, 16 June 1955; *The State* (Columbia), 24 February 1957.

11. HCF Minutes, 15 April 1955, 16 June 1955.

12. HCF Minutes, 15 April 1955, 16 June 1955; Samuel G. Stoney to Francis T. Carmody, 15 April 1955, Simons Papers, SCHS; Ridout and Graham, *Architectural and Historical Analysis,* 65–71.

13. *Charleston News and Courier,* 26 February 1956.

14. *Charleston News and Courier,* 3 March 1956, 28 February 1957. In this and subsequent years the foundation offered an annual free admission day to express gratitude for the outpouring of local support that had allowed it to purchase the property.

15. HCF Minutes, 31 January 1956.

16. *Charleston News and Courier,* 8 June 1956.

17. *Charleston News and Courier,* 26 February 1956, 9 December 1956; J. Thomas Savage, "The Nathaniel Russell House Forty Years On," *Historic Charleston* 1 (Summer 1995): 4–7.

18. *Charleston News and Courier,* 26 February 1956.

19. *Los Angeles Times Magazine,* 25 October 1959; *Charleston News and Courier,* 7 July 1960.

20. Initially the third floor and part of the rear of the house were rented out as apartments.

21. *Charleston News and Courier,* 13 December 1959, 3 July 1967, 23 November 1975; Nathaniel Russell House New Acquisitions, 1 March 1962–1 March 1963, HCF scrapbooks; *Charleston Evening Post,* 29 April 1965, 23 June 1965. The painting of Mrs. Roger (Mary Rutledge) Smith and the one-year-old Edward Nutt Smith (1786) was purchased in London for $41,000 through anonymous out-of-state donations.

22. Dedication in *Charleston's Historic Houses* (1956), the pamphlet for the foundation's ninth annual tour of houses.

23. *Los Angeles Times Magazine,* 25 October 1959; *Christian Science Monitor,* 19 October 1962; *Newport News Times-Herald,* 21 March 1966; *Antiques* 97 (April 1970): Special Charleston Issue.

24. Savage, "The Nathaniel Russell House Forty Years On," *Historic Charleston* 1 (Summer 1995): 4–7; "Recent Additions to the Nathaniel Russell House Collection," *Historic*

*Charleston* 1 (Summer 1995): 18; *Charleston Post and Courier,* 6 March 1993; Interview with J. Thomas Savage, 9 May 1996.

25. With the recently expanded mandate for the museums division to operate the Aiken-Rhett House and the Powder Magazine, as well as the Russell House, consideration is now being given to seeking accreditation for these additional historic properties. For a discussion of the Aiken-Rhett House and the Powder Magazine, see chapter 10.

26. "Russell House Recovers from Hurricane Hugo," *Charleston* 7 (Spring 1990): 2; Charles H. Bentz Associates, Inc., *Historic Charleston Foundation Marketing/Feasibility Study* (1991), 13–14, 25–26; Ridout and Graham, *Architectural and Historical Analysis,* 70–74.

27. Bentz Associates, *Historic Charleston Foundation Marketing/Feasibility Study,* 26.

28. Offices were established in leased quarters at 11 Fulton Street for four years, until the foundation moved into the Missroon House at 40 East Bay Street in 1996.

29. Scott Lane to Friends of Historic Charleston, 3 December 1997.

30. HCF, *Heritage Campaign* (1992).

31. "Russell Descendants Enjoy Reunion Weekend," *Charleston* 9 (Winter 1993): 2; "Russell Family Reunion Yields Important Artifacts," *Charleston* 10 (Spring 1993): 1–2; Catherine C. Abbot, "The Russell Family Reunion: A Personal Memoir," *Historic Charleston* 1 (Summer 1995): 12–13.

32. The $35,000 challenge grant from the Getty Foundation was matched with $15,000 from Norfolk Southern Corporation and $20,000 from the Foundation's Heritage Campaign.

33. Preface, in *Historic Charleston Foundation Report to the Getty Grant Program* (April 1995), 4 vols.; Martha Zierden, "Going Underground at the Nathaniel Russell House," *Historic Charleston* 1 (Summer 1995): 14–15; Robert A. Leath, "Recovering the Past at the Russell House," *Historic Charleston* 1 (Summer 1995): 8–11; "Getty Grant Funds Russell House Archaeology," *Charleston* 11 (Summer 1994): 2.

34. Ridout and Graham, *Architectural and Historical Analysis,* 75–82.

35. On recent institutional initiatives, see the discussion in chapter 10.

## CHAPTER 4. ANSONBOROUGH

1. Frances Edmunds to Albert Simons et al., 25 January 1957, Simons Papers, SCHS; Albert Simons to Frances Edmunds, 28 January 1957, Simons Papers, SCHS; Plan as Adopted at a Meeting of the Board of Trustees of Historic Charleston Foundation, 6 February 1957, file 30-14-37, SCHS; HCF, *Charleston, South Carolina: An Historic City Worth Saving* [1957].

2. *Charleston News and Courier,* 12 March 1957.

3. *Charleston News and Courier,* 10 March 1957; HCF, *Charleston: Worth Saving.*

4. *Charleston News and Courier,* 10 March 1957.

5. H. S. Richardson to Frances Edmunds, 2 January 1957, Simons Papers, SCHS; Frances Edmunds et al. to the President and Board of Trustees, 22 February 1957; *Charleston News and Courier,* 14 April 1957; *Preservation Progress* 2 (May 1957); HCF, *Charleston: Worth Saving; Baltimore Sun,* 17 December 1967.

6. Albert Simons, Report to Revolving Fund Committee, 8 December 1958, Simons Papers, SCHS.

7. HCF, *Ansonborough, An Historic Residential Area in Old Charleston: Area Rehabilitation Project of Historic Charleston Foundation* (1967); Peter J. McCahill, "Saving a Neighborhood through Historic Preservation," *Journal of Housing* 3 (1967): 169–72. The latter article is a retrospective assessment prepared by an urban planner hired by the foundation in 1966.

8.  HCF, *Ansonborough, An Historic Residential Area.*

9.  HCF Minutes, 21 July 1959.

10. *Charleston News and Courier,* 21 June 1958. Recent research suggests that the house at 329 East Bay was not associated with Christopher Gadsden; it was built on his former property by his son-in-law. See Poston, *Buildings of Charleston,* 434–35.

11. The Woodwards eventually purchased three other properties near the Gadsden House and donated them to Historic Charleston Foundation. In addition to these, they purchased and restored the Isaac Jenkins Mikell House at 94 Rutledge Avenue, the Joseph Jenkins House at 59 Smith Street, the Bernard Wohlers House at 40 Montagu Street, and the Charles Drayton House at 25 East Battery. Their gifts in the 1970s also made possible land acquisition for what became the Cooper River Waterfront Park. See David R. Contosta, *A Philadelphia Family: The Houstons and Woodwards of Chestnut Hill* (Philadelphia: University of Pennsylvania Press, 1988), 123–39; Sarah Elisa Venezian, "The Development of a Local Preservation Group: The Chestnut Hill Historical Society, 1966–1995" (M.A. thesis, University of South Carolina, 1996), 8–18.

12. *Charleston News and Courier,* 18 December 1958; *Charleston Evening Post,* 21 May 1959, 27 May 1959, 17 March 1960.

13. HCF Minutes, 9 December 1958; *Charleston Evening Post,* 20 July 1959; Tobias & Company, Anson-Society Street Rehabilitation, undated typescript report to HCF.

14. *Charleston News and Courier,* 19 July 1959.

15. *Charleston Evening Post,* 19 July 1960; *Preservation Progress* 5 (January 1960); *Charleston News and Courier,* 30 April 1961.

16. *Charleston News and Courier,* 8 July 1960, 30 January 1961; *Charleston Evening Post,* 1 May 1961.

17. *Charleston News and Courier,* 19 July 1959, 14 July 1960, 4 March 1962, 19 March 1972; *Charleston Evening Post,* 20 July 1959, 1 May 1961.

18. *Charleston News and Courier,* 14 July 1960.

19. HCF Minutes, 11 June 1959; *Charleston News and Courier,* 14 July 1960; *Charleston Evening Post,* 4 May 1961.

20. *Charleston News and Courier,* 30 April 1961, 6 May 1961; *Charleston Evening Post,* 4 May 1961. On these and many subsequent projects for Historic Charleston Foundation, the H. A. DeCosta Company was the contractor for the restoration.

21. *Charleston News and Courier,* 1 October 1961.

22. *Charleston News and Courier,* 20 January 1963.

23. HCF Minutes, 21 July 1959. In subsequent years covenants were occasionally used to protect historically significant interiors.

24. HCF, *Progress in Ansonborough: Highlights of the Annual Report of the Area Projects Committee to the Board of Trustees,* April 1965. The racial calculus is clear in the minutes of foundation board meetings, which contain references to the problem of properties "teeming with undesirable Negro tenants," efforts to evict "negro tenants" and to recruit whites, and a decision to purchase property to prevent it "being used as a negro tenement." See, for example: HCF Minutes, 21 July 1959, 11 July 1961, 18 September 1962.

25. *Charleston News and Courier,* 27 October 1962.

26. *Charleston News and Courier,* 12 October 1962, 16 August 1963, 8 September 1963, 19 November 1963.

27. *Charleston Evening Post,* 15 March 1965.

28. This general area was known historically as Middlesex; it was laid out by Christopher Gadsden in the late eighteenth century.

29.	*Charleston News and Courier,* 29 May 1964; *Charleston Evening Post,* 2 October 1964, 4 November 1964.

30.	*Charleston Evening Post,* 29 May 1964.

31.	*Charleston Evening Post,* 18 August 1964.

32.	*Charleston Evening Post,* 29 May 1964.

33.	*Charleston News and Courier,* 2 July 1964, 18 August 1964, 22 October 1964, 25 April 1965, 11 June 1965.

34.	*Charleston News and Courier,* 29 May 1964.

35.	*Charleston News and Courier,* 21 August 1964.

36.	Ben Scott Whaley, quoted by *Charleston Evening Post,* 29 May 1964.

37.	*Charleston Evening Post,* 23 November 1965, 6 December 1965, 1 June 1966; *Charleston News and Courier,* 7 December 1965, 2 March 1966.

38.	*Charleston Evening Post,* 1 June 1966, 27 February 1973; *Charleston News and Courier,* 4 July 1967; Frances Edmunds to Glenn Cole, 21 September 1970; Frances Edmunds to Owners and Residents of Ansonborough, 31 May 1972.

39.	Both men are quoted in Philip J. Johnson, "Contemporary Building in Historic Districts: A Charleston Critique," *Historic Preservation* 23 (January–March 1971): 17–18.

40.	*Charleston News and Courier,* 2 January 1972; Arthur P. Zeigler Jr. et al., *Revolving Funds for Historic Preservation: A Manual of Practice* (Pittsburgh: Park Associates, 1975), 57–61; Gregory B. Paxton to Milton Herd, 5 September 1978.

41.	Director's Report for the Thirtieth Annual Meeting.

42.	*Charleston News and Courier,* 19 March 1972; Frances Edmunds, Tally Sheet: Progress Report on Ansonborough, 5 June 1969; Frances Edmunds to Harold L. Kennedy, 14 July 1980; Frances Edmunds, Remarks to the National Trust for Historic Preservation, 18 October 1990; HCF Minutes, 11 October 1966.

43.	*Charleston News and Courier,* 19 March 1972. Enhanced municipal protection for the neighborhood came in 1966, when Charleston's zoning ordinance was revised to expand the Old and Historic Charleston District (with its preservation restrictions) to include Ansonborough.

44.	Frederick M. Ehni to Thomas C. Stevenson, 9 January 1970; Glenn Cole to Historic Charleston Foundation, 10 September 1970; Mrs. John D. Doran to Thomas E. Thornhill, 30 April 1973.

45.	R. Angus Murdoch, quoted in Daniel Cohen, "Charleston's Restoration Challenge," *Historic Preservation* 39 (January–February 1987): 38.

46.	The *Oxford English Dictionary* gave a first usage of the verb "gentrify" in 1972. The *American Heritage Dictionary,* third edition, defines gentrification as "the restoration and upgrading of deteriorated urban property by the middle classes, often resulting in displacement of lower-income people."

47.	The history of this initiative in the uptown boroughs of Wraggborough and Radcliffeborough is discussed in chapter 7.

48.	See, for example, *New York World-Telegram and Sun,* 7 June 1962; article from *Greater Boston Business,* reprinted in *Charleston News and Courier,* 25 November 1962; Barbara Snow Delaney, "Preservation 1966," *Antiques* 90 (October 1966): 526–33; *Kansas City Times,* 4 November 1966; *Baltimore Sun,* 17 December 1967; *Miami Herald,* 12 February 1967; *New York Times,* 4 April 1971; *Detroit Free Press,* 3 April 1973.

49.	*With Heritage So Rich: A Report of a Special Committee on Historic Preservation under the Auspices of the United States Conference of Mayors* (New York: Random House, 1966), 46, 59.

50. National Trust for Historic Preservation, *Program for the Twenty-Fourth Annual Meeting and Preservation Conference, November 4–8, 1970, Charleston, South Carolina,* 10; *Charleston News and Courier,* 13 October 1970; *Charleston Evening Post,* 6 November 1970; National Trust, *Preservation News* 10 (December 1970).

51. National Trust for Historic Preservation, *Adaptive Use and Area Preservation Tours, November 5–6, 1970.*

52. National Trust, *Twenty-Fourth Annual Meeting,* 18–25.

53. Whaley, *Mrs. Whaley and Her Charleston Garden,* 181–82.

54. See, for example, the informal poll cited in the *Charleston Post and Courier,* 21 June 1985.

55. Mrs. St. Julien (Harriott Horry Rutledge) Ravenel, author of *Charleston: The Place and the People* (New York: Macmillan, 1906).

56. The history of the annual spring tours is discussed in chapter 9 as part of a general assessment of how the foundation has funded its wide-ranging preservation activities.

57. A subsequent article that received wide distribution was her essay on "The Adaptive Use of Charleston Buildings in Historic Preservation," *Antiques* 97 (April 1970): 590–95.

58. In the course of her distinguished career with the foundation between 1948 and 1985, Frances Edmunds received a number of honors that reflected both her success in Charleston and her influence nationally. These included, among others, awards from the United States Department of the Interior, the National Trust for Historic Preservation, the American Institute of Architects, the Historic Savannah Foundation, the Charleston Federation of Women's Clubs, the Rotary Club of Charleston, and the Greater Charleston Board of Realtors; an honorary degree and the Founders' Medal from the College of Charleston; appointment as trustee at Monticello and appointment by President Carter to the Advisory Council on Historic Preservation. The life and work of Frances Edmunds warrant the attention of a book-length study from a future biographer.

## Chapter 5. Let the Old Exist in Harmony with the New

1. The architectural survey of 1941 is discussed in chapter 2. In its obituary of Carl Feiss on 27 October 1997, the *New York Times* called him "a visionary architect and pioneering urban planner who helped transform the science of clearing slums into the art of historic preservation." Feiss held a degree in architecture from the University of Pennsylvania and a master of arts in urban planning from the Massachusetts Institute of Technology. He was active in New York, Denver, Annapolis, Alexandria, and Savannah, among other cities, as well as Charleston.

2. HCF Minutes, 9 December 1958, 16 December 1958, 2 February 1959, 19 January 1960.

3. While voters within the city of Charleston favored the change, suburban voters in Charleston County were able to defeat the measure. Finally in 1970 voters ratified an amendment to the state constitution that permitted Charleston, as well as other cities, to begin an urban renewal program. See *Charleston News and Courier,* 18 February 1957, 1 May 1957, 30 August 1958, 27 January 1959, 10 February 1960, 9 February 1964, 12 April 1964, 16 August 1966, 7 November 1966, 10 November 1966; *Charleston Evening Post,* 31 October 1958, 1 November 1958; Joseph H. McGee, "Legal Aspects of Preservation," *Historic Preservation* 23 (January–March 1971): 14–15.

4. *Charleston News and Courier,* 30 August 1966; *Charleston Evening Post,* 22 November 1966; HCF Minutes, 8 March 1966, 28 July 1966.

5. Statement of Ben Scott Whaley to City Council, 9 November 1966, Simons Papers, SCHS; *Charleston News and Courier,* 25 January 1967; *Charleston Evening Post,* 6 December 1968.

6. The extension of the area rehabilitation program into Wraggborough and Radcliffeborough is the subject of chapter 7.

7. As originally proposed by the mayor, the modification adopted in 1959 had sought to expand Board of Architectural Review oversight to all buildings erected prior to 1875, but this cut-off date was scaled back to antebellum buildings. At the time, BAR members also suggested a requirement for "preliminary approval," as a way to provide guidance for owners contemplating large projects involving more than $5,000 in repairs and alterations. See: A. J. Tamsberg to Robert M. Hollings, 13 March 1958, Simons Papers, SCHS; *Charleston News and Courier,* 9 October 1958.

8. Outside the Old and Historic Charleston District, the Board of Architectural Review was given authority to delay demolition and exterior alteration of pre-1860 buildings for up to 180 days, double the previous time frame.

9. City Council of Charleston, *Proceedings,* Regular Meeting of 16 August 1966, 510–43; *Charleston News and Courier,* 17 August 1966, 18 August 1966; *Charleston Evening Post,* 17 August 1966.

10. Joseph H. McGee, Summary of Remarks to Board of Directors, Historic Charleston Foundation, 1966.

11. McGee, Summary of Remarks; Delaney, "Preservation 1966," *Antiques* 90 (October 1966): 527–30.

12. McGee, Summary of Remarks; McGee, "Legal Aspects of Preservation," *Historic Preservation* 23 (January–March 1971): 14–15.

13. Historic Charleston Foundation, *Broad Street Beautification Plan,* undated pamphlet; *Charleston News and Courier,* 26 January 1969; National Trust for Historic Preservation, *Broad Street, Charleston, South Carolina: A Walking Adventure,* tour brochure for the 1970 annual meeting; *New York Times,* 4 April 1971.

14. City Planning and Architectural Associates, Russell Wright, Carl Feiss, and National Heritage Corporation, *Historic Preservation Plan,* June 1974; *Charleston News and Courier,* 4 November 1973; *Charleston Evening Post,* 10 April 1974.

15. The area south of Line Street, which was roughly the route of the Crosstown Expressway, had been designated the Old City Historic District in April 1973. This was an entirely new district, separate from the Old and Historic Charleston District established in 1931 and subsequently expanded.

16. The jury consisted of William J. Murtagh, Keeper of the National Register of Historic Places; Bernard Lemman, School of Architecture, Tulane University; Charles E. Lee, State Historic Preservation Officer and Director of the South Carolina Department of Archives and History; and Carl Feiss and Russell Wright, consultants to the project. See *Charleston News and Courier,* 9 June 1972; *Charleston Evening Post,* 8 September 1973, 11 April 1974.

17. Joseph H. McGee, quoted in *Charleston News and Courier,* 18 June 1975.

18. Adoption of the historic architecture inventory in June 1975 (and a doubling of the size of the Old and Historic Charleston District in July) were connected with the politics that surrounded the hotly debated location of the Charleston terminus of the James Island Bridge, a subject discussed in chapter 8.

19. *Charleston News and Courier,* 15 April 1974; *Charleston Evening Post,* 16 April 1974.

20. *Charleston Evening Post,* 13 July 1973, 27 June 1978; *Charleston News and Courier,* 7 July 1973, 15 July 1973, 22 July 1973, 16 August 1973, 4 November 1973, 14 April 1974, 2 July 1978; *Charlotte Observer,* 22 July 1973.

21. *Charleston News and Courier,* 7 July 1973.

22. *Charleston News and Courier,* 2 March 1978, 13 September 1978, 10 October 1978.

23. *Charleston Evening Post,* 17 April 1974.

24. *Charleston News and Courier,* 2 July 1978, 19 October 1978, 6 December 1978, 20 December 1978; *Charleston Evening Post,* 13 September 1978, 19 October 1978, 20 December 1978; *Preservation Progress* 23 (February 1979).

25. Letter to the editor, *Charleston News and Courier,* 11 September 1984.

26. The architectural inventory adopted in 1975 was based on a survey in 1972–73 and had been unofficially updated by Historic Charleston Foundation and others in the late 1970s; under contract with the city, the Geier Brown Renfrow firm of Washington, D.C., undertook a resurvey in 1984–85.

27. Rhoad, "The Board of Architectural Review in Charleston, 1931–1993," *Preservation Progress,* special edition (Spring 1993): 13–18.

28. *Charleston News and Courier,* 17 August 1962, 29 May 1967, 30 May 1967, 8 June 1967; *Charleston Evening Post,* 2 April 1986.

29. *The State* (Columbia), 18 June 1978.

30. HCF Minutes, 18 March 1975; *Charleston News and Courier,* 28 October 1978, 24 November 1978, 11 May 1983, 28 October 1984; *Charleston Evening Post,* 27 February 1979, 31 October 1984; *Hilton Head Island Packet,* 11 December 1986.

31. Barton-Aschman Associates, *Tourism Impact and Management Study, Charleston, South Carolina, Summary Report* (Prepared for Charleston County Park, Recreation and Tourist Commission, February 1978).

32. The Arch Building at 85 Calhoun Street had been spared demolition when the municipal auditorium was constructed in the late 1960s. It was subsequently restored with funds from Historic Charleston Foundation and the federal government and operated by the Chamber of Commerce as a tourist information center beginning in 1972. See *Charleston Evening Post,* 4 February 1966, 26 May 1970; *Charleston News and Courier,* 13 April 1966, 24 January 1972.

33. *Charleston Evening Post,* 27 September 1978; *Charleston News and Courier,* 10 October 1980, 3 December 1980, 9 December 1982; *Charleston News and Courier/Charleston Evening Post,* 19 July 1983.

34. *Charleston Evening Post,* 25 October 1978, 4 January 1979; *Charleston News and Courier/Charleston Evening Post,* 6 October 1987, 5 November 1988.

35. The debate over the hotel and convention center is the subject of chapter 6.

36. *Charleston News and Courier,* 3 May 1981, 11 March 1983; *Charleston Evening Post,* 28 October 1984.

37. HCF Director's Reports, 29 July 1980, 18 November 1980; Report of the Planning and Zoning Committee to HCF, 11 May 1982; HCF Minutes, 26 October 1982. Mr. and Mrs. Charles H. Woodward were important benefactors of Waterfront Park, as they had been in the Ansonborough project and other foundation ventures.

38. Joseph P. Riley Jr. to Norman Olsen Jr., 30 October 1980, file 30-25-1C, SCHS.

39. Memo from Frances Edmunds, 9 September 1980; *Charleston News and Courier,* 7 November 1980; HCF Director's Reports, 18 November 1980, November 1980–January 1981; Statement of Historic Charleston Foundation Concerning Proposed Visitor Reception/Transportation Center, 22 January 1981; HCF Zoning and Planning Committee Report, [March 1981]; HCF Minutes, 19 March 1981, 16 April 1981; Statement Concerning Visitor Reception/ Transportation Center, 27 March 1981; untitled pamphlet urging support of the visitor center bond issue [1987], file 30-25-13, SCHS.

40. *Charleston News and Courier,* 23 January 1981, 3 October 1981, 22 July 1988.

41. *Charleston News and Courier,* 17 September 1990, 13 May 1991, 14 May 1991.

42. *Charleston News and Courier/Charleston Evening Post,* 10 November 1988. The controversy over the James Island Bridge is discussed in chapter 8.

43. Buckhurst Fish Hutton Katz Inc. and Thomas & Means Associates, *Calhoun Street Corridor Study: Final Report* (Prepared for the City of Charleston, January 1989); *Charleston News and Courier/Charleston Evening Post,* 29 January 1989; *Charleston News and Courier,* 16 July 1990, 12 September 1991.

44. *Charleston News and Courier,* 5 February 1980, 11 February 1980.

45. Frances Edmunds to the Trustees of Historic Charleston Foundation, 26 May 1980.

46. *Charleston News and Courier,* 23 April 1982.

47. *Charleston News and Courier,* 23 April 1982.

48. *Charleston Evening Post,* 8 July 1983.

49. *Charleston Evening Post,* 18 July 1983.

50. Advisory Council actions do have the force of law when a formal memorandum of agreement can be negotiated among the parties, as happened at one point in the case of the controversial hotel and convention center discussed in chapter 6.

51. *Charleston News and Courier,* 3 November 1983, 4 November 1983, 2 February 1984, 24 May 1984; *Charleston Evening Post,* 12 December 1983, 13 December 1983, 11 January 1984, 27 March 1984.

52. *Charleston News and Courier,* 1 June 1984, 8 June 1984, 22 November 1984; *Charleston Evening Post,* 29 June 1984, 2 July 1984, 27 September 1984; *Charleston News and Courier/Charleston Evening Post,* 1 September 1984; *Preservation Progress* 30 (September 1986). The annex was formally dedicated in November 1988.

53. *Charleston News and Courier,* 8 December 1988.

## CHAPTER 6. THE "BATTLE OF CHARLESTON"

1. John Sherwood to Barton-Aschman Associates, Work Memorandum, 8 July 1976; Barton-Aschman Associates, *Charleston Commercial Revitalization Program* (Prepared for City of Charleston, March 1977), in files at City of Charleston Department of Economic Development; *Charleston News and Courier,* 26 July 1977; Kenneth A. Gifford to J. Rutledge Young Jr., 25 October 1977.

2. *Charleston News and Courier,* 19 October 1977; *Charleston Evening Post,* 19 October 1977.

3. In the environmental impact statement prepared by the city and released in August 1978, the claim was made that the project would increase annual tax revenues to the city by $280,000 and to the county by $200,000, provide two hundred construction jobs and nine hundred permanent jobs, and reverse the prospects of downtown within three years of completion. See *Charleston News and Courier,* 15 August 1978.

4. *Charleston News and Courier,* 19 October 1977, 26 October 1977.

5. Letterbook of Frances Edmunds, 28 October 1977; *Charleston News and Courier,* 9 November 1977, 11 November 1977, 12 December 1977.

6. *Charleston News and Courier,* 12 December 1977.

7. HCF, Statement [on] Proposed Market Street Development, [15 December 1977]. On the evolution of the foundation's position, see Joseph H. McGee to HCF, 14 November 1977; Joseph H. McGee to HCF Committee to Study Market Street Hotel and Convention Complex, 23 November 1977; HCF Minutes of Ad Hoc Committee, 15 December.

8. The Save Historic Charleston Fund was established in January 1978 to oppose the hotel and convention center. It was distinct from the Save Charleston Foundation founded in

the early 1970s to oppose a condominium development at East Bay and Cumberland Streets. Neither was affiliated with Historic Charleston Foundation. The Charlestown Neighborhood Association represented the area south of Broad Street and had been formed in November 1977.

9. Subsequently the city proposed a public-use garage, and it began negotiating the purchase of private property, rather than seeking to condemn it. On coverage of the suit in local newspapers, see *Charleston News and Courier,* 26 January 1978, 20 June 1978, 1 September 1978, 6 September 1978; *Charleston Evening Post,* 17 February 1978, 10 April 1978, 11 April 1978, 19 April 1978, 22 May 1978, 1 September 1978.

10. To acquire the portion of the site to be owned by municipal government and used as a convention center and parking garage, the city had applied for and received an Urban Development Action Grant in the amount of $4.1 million from the United States Department of Housing and Urban Development.

11. *Charleston News and Courier/Charleston Evening Post,* 21 January 1979.

12. HCF Minutes, 19 March 1979. The architects were Jean Paul Carlhian of Shepley Bullfinch Richardson Abbott of Boston, Malcolm Holzman of Hardy Holzman Pfeiffer Associates of New York, and Hugh Newell Jacobsen of Washington, D.C.

13. *Charleston News and Courier,* 21 February 1979, 22 March 1979; *Charleston News and Courier/Charleston Evening Post,* 25 February 1979; *Charleston Evening Post,* 26 February 1979; Hugh Newell Jacobsen et al., Report to Historic Charleston Foundation on Charleston Center, 16 February 1979; Statement of Mrs. S. Henry Edmunds to Public Meeting, 24 February 1979.

14. *Charleston News and Courier,* 2 March 1979.

15. The affected structures were 209, 211, 215, 217, 223, 225, 227, 229, and 231 Meeting Street. In addition, the facades of buildings at 244 and 246 King Street were to be donated by the developer to the city and moved to 219 and 221 Meeting Street as infill.

16. *Charleston News and Courier,* 7 June 1979; *Charleston Evening Post,* 20 June 1979, 21 June 1979, 20 August 1979; *Charleston News and Courier/Charleston Evening Post,* 22 July 1979.

17. The suit contended that the city should not be allowed to receive about $7.1 million of federal grants from the Department of Housing and Urban Development and the Department of Commerce because the environmental impact statement for the hotel-convention complex was defective.

18. *Charleston News and Courier,* 29 May 1981, 30 May 1981, 4 March 1983, 31 March 1983, 18 May 1983, 25 August 1983, 13 December 1984, 23 October 1986, 16 November 1986; *New York Times,* 17 February 1985. Architect John Carl Warnecke designed the building for developers A. Alfred Taubman of Troy, Michigan, and the Rainbow Square firm of Baltimore.

19. *Charleston Evening Post,* 24 July 1985.

20. *Charleston News and Courier,* 9 December 1986, 16 June 1988; *This Week in Peninsular Charleston,* 17 August 1989.

21. *Los Angeles Times,* 11 May 1979.

22. *Charleston News and Courier,* 12 December 1977.

23. *Los Angeles Times,* 11 May 1979.

24. *Christian Science Monitor,* 29 January 1979; *Charleston News and Courier,* 28 November 1979.

25. Preservation Society of Charleston, "In Defense of Charleston: 1980," typescript press release, file 30-25-1C, SCHS.

26. *Charleston News and Courier,* 19 February 1979, 7 March 1979, 8 March 1979, 9 March 1979, 11 May 1979, 16 May 1979; *Charleston News and Courier/Charleston Evening Post,* 11 March 1979, 22 April 1979.

27. *Charleston News and Courier*, 15 April 1981.
28. *Charleston News and Courier*, 31 January 1979.
29. *Los Angeles Times*, 11 May 1979; *The State* (Columbia), 9 November 1980.
30. John Hamilton to Friends of the Cause of Historic Preservation, 9 March 1978, file 30-25-1C, SCHS; *Charleston News and Courier*, 18 February 1978.
31. R. de Treville Lawrence to Joseph P. Riley Jr., 18 January 1978, file 30-25-1A, SCHS.
32. *Los Angeles Times*, 11 May 1979. Over time R. de Treville Lawrence became especially outspoken in his opinion of Mayor Riley and the role of Historic Charleston Foundation in the controversy, suggesting that the mayor had used the foundation as a front in "a communist tactic," hiding behind the foundation's national prestige in order "to do bad work." See *Charleston News and Courier*, 5 April 1981.
33. *Winston-Salem Journal*, 12 March 1978.
34. Save Historic Charleston Fund to Friends, 5 February 1979, file 30-25-1C, SCHS. For some of the national publicity, see *New York Times*, 27 January 1979; *Charlotte Observer*, 18 February 1979; *Washington Post*, 3 March 1979; *Christian Science Monitor*, 12 March 1979; *Winston-Salem Journal*, 12 March 1979; *Los Angeles Times*, 11 May 1979.
35. *Charleston* (West Virginia) *Daily Mail*, 7 March 1979.
36. Tom Huth, "Should Charleston Go New South?," *Historic Preservation* 31 (July–August 1979): 32–38.
37. [Downtown Residents for Charleston Center], Charleston Center [1978]; *Charleston Evening Post*, 10 November 1978, 15 December 1978; *The State* (Columbia), 9 November 1980.
38. Preservation of the Riviera inspired a small battle all its own, as various ideas for the vacant theater were proposed and debated during the 1980s. Eventually the property was sold and stabilized, then conveyed to the city and sold to Charleston Place. Historic architectural details have been boxed in (so they can be recovered in the future) on the ground floor, which has been converted into shops and offices; an auditorium occupies the upper floor.

## CHAPTER 7. KEEPING SOUND THE LEGACY

1. Poston, *Buildings of Charleston*, 221–22.
2. Charles H. P. Duell to Thomas C. Stevenson, 9 September 1971.
3. *Charleston Evening Post*, 20 December 1972, 8 January 1990; *Charleston News and Courier*, 22 March 1973, 8 December 1973.
4. Poston, *Buildings of Charleston*, 276–78.
5. It had been owned since 1928 by the Roebling family.
6. *Charleston News and Courier*, 9 May 1984.
7. Reports of the Area Projects Committee, 12 November 1985, 25 March 1986.
8. HCF, *Preservation and Conservation Easements*, undated informational brochure; *Charleston Evening Post*, 2 March 1983. See also Elizabeth Watson and Stefan Nagel, *Establishing an Easement Program to Protect Historic, Scenic, and Natural Resources* (Washington, D.C.: National Trust for Historic Preservation, 1995).
9. A list of easements held by Historic Charleston Foundation can be found in the appendix. The first easement was actually donated to the foundation in 1979, even before it had established a formal program, by a citizen who had learned about easements and wanted to protect a property in the vicinity of the controversial hotel and convention center then under discussion in Charleston. Changes in federal tax law that discouraged the use of investment tax credits for historic preservation in the late 1980s also discouraged donation of conservation easements as part of investment incentive packages. In addition in 1986 the regional

office of the Internal Revenue Service began "studying" the deductions taken by easement donors in Charleston, eventually devaluing them by as much as 100 percent. Appeals over the next two years restored some or most of the declared value, but the IRS action exerted a chilling effect for a number of years.

10. The two houses on East Bay Street were Presqu'ile (2 Amherst Street), purchased in 1962, and the Faber House (631 East Bay), purchased in 1965. The property at 44 Charlotte Street was donated to the foundation in 1966.

11. HCF Minutes, 20 September 1972.

12. HCF Minutes, 20 September 1972.

13. Director's Report for the Thirtieth Annual Meeting; HCF Minutes, 19 March 1979; Report of the Area Projects Committee, 12 November 1985.

14. Director's Report for the Thirtieth Annual Meeting.

15. HCF Minutes, 19 March 1979. Gregory Paxton was a graduate of the University of Vermont who played a key role in inaugurating these uptown initiatives.

16. HCF Minutes, 19 March 1979.

17. Frances Edmunds to Charles E. Lee, 30 November 1977.

18. *Charleston Chronicle,* 28 June 1989. A court of freedmen's cottages was razed to make way for the new construction. A hiatus again followed after 1989, with renewed activity in the mid 1990s focused on detached single-family houses. All of the lots have now been sold. Fourteen houses have been completed and are owner-occupied. There is only one unimproved lot left.

19. HCF, Eighth Year Community Development Block Grant, Request for Funding to City of Charleston, December 1981.

20. HCF Minutes, 19 March 1979; Report of the Area Projects Committee, January 1980.

21. Edmunds to Lee, 30 November 1977.

22. Frances Edmunds to Ernest Allen Connally, 5 December 1977.

23. *Charleston News and Courier,* 11 March 1973.

24. Reports of the Area Projects Committee, January 1980, 23 July 1986; *Charleston News and Courier,* 18 August 1983; Frances Edmunds, Remarks to the National Trust for Historic Preservation, 18 October 1990. Making use of its regular revolving fund, the foundation also purchased Radcliffeborough properties at 62–64 and 86–88 Warren Street.

25. "Charleston Heritage Housing, Inc.," located with HCF Minutes, 24 November 1987.

26. *Charleston News and Courier/Charleston Evening Post,* 26 March 1989; HCF Minutes, 28 November 1989; "Charleston Heritage Housing Established," *Charleston* 6 (Spring 1989): 2; interview with Charles E. Chase, 19 August 1998.

27. See, for example, *Charleston Post and Courier,* 30 March 1994, 22 June 1994, 8 February 1996.

28. Annual Report of the Executive Director, 27 January 1987; Reports of the Area Projects Committee, 19 May 1987, 31 October 1988, 15 September 1989, 31 October 1990, 31 October 1991; HCF Minutes, 25 September 1990. The corner grocery store with upstairs apartment at 14 Amherst was donated to the city in 1990 for development of the Charleston Crafts Project, funded by a grant from the Getty Foundation. The three rental units at 70 Nassau were rehabilitated by the foundation and sold in 1996.

29. See, for example, *Charleston News and Courier/Charleston Evening Post,* 11 November 1979. See chapter 5 for a discussion of the Historic Preservation Plan of 1974.

30. *Charleston News and Courier,* 10 December 1982.

31. *Charleston Evening Post,* 1 February 1985; *Charleston News and Courier,* 27 June 1986.

32. *Charleston News and Courier,* 18 January 1983, 27 June 1986, 18 November 1986, 21 November 1986, 18 December 1986; *Charleston Evening Post,* 28 September 1983.

33. *Charleston Chronicle,* 6 December 1986.
34. Quoted in Cohen, "Charleston's Restoration Challenge," *Historic Preservation* 39 (January–February 1987): 31–39.
35. *Charleston News and Courier,* 16 December 1988.
36. *Charleston News and Courier/Charleston Evening Post,* 4 December 1988.
37. *Charleston News and Courier,* 4 December 1988, 29 December 1988, 27 January 1989; *Charleston Chronicle,* 14 December 1988; *Charleston Evening Post,* 25 January 1989, 27 January 1989; National Trust for Historic Preservation, "Charleston Surprise," *Preservation News* 29 (October 1989).
38. *Charleston News and Courier,* 16 December 1988.
39. *Charleston Chronicle,* 14 December 1988.
40. Jim French in *Charleston Chronicle,* 1 March 1989, 28 June 1989.

## CHAPTER 8. A REGIONAL AND ENVIRONMENTAL AGENDA

1. *Charleston Evening Post,* 19 December 1969.
2. Thomas C. Stevenson Jr., Open Letter from Historic Charleston Foundation to Silas N. Pearman et al., 10 February 1969.
3. *Charleston Evening Post,* 4 February 1971.
4. Because construction of the highway involved the use of federal funds, the controversy over its location was reviewed by the Advisory Council on Historic Preservation, a presidentially appointed agency charged with oversight of the impact of federally funded or licensed projects on historic structures. Advisory Council actions can have the force of law when a formal memorandum of agreement can be negotiated among the parties, as happened in the case of the Charleston Place hotel-convention complex in 1979 (see the discussion in chapter 6). At other times Advisory Council findings are essentially recommendations to the affected federal agencies, as in its comments on the Federal Courthouse Annex in 1983 (see chapter 5).
5. *Charleston News and Courier,* 29 January 1970, 6 February 1971, 17 November 1971, 24 November 1971, 29 December 1974; *Charleston Evening Post,* 10 February 1970, 4 February 1971, 9 August 1974; *New York Times,* 2 April 1971.
6. Thomas E. Thornhill, Statement to the President's Advisory Council on Historic Preservation, 21 January 1975.
7. *Charleston News and Courier,* 16 November 1974, 20 November 1974, 22 January 1975; *Charleston Evening Post,* 25 July 1975.
8. *Charleston News and Courier,* 7 February 1971, 7 May 1975, 29 May 1975, 30 May 1975, 18 June 1975.
9. See the previous discussion in chapter 5.
10. *Charleston News and Courier,* 3 April 1976, 19 July 1978, 15 March 1979, 15 September 1983; *Charleston Evening Post,* 19 July 1978; Thomas E. Thornhill to Joseph H. McGee, July 1978; Frances Edmunds to E. S. Coffey, 28 July 1978.
11. *Charleston News and Courier,* 17 September 1983.
12. *Charleston Evening Post,* 20 June 1985, 21 June 1985; *Charleston Post and Courier,* 24 February 1996. Design engineers for the James Island Expressway were Wilbur Smith & Associates of Columbia.
13. Since the early 1970s the city had been in the process of annexing pieces of James Island.
14. For a comparative analysis of the protection afforded by Section 106 of the National Historic Preservation Act of 1966, Section 4(f) of the Transportation Act of 1966, and the National Environmental Policy Act of 1969, see the discussion in Robert E. Stipe and

Antoinette J. Lee (eds.), *The American Mosaic: Preserving a Nation's Heritage* (Washington, D.C.: Preservation Press, 1987), 40–61.

15. *Charleston News and Courier,* 5 November 1971, 30 December 1971; Thomas C. Stevenson Jr. to Charleston County Council, 28 December 1971.

16. *Charleston Evening Post,* 9 August 1978, 1 August 1979; *Charleston News and Courier,* 23 January 1980, 28 March 1981, 21 February 1985.

17. *Charleston News and Courier/Charleston Evening Post,* 1 June 1985; *Charleston News and Courier,* 30 July 1985; *61 Corridor Growth Management Plan* (Prepared for Charleston City Council, Charleston County Council, and Dorchester County Council, [1986]); *61 Corridor Study Area: A Development Standards Guidebook* (Prepared by John Rahenkamp Consultants for Charleston City Council, Charleston County Council, and Dorchester County Council, [n.d.]); interview with George W. McDaniel, 19 August 1998. In addition, in the early 1990s Charleston County commissioned a survey of its historic and archaeological properties, with support from Historic Charleston Foundation and others, designed to facilitate countywide preservation planning of historic resources.

18. *Charleston Evening Post,* 13 September 1978, 2 October 1978, 20 October 1978; *Charleston News and Courier,* 13 September 1978, 20 September 1978, 20 October 1978.

19. *Charleston News and Courier,* 26 September 1978.

20. *Charleston News and Courier,* 10 June 1987; *Charleston Evening Post,* 15 June 1987, 19 November 1987; Dana Beach, "An Environmental View of 61 Expressway," *Preservation Progress* 31 (July 1987).

21. South Carolina Coastal Council and South Carolina Department of Archives and History, *Ashley River Special Area Management Plan* (February 1992); McDaniel interview. For an earlier planning document also developed with the encouragement and funding of the state historic preservation office, see Berkeley Charleston Dorchester Council of Governments, *Ashley River Study* (August 1980). The South Carolina Coastal Council is a state agency charged with "the proper management of the natural, recreational, commercial and industrial resources of the State's coastal zone" by the Coastal Management Act of 1977.

22. The Lowcountry Open Land Trust, *Preserving the Natural Heritage of the Lowcountry,* undated brochure, file 30-25-17, SCHS.

23. *Charleston News and Courier,* 28 October 1986; *Charleston Post and Courier,* 15 November 1993.

24. *Charleston Post and Courier,* 6 June 1995.

25. Jane Brown Gillette, "American Classic," *Historic Preservation* 43 (March–April 1991): 22–29, 71–72; Poston, *Buildings of Charleston,* 25.

26. *Charleston News and Courier,* 31 October 1971.

27. Lease with Option to Purchase [Drayton Hall], 1 January 1973.

28. *Charleston News and Courier,* 6 August 1975; excerpts from Drayton Hall acquisition grant report, Drayton Hall files.

29. *Charleston Evening Post,* 17 April 1974; *Charleston News and Courier,* 18 April 1974, 22 April 1974.

30. Hugh C. Lane and Rufus C. Barkley Jr. to Roderick K. Shaw Jr., 18 April 1974.

31. HCF, *Drayton Hall,* fund-raising booklet [ca. March 1974], Drayton Hall files.

32. *Charleston News and Courier,* 14 July 1974. Shortly after the fund-raising campaign to purchase the property was completed, the National Trust announced an ambitious $2 million restoration and endowment campaign.

33. A summary of early planning reports can be found in Robert Lamb Hart, *Drayton Hall Property Development Plan* (Prepared for the National Trust for Historic Preservation and the State of South Carolina, November 1979), Drayton Hall files.

34. John M. Dickey, Richard C. Frank, Frederick D. Nichols, F. Blair Reeves, *Initial Report on the Preservation of the John Drayton House to the National Trust for Historic Preservation,* 11 March 1975, Drayton Hall files.

35. *Charleston News and Courier,* 12 April 1976.

36. For an extended discussion of these issues, see Gerald George, "The Great Drayton Hall Debate," *History News* 39 (January 1984): 7–12.

37. *Charleston Post and Courier,* 17 December 1994, 6 June 1995, 25 August 1995, 6 February 1996. See also Wade Lawrence, "Preserving the Visitor Experience," *Preservation Forum* 12 (Summer 1998): 15–21.

38. For the specifics of the foundation's participation with the Friends of Historic Snee Farm, see "Historic Charleston Foundation's Role in the Establishment of the Charles Pinckney National Historic Site," *Charleston* 7 (Summer 1990): 2.

39. Initial skirmishes over Snee Farm had involved the permit process at meetings of the South Carolina Coastal Council.

40. Report of the Executive Director, 24 November 1987.

41. Lots had been laid out and grading had begun when bulldozers hit the archaeological remains of the slave row.

42. *Charleston News and Courier,* 24 November 1987, 22 January 1988, 9 February 1988; *Charleston Evening Post,* 10 December 1987; Friends of Historic Snee Farm, Media Advisory, 11 December 1987; Friends of Historic Snee Farm Minutes, 7 January 1988, 20 January 1988, 22 February 1988, 7 March 1988, 15 July 1988, 3 October 1988, 16 January 1989; Richard L. Jones to Brien Varnado, 26 May 1988. The correspondence and minutes of the Friends of Historic Snee Farm cited in this chapter are located at the Fort Moultrie offices of Fort Sumter National Monument.

43. Public Law 100-421, 102 Stat. 1581, 100th Congress, 8 September 1988.

44. Congress, House, Representative Vento of Minnesota, H. R. 3960, 100th Congress, *Congressional Record,* 20 June 1988.

45. *Charleston News and Courier,* 13 September 1989, 8 May 1990; Corporate Offer to Sell Real Property, 27 April 1990, Fort Moultrie files.

46. *Charleston Post and Courier,* 14 December 1991. The work was carried out by a team assembled by the Friends of Historic Snee Farm, with technical assistance from Jonathan Poston of Historic Charleston Foundation. Snee Farm had returned to Pinckney's estate sometime in the 1820s, following his death in 1824.

47. For a view of management thinking about the site in the wake of discoveries about the house, see National Park Service, Southeast Regional Office, *Draft General Management Plan, Development Concept Plan, Environmental Assessment, Charles Pinckney National Historic Site,* March 1994.

48. *Charleston News and Courier,* 18 June 1987, 26 July 1987.

49. *Charleston News and Courier,* 26 July 1987; *Charleston Evening Post,* 3 August 1987, 19 December 1988.

50. *Charleston News and Courier,* 25 August 1988.

51. Report of the Area Projects Committee, 8 May 1984.

52. For a discussion of the easements program, see chapter 7; for a list of easements held by Historic Charleston Foundation, see the appendix.

## CHAPTER 9. FINANCING PRESERVATION

1. The following discussion is a summary review of material presented previously; for a fuller analysis of individual topics, refer to the appropriate chapters.

2. For recent recognition of the role of the Woodwards in foundation activities, see Jonathan H. Poston, "Mr. and Mrs. Charles Woodward Receive Frances R. Edmunds Award," *Historic Charleston* 1 (Summer 1995): 20.

3. The foundation's role at the Aiken-Rhett House and the Powder Magazine is discussed in chapter 10.

4. Mary Pope Waring, "Foundation Concludes Most Successful Festival of Houses and Gardens," *Historic Charleston* 1 (Summer 1995): 19.

5. Chorley, *The Challenge to Charleston;* Minutes of the Civic Services Committee, 30 July 1946, 6 November 1946, Simons Papers, SCHS.

6. HCF Minutes, 9 April 1947, 15 April 1947; *Charleston News and Courier,* 10 April 1947. On the history of the "Natchez Pilgrimages" created in 1932 by the Natchez Garden Club see Mary Warren Miller, "Paying Homage in Natchez," *Reckon: The Magazine of Southern Culture* 1 (Fall 1995): 62–71. Dorothy Haskell Porcher Legge was a founding trustee of Historic Charleston Foundation who had pioneered the revitalization of Rainbow Row; see the discussion in chapters 1–2.

7. *Charleston Evening Post,* 10 March 1948; *Charleston News and Courier,* 14 March 1948.

8. *Charleston News and Courier,* 1 February 1948; *Charleston Evening Post,* 10 March 1948. In subsequent years historic house museums routinely open to the public were dropped from the tour schedule.

9. C. Bissell Jenkins Jr., President's Report to the Annual Meeting, 19 May 1948.

10. *Charleston Evening Post,* 15 June 1948; HCF Minutes, 22 November 1954.

11. Annual Reports of the Tours Director, 1949 and 1950; *Charleston Evening Post,* 3 February 1950; "Three Southern States Complete Plans for Progressive 1950 Spring House and Garden Tours," undated press release; *Richmond* (Virginia) *News Leader,* 31 January 1951.

12. Quoted in *Charleston News and Courier,* 6 March 1949.

13. Thomas R. Waring, *New York Times,* 6 March 1949.

14. *Charleston News and Courier,* 16 January 1949.

15. Annual Report of the Tour Director, 1950; "Festival Comparison" statistics provided by Mary Pope Waring, Division of Tours and Special Programs.

16. Between 1976 and 1996 the number of patrons has averaged almost 11,500 per year. Alicia Rudolf was a Charlestonian who worked as Frances Edmunds's assistant for ten years, with responsibilities for all aspects of foundation operations and projects.

17. "Festival Comparison" statistics provided by Mary Pope Waring, Division of Tours and Special Programs; HCF Minutes, 28 July 1966; *Charleston News and Courier,* 31 March 1967, 29 August 1977.

18. Interview with Mary Pope Waring, 9 May 1996.

19. Initially the foundation did compensate property owners, but now it offers discounts in its shops, invitations to events, and passes to its house museums.

20. Interview with Cornelia H. Pelzer, 9 May 1996.

21. Interview with Thomas E. Thornhill, 9 May 1996; *Charleston Evening Post,* 31 March 1964; *Charleston News and Courier/Charleston Evening Post,* 8 December 1990; *Charleston Post and Courier,* 30 April 1994. Historic Charleston Foundation was an investor with Richard Jenrette in the Mills House project, an effort at downtown revitalization through restoration of the old hotel.

22. HCF Minutes, 20 September 1972.
23. *Charleston Evening Post,* 16 October 1973, 20 October 1973, 17 November 1977, 6 November 1984; *Charleston News and Courier,* 16 October 1973, 22 September 1974, 22 December 1974; *New York Times,* 12 May 1974, 27 March 1978.
24. HCF, *Reproduction Furniture & Accessories* (1992).
25. HCF, *Reproduction Furniture & Accessories.*
26. HCF, *Heritage Campaign* (1992).
27. Interview with Lawrence A. Walker, 10 May 1996; Bentz Associates, *Historic Charleston Foundation Marketing/Feasibility Study; Charleston Post and Courier,* 18 June 1992.

## CHAPTER 10. CONTINUITIES AND NEW DIRECTIONS

1. Lawrence Walker and Jonathan Poston of Historic Charleston Foundation were approached by the circuit solicitor to help push for a quality restoration of the building; subsequently Poston became actively involved in the Friends of the Courthouse.
2. *Charleston News and Courier,* 7 March 1991, 8 March 1991; *Charleston Evening Post,* 12 March 1991; *Charleston Post and Courier,* 14 July 1996, 3 August 1996.
3. *Charleston News and Courier/Charleston Evening Post,* 16 March 1991; *Charleston News and Courier,* 21 June 1991; "County Courthouse Restoration Approved," *Charleston* 8 (Fall 1991): 6; Rutledge Young, "Keeping Law at the Four Corners," *Historic Charleston* 3 (Autumn 1996): 11.
4. "County Courthouse Restoration Approved," *Charleston* 8 (Fall 1991): 6. On the architectural analysis of the building, see John Milner Associates, *Charleston County Courthouse: A Historic Structure Report on the Architectural Development and Historical Alterations to the Building* (Prepared for Liollio Associates, Inc., January 1991); Carl Lounsbury, Willie Graham, Mark R. Wenger, and W. Brown Morton III, *An Architectural Analysis of the Charleston County Courthouse,* 15 August 1991.
5. "The Charleston County Courthouse," *Charleston* 9 (Fall 1992): 2; "Charleston County Courthouse Update," *Charleston* 9 (Winter 1993): 2; *Charleston Post and Courier,* 15 April 1993, 23 June 1993, 7 July 1995, 21 December 1995, 18 February 1996, 12 March 1996, 13 March 1996, 1 May 1996, 3 May 1996, 4 June 1996, 14 July 1996, 3 August 1996.
6. Addison Ingle, "HCF's Position on the Charleston County Courthouse," *Historic Charleston* 4 (Summer 1997): 8.
7. Young, "Keeping Law at the Four Corners," *Historic Charleston* 3 (Autumn 1996): 11.
8. Poston, *Buildings of Charleston,* 89–90.
9. *Charleston News and Courier,* 27 October 1989; *Charleston Post and Courier,* 25 June 1993; "Foundation Leases City's Oldest Public Building," *Charleston* 10 (Summer 1993): 1–2.
10. Carter L. Hudgins, quoted in *Charleston Post and Courier,* 1 September 1996.
11. "Powder Magazine Work Progresses," *Historic Charleston* 3 (Autumn 1996): 7.
12. The estimate of the number of endangered structures is based on research by the City of Charleston; see "Neighborhood Impact Initiative," *Historic Charleston* 1 (Fall 1994): 7.
13. "Neighborhood Impact Initiative," *Historic Charleston* 1 (Fall 1994): 7; *Charleston Post and Courier,* 24 June 1995.
14. The building crafts training program is discussed later in this chapter, as a "new direction" for the foundation.
15. *Charleston Post and Courier,* 31 December 1992, 3 May 1993, 30 May 1994; "Foundation Selected for South Carolina National Bank Affordable Housing Challenge Grant,"

*Charleston* 10 (Summer 1993): 4; Bernett W. Mazyck, "Preservation Is for People," *Historic Charleston* 1 (Fall 1994): 4–7.

16. *Charleston Post and Courier,* 24 June 1995.

17. Mazyck, "Preservation Is for People," *Historic Charleston* 1 (Fall 1994): 6.

18. *Charleston Post and Courier,* 3 July 1995.

19. See, for example, HCF, *Neighborhood Impact Initiative: Elliottborough Home Ownership Project,* May 1996; HCF, *The Neighborhood Impact Initiative,* October 1997.

20. *Charleston News and Courier,* 14 May 1990, 20 February 1991; HCF, *Trustee Handbook* [1996], 21.

21. George L. Vogt, quoted in "Foundation Inherits Partial Interest in McLeod Plantation," *Charleston* 7 (Summer 1990): 1.

22. Bentz Associates, *Historic Charleston Foundation Marketing/Feasibility Study,* 11–13.

23. *Charleston Post and Courier,* 30 May 1993, 6 June 1993, 12 June 1994; *New York Times,* 6 June 1993; "A Future for McLeod Plantation," *Charleston* 11 (Fall 1994): 1.

24. Quoted in Patricia L. Hudson, "The Steeple Still Stands," *Americana* (April 1990): 30.

25. "Hugo Recovery," *Charleston* 7 (Fall 1990): 2; Thomas W. Sweeney, "Charleston on the Mend," *Historic Preservation* 42 (September–October 1990): 25–31, 80; *Chicago Tribune,* 4 August 1991.

26. Report of the Area Projects Committee, 24 October 1989; "Hugo Recovery," *Charleston* 7 (Fall 1990): 2; Bentz Associates, *Historic Charleston Foundation Marketing/Feasibility Study,* 8–9.

27. *Charleston Evening Post,* 3 October 1989; *Charleston News and Courier,* 30 October 1989, 29 March 1990, 7 May 1990; *Chicago Tribune,* 4 August 1991; Bentz Associates, *Historic Charleston Foundation Marketing/Feasibility Study,* 9.

28. Hudson, "The Steeple Still Stands," *Americana* (April 1990): 30; "Hugo Recovery," *Charleston* 7 (Fall 1990): 2; Bentz Associates, *Historic Charleston Foundation Marketing/Feasibility Study,* 9.

29. *Charleston Evening Post,* 22 April 1986; *Charleston News and Courier/Charleston Evening Post,* 26 April 1986, 20 May 1990; *Charleston News and Courier,* 6 March 1987, 23 May 1990, 16 August 1990; *Charleston Post and Courier,* 4 March 1995; Bentz Associates, *Historic Charleston Foundation Marketing/Feasibility Study,* 8–9.

30. *Charleston Post and Courier,* 19 November 1995. M. E. Van Dyke was a Charlestonian, retired from the lumber business, who had inaugurated the crafts training program.

31. *Charleston News and Courier,* 14 May 1987; *Charleston Evening Post,* 15 November 1987; *Charleston News and Courier/Charleston Evening Post,* 21 April 1990; "Foundation Fosters French Connection," *Charleston* 6 (Summer 1989): 1; Sweeney, "Charleston on the Mend," *Historic Preservation* 42 (September–October 1990): 30.

32. "Preservation Crafts Training Program," *Charleston* 9 (Spring 1992): 7; *Charleston Post and Courier,* 21 July 1992, 25 July 1992; *Charleston Chronicle,* 26 August 1992; Program for the Presentation of Certificates, Historic Preservation Building Crafts Training Program, 27 August 1992.

33. *Charleston Post and Courier,* 21 July 1992.

34. *Charleston Post and Courier,* 2 September 1993.

35. *Charleston Post and Courier,* 2 September 1993.

36. *Charleston Post and Courier,* 24 June 1995.

37. *Charleston Post and Courier,* 19 November 1995, 25 July 1996; "Back on the Scaffolds Again," *Historic Charleston* 3 (Autumn 1996): 10.

38. *Charleston Evening Post,* 8 December 1975; *Charleston News and Courier,* 20 March 1979, 4 January 1982; *Charleston Post and Courier,* 17 December 1993, 12 December 1995.

39. HCF, Prospectus for Aiken-Rhett House [undated]; Allen Freeman, "Faded Glory," *Historic Preservation* 47 (September–October 1995): 72–79, 117–18.
40. "Foundation Acquires Aiken-Rhett House," *Charleston* 11 (Spring 1996): 2. Carter Lee Hudgins was the first executive director of Historic Charleston Foundation to hold a Ph.D.; he came to the foundation in January 1994 from Mary Washington College in Fredericksburg, Virginia, where he had been director of its Center for Historic Preservation and Prince B. Woodard Professor of Historic Preservation.
41. Interpretive sheets distributed at Aiken-Rhett House. See also Michael Laws, "The Aiken-Rhett House: Historic Charleston Foundation Looks at Its Past and Sees Its Future," *CRM: Cultural Resource Management* 22 (1999): 28–30.
42. For an example of current thinking, see "Facing the Past," *The State* (Columbia), 27 February 1997.

# FOR FURTHER READING

## CHARLESTON ARCHITECTURE, PRESERVATION, AND HISTORY

Bland, Sidney R. *Preserving Charleston's Past, Shaping Its Future: The Life and Times of Susan Pringle Frost*. 2nd ed. Columbia: University of South Carolina Press, 1999.

Chase, Charles Edwin. "Charleston: Guarding Her Customs, Buildings, and Laws," *Preservation Forum* 13 (Fall 1998): 6–14.

Cothran, James R. *Gardens of Historic Charleston*. Columbia: University of South Carolina Press, 1995.

Datel, Robin Elisabeth. "Southern Regionalism and Historic Preservation in Charleston, South Carolina, 1920–1940," *Journal of Historical Geography* 16 (April 1990): 197–215.

Doyle, Don H. *New Men, New Cities, New South: Atlanta, Nashville, Charleston, Mobile, 1860–1910*. Chapel Hill: University of North Carolina Press, 1990.

Fraser, Walter J., Jr. *Charleston! Charleston! The History of a Southern City*. Columbia: University of South Carolina Press, 1989.

Poston, Jonathan H. *The Buildings of Charleston: A Guide to the City's Architecture*. Columbia: University of South Carolina Press, 1997.

Powers, Bernard E., Jr. *Black Charlestonians: A Social History, 1822–1885*. Fayetteville: University of Arkansas Press, 1994.

Preservation Society of Charleston. *Preservation Progress*. Charleston, S.C.: Preservation Society of Charleston, 1956– .

Ravenel, Beatrice St. Julien. *Architects of Charleston*. Charleston, S.C.: Carolina Art Association, 1945; reprint, 1992.

Rhoad, Debbi. "The Board of Architectural Review in Charleston, 1931–1993," *Preservation Progress,* special edition (Spring 1993): 13–18.

Severens, Kenneth. *Charleston Antebellum Architecture and Civic Destiny*. Knoxville: University of Tennessee Press, 1988.

Simons, Albert, and Samuel Lapham Jr., eds. *Charleston, South Carolina*. New York: American Institute of Architects, 1927. Reprinted as *The Early Architecture of Charleston*, 1970.

————, eds. *Plantations of the Carolina Low Country.* Charleston, S.C.: Carolina Art Association, 1938.

Stockton, Robert P. *The Effects of the 1886 Earthquake on the Built Environment of Charleston, South Carolina.* Easley, S.C.: Southern Historical Press, 1986.

Vlach, John Michael. *Back of the Big House: The Architecture of Plantation Slavery.* Chapel Hill: University of North Carolina Press, 1993.

Wade, Richard C. *Slavery in the Cities: The South, 1820–1860.* New York: Oxford University Press, 1964.

## Preservation History in the United States

Hosmer, Charles B., Jr. *Presence of the Past: A History of the Preservation Movement in the United States before Williamsburg.* New York: G. P. Putnam's Sons, 1965.

————. *Preservation Comes of Age: From Williamsburg to the National Trust, 1926–1949.* 2 vols. Charlottesville: University Press of Virginia, 1981.

Kammen, Michael. *Mystic Chords of Memory: The Transformation of Tradition in American Culture.* New York: Alfred A. Knopf, 1991.

Lindgren, James M. *Preserving Historic New England: Preservation, Progressivism, and the Remaking of Memory.* New York: Oxford University Press, 1995.

————. *Preserving the Old Dominion: Historic Preservation and Virginia Traditionalism.* Charlottesville: University Press of Virginia, 1993.

Murtagh, William J. *Keeping Time: The History and Theory of Preservation in America.* Rev. ed. New York: John Wiley and Sons, 1997.

Runte, Alfred. *National Parks: The American Experience.* 3rd ed. Lincoln: University of Nebraska Press, 1997.

Savage, Beth L., ed. *African American Historic Places: National Register of Historic Places.* Washington, D.C.: Preservation Press, 1994.

Stipe, Robert E., and Antoinette J. Lee, eds. *The American Mosaic: Preserving a Nation's Heritage.* Detroit: Wayne State University Press, 1997. Originally published, 1987.

Stokes, Samuel N., A. Elizabeth Watson, Genevieve P. Keller, and J. Timothy Keller. *Saving America's Countryside.* Baltimore: Johns Hopkins University Press, 1989.

# INDEX

Adam, Robert, 48

Adams, Franklin O., 221n. 17

adaptive use of buildings: Ansonborough, 56, 60–61, 69; early efforts, 11–13; Edmondston-Alston House, 106; Frances Edmunds as commentator, 71, 231n. 57; Visitor Reception and Transportation Center, 88

Advisory Council on Historic Preservation: Frances Edmunds appointment to, 231n. 58; role with Federal Courthouse Annex, 90–91; role with hotel and convention center, 98–99, 101, 103, 104, 234n. 50, 238n. 4; role with James Island Bridge, 125–27

African-American heritage, preservation and interpretation of, xvii; at Aiken-Rhett House, 158, 174–78; at McLeod Plantation, 166–70; at Nathaniel Russell House, 41, 53–54; at Snee Farm, 140–41

African-American neighborhoods, xix, 85, 92, 104–5, 106, 145, 146, 157, 179; area rehabilitation in, 110–23; Neighborhood Impact Initiative, 163–67

Aiken, William, Jr., 175

Aiken-Rhett House, 87, 147, 158, 174–78, 179

Albemarle Point, 127

Alexander Street, 64

Alexandria, Va., 19

Allston, R. F. W., 42

Alston, Charles, 107–8

American Association of Museums, 50

American Institute of Architects (AIA), 10, 16, 34, 35, 221n. 17, 231n. 58

American Society of Civil Engineers, 16

America the Beautiful Fund, 81, 146

Amherst Street, 119

Andreini, Mrs. Cesare, 221n. 17

Andrew Moffett House, 64

Annapolis, Md., 19

annual spring tours: Ansonborough, 61; role of Frances Edmunds, 71; first use of revenue, 37; compared with Historic Charleston Reproductions, 153; history and operation, 147–52; role of Dorothy Haskell Porcher Legge, 36; use of local museums, 241n. 8

Anson Street, 60, 61, 64, 66, 67

Ansonborough area rehabilitation project, xiii, xiv, xix; annual spring tours, 61, 150; considered as municipal model, 83; implementation, 55–71; inclusion in Old and Historic Charleston District, 79; legacy, 106, 110, 119–20, 121, 163; origins, 27; role of Woodwards, 145

Arch Building, 86, 233n. 32

archaeological research and preservation: Drayton Hall, 137; Nathaniel Russell House, 50, 52–54, 146; McLeod Plantation, 168; Powder Magazine, 162; Snee Farm, 139, 141

architectural surveys and inventories: Charleston County, 239n. 17; Feiss-Wright-Anderson survey of 1974, 73, 82–83, 120, 126–27,